The Mystery of the Katyn Massacre
The Evidence
The Solution

By Grover Furr

Erythros Press and Media, LLC
Corrected Edition April 2019

The Mystery of the Katyn Massacre: The Evidence, the Solution

First Edition: 2018

Published by Erythros Press and Media, 2018
PO Box 291994
Kettering, Ohio 291994
media@erythrospress.com

Badge and shell casing artwork by Shahin Shayegan
www.nuclearheatgraphics.com

Locally Assigned LC-type Call Number D804.R9 F872 2018
Furr, Grover C. (Grover Carr)

The Mystery of the Katyn Massacre: The Evidence, the Solution /
Grover C. Furr; translations by Grover C. Furr

ISBN: 978-0-692-13425-2

268 pp. Includes index.

1. Katyn Massacre, Katyn', Russia, 1940. 2. World War, 1939-1945
– Poland. 3. Polish people – Crimes against – Russia (Federation) –
Katyn' – History – 20th century. 4. Prisoners of war – Crimes
against – Russia (Federation) – Katyn' – History – 20th century. 5.
Poland – Foreign relations – Soviet Union. 6. Soviet Union – For-
eign relations – Poland.

Table of Contents

Acknowledgements and Dedication

I would like to express my thanks to the dedicated staff of Harry S. Sprague Library, Montclair State University.

I am especially grateful for the invaluable work of the Inter-Library Loan librarians Kevin Prendergast, Arthur Hudson, and Siobhan McCarthy. Without their hard work I simply could not obtain the many hard-to-find books and articles, in many languages, that make my research possible.

My publisher, cover designer, cogent critic, and friend Mike Bessler of Erythros Press and Media, LLC, has given me encouragement, inspiration, and help whenever I needed it, often at late night hours. I could not ask for a better publisher.

Professor Susana M. Sotillo, Ph.D., my camarada and compañera, has helped me immeasurably with her patience and affectionate encouragement more than any words of mine can express.

Yet again my colleague and friend Vladimir L'vovich Bobrov, of Moscow, Russia, has given unstintingly of his time and help to make this book a reality. I cannot do justice to the contribution he has made to this book, as to all my research and our joint research, in the field of history of the Stalin period.

My deepest thanks to each one of you.

Dedication

I dedicate this book to my friend Bill Sacks. Bill has proofread this and several other books of mine with great care, and made excellent suggestions that have improved my work immeasurably. No one has been more encouraging, supportive, and helpful. Thank you, Bill!

Preface

Many a reader will wonder: "Why another book on the Katyn Massacre?" "And, particularly, why call it a "mystery"? For (they will think) the mystery – if there ever really was one – was solved long ago, in the early 1990s when the Soviet, then the Russian governments admitted guilt and produced the "smoking gun" documents of "Closed Packet No. 1", the primary source evidence of Soviet guilt in that atrocity.

I used to think the same thing. When I read in the *New York Times* that President Gorbachev of the USSR had admitted the guilt of the Stalin government at Katyn, I had no cause to doubt it. The revelation in the same newspaper a couple of years later that President Yeltsin of Russia had given these "smoking gun" documents to Lech Walesa, President of Poland, confirmed what I already thought.

I did not care very much. To me, the Katyn Massacre seemed long ago and far away. Meanwhile the number of mass murders committed by the Germans and Japanese, and the scale of mortality in the Second World War, were so great that Katyn hardly added to it. Nor were my sympathies engaged by the fates of the Polish POWs said to have been murdered at the places which, collectively, came to be known as the Katyn Massacre, or "Katyn." Why sympathize with them rather than with the tens of millions of others murdered in that war? It is simply impossible, overwhelming, even crippling, to try to truly feel for all those long-dead people.

But since the mid-1990s there has appeared research claiming that this is all wrong. That "Katyn" is a frame-up, anti-Soviet, anti-Russian and anticommunist. I was not convinced – but thinking back, I realize today that I still did not care enough to be either truly convinced or truly unconvinced.

I did become intrigued, however. "Katyn" – a term I will use in this book without scare quotes from now on as shorthand for "the

Katyn massacre" – was now a mystery. And I like mysteries! Especially historical ones.

There was more to my attraction to Katyn than just liking a good mystery. Since my student days, when I became involved in the protest movement against the American war in Vietnam, I have been attracted to Marxism. I sympathized with the Vietnamese struggle for independence. I learned that anticommunism was not exactly a fraud – the United States government was genuinely anticommunist – but that anticommunism also served as camouflage for imperialism and for ordinary capitalist exploitation. France, then Japan, and then the United States, wanted to dominate Vietnam. In the cases of France and the United States anticommunism became the rationale for a war to preserve empire. In Vietnam and around the world it was the communists who were the major force organizing opposition to this imperialist war by the United States.

At a huge antiwar demonstration in Manhattan in 1967 an older person – an onlooker, not a participant – told me in a friendly manner that I should not be supporting the National Liberation Front of South Vietnam. Why not? I asked. Because the NLF was really led by the Vietnamese Communist Party, which was led by Ho Chi Minh. Ho had been trained by Joseph Stalin. And Stalin, he said, had murdered 40 million people.

I did not just "believe" what he said. But I did not disbelieve it either. I determined that I would look into this matter seriously once I had the time to do so, once I had my feet on the ground in teaching and my doctoral dissertation was well on the way to completion.

I was confident that I possessed the tools to do this. I could read the Russian language well; it was one of my languages for my degree in Comparative Literature (Medieval English, German, Russian) at Princeton University.

I also knew that to do valid historical research the student must identify, locate, obtain, study, and draw the logical conclusions from, primary sources. I had learned this from a master teacher, D. W. Robertson, Jr. In the early 1960s his insistence on primary source research had shaken the staid field of medieval literary research to its foundations. Robertson – his students called him "Robby" – had been attacked as an enemy of scholarship, even of the Enlightenment itself, because he dared to question "received knowledge."

Robby's publications had changed the field in a definitive way. And, as he informed us, he had done it by insisting on the primacy of primary sources. He told us what that meant: to never be afraid to question, and in fact to challenge, the prevailing orthodoxy within the field, no matter how monolithic, how indestructible it appeared to be – if the primary source evidence demands it.

I also embarked on the study of Soviet history as a project in self-clarification. I had questions about the Stalin period in the Soviet Union that challenged my opposition to the Vietnam War, to American imperialism, and to the conventionally accepted Cold War paradigm of understanding history and politics. I had the tools. I had a little courage, learned from my participation in the antiwar movement. So I began to research the Stalin years in the USSR.

By 2006 I had read enough on Katyn to know that there was a critical mass of research that rejected what I call the "official" version of Katyn – that the Soviets were guilty. So I created a web page to which I gave the title "The Katyn Forest Whodunnit."[1] At that time it was the only resource in the English language where one could learn about the research that challenged the "official" version. I did not endorse either version: the "official", Soviets-did-it, or the "oppositional", Germans-did-it-Soviets-were-framed. I was agnostic.

I also determined that I myself would never write anything about Katyn. For almost seven years I concluded my Katyn web page with these words:

---

[1] At http://tinyurl.com/Katyn-the-truth

So here is my last thought, for now: SO WHAT?

I'm serious. I do not think it matters to very many people, and maybe to nobody.

"The Katyn Massacre" is not an historical question – it is a WEAPON, a CUDGEL. You use it to make war on "the other side", and that's it.

Those who say "the Soviets did it" are NEVER going to accept that they did not, no matter what the evidence.

Those who say and / or hope: "The Soviets did NOT do it" are NEVER going to shed their respect and admiration for the USSR, EVEN IF you managed to convince them that the Soviets did it. And I do not think that's going to happen either!

It's like convincing a Christian that Jesus never existed. That is, it's no longer history, it's religion.

Good luck!

* * * * *

So it is interesting. But at this point I confine myself to (a) reading about it; and (b) reminding those who "know" (= are sure they know, and do not want to hear otherwise) of their bad faith.

You can imagine how popular THAT makes me! But being unpopular in this way is something I'm very content to be.

I hope this has been interesting, maybe even helpful. Believe me, there is so much more to say that you do not even want to know!

("The Katyn Forest Whodunnit" April 3, 2007)

In 2006 and 2007 my conclusions were sharply challenged by Sergei Romanov. Mr. Romanov proved to me that I had made some errors in my page. I corrected them, and thanked him explicitly on that page. He also put our exchange online on his own website.[2]

Mr. Romanov also made a significant error in historical method. At the time I had not studied Katyn enough, or thought deeply enough about it, to be able to recognize his error. So I thanked him, but I refused to do what he demanded: acknowledge that the Soviets were indeed guilty.

I remained agnostic about Katyn. As it turns out, I was correct to do so. But I did not fully understand that then.

In 2010 I learned about Duma member Viktor Iliukhin's announcement that he had evidence that the documents presented by Yeltsin to Walesa, known as "Closed Packet No. 1", were forgeries. I summarize this briefly in Chapter One, below.

In January 2013 I learned about excavations by a joint Polish-Ukrainian archeological team of a mass murder site at Volodymyr-Volyns'kiy, Ukraine. I found the Polish archeologist's report on it online and studied it. I recognized the importance of the discoveries made there for any objective understanding of Katyn. Violating my own promise to myself never to write anything on Katyn (other than my web page) I set about doing some intensive study.

I found a journal willing to accept an article, which was published in August 2013. I also realized that, unless I did something to publicize it, this discovery and its importance for our understanding of Katyn would remain almost entirely unknown. So during the next eighteen months I printed up several hundred offprints of this article and mailed them around the world. After 18 months I put a link to that article on my Home Page.

---

[2] Where it remains as of this writing (January 2017) -
http://holocaustcontroversies.blogspot.com/2007/03/and-now-for-something-not-completely.html

The title of my article is:

> "The 'Official' Version of the Katyn Massacre Disproven? Discoveries at a German Mass Murder Site in Ukraine." [3]

During the pre-publication process my very helpful editor asked me: "Why the question mark?" Once the article had been published a few other people asked me the same question. I did not have a good answer. In truth, I did not know why, except that "it felt right." Once the article was published I concentrated on mailing offprints and on researching and writing another book. When that book was published, I went on to research and write two more. It was a very busy time.

But that question mark nagged at me! Why had I put it there? At length I understood: I was still not fully convinced that the "official" version of Katyn had indeed been disproven. As much as I knew about Katyn – and I already knew more than most specialists in Soviet history – I realized that I still did not know enough.

When confronted with a mystery a detective sets out to solve it. If a crime is involved – Katyn is surely a massive crime – he, or she, doesn't care who is guilty. The detective approaches the task of solving the crime objectively, for the sake of the thing itself – that is, for him- or herself. In "The Adventure of the Red Circle" we find the following exchange between Sherlock Holmes and Dr. Watson:

> "It is art for art's sake. Watson, I suppose when you doctored you found yourself studying cases without a thought of a fee?"
>
> "For my education, Holmes."
>
> "Education never ends, Watson. It is a series of lessons with the greatest for the last. This is an instructive

---

[3] *Socialism and Democracy* 27(2) (August 2013): 96-129.

case. There is neither money nor credit in it, and yet
one would wish to tidy it up."

Holmes' words – that is, Conan Doyle's – precisely express my
deeper motive in researching and writing this book. For there is
"neither money nor credit in it." On the contrary, I can be assured
that I will be attacked and slandered by those who are horrified to
look the truth in the face and discover that it is not at all what they
want it to be. Yet "one would wish to tidy it up" – to solve the mystery.

To solve any mystery we must first identify the relevant evidence.
And concerning Katyn, there is a mountain of material that is often
taken to be evidence. Holmes can help here too:

> It is one of those cases where the art of the reasoner
> should be used rather for the sifting of details than for
> the acquiring of fresh evidence. The tragedy has been
> so uncommon, so complete and of such personal im-
> portance to so many people, that we are suffering
> from a plethora of surmise, conjecture, and hypothe-
> sis. ("Silver Blaze")

Maria Konnikova explains:

> In other words, there is too much information to begin
> with, too many details to be able to start making them
> into any sort of coherent whole, separating the crucial
> from the incidental. When so many facts are piled to-
> gether, the task becomes increasingly problematic.
> You have a vast quantity of your own observations
> and data but also an even vaster quantity of potential-
> ly incorrect information from individuals who may not
> have observed as mindfully as you have.[4]

---

[4] Maria Konnikova, *Mastermind. How To Think Like Sherlock Holmes*. New York: Viking Pen-
guin, 2013. "Learning to Tell the Crucial from the Incidental."

This is exactly the situation that faces us in the case of Katyn.

Holmes concludes:

> The difficulty is **to detach the framework of fact—of absolute undeniable fact — from the embellishments** of theorists and reporters. Then, having established ourselves upon this sound basis, it is our duty to see what inferences may be drawn and **what are the special points upon which the whole mystery turns**.

As it happens, this is a good, succinct outline of the proper method of doing historical research too. In the case of Katyn there is "too much information," "too many details."

A bigger problem is that very few of the persons involved in studying Katyn are objective. They have decided that the "official" version is correct; that the Soviets killed the Polish POWs and that there is no doubt remaining about this. Moreover, they have decided that it is perverse to even raise the question. That simply to approach Katyn as a mystery implies that the solution has not been definitively determined for all time, and is therefore a dishonest thing to do, since it implies the possibility that the Soviets *might not* have done it. This attitude has discouraged objective study of Katyn.

So I have undertaken to solve the Katyn mystery more for self-clarification than for any other reason. "For my education, Holmes." Can I apply my own principles? Am I capable of approaching this important topic with objectivity?

Can I look with especial suspicion on all evidence that tends to support my preconceived ideas while giving an especially generous reading to evidence that tends to contradict my own ideas? In my case, can I discover the truth, even if the truth is that the Soviets – the communists, with whom I have been in sympathy ever since the Vietnam War – were indeed guilty?

At a debate in October 2012 I said that I had researched alleged "crimes of Stalin" for many years and had yet to find one crime that Stalin committed. At that time I was still agnostic, undecided, about Katyn. But if the evidence demands it, am I capable of concluding that Stalin and the Soviet leadership did indeed kill the Polish POWs, as the "official" version states?

Yes, I am. I am much more interested in the mystery itself than in what the solution might be. Besides, it is more satisfying to demand objectivity of oneself than to take the coward's way out and either decide for the stronger side (and thus win a dishonest approbation) or to assert the unpopular side out of bias and prejudice, and thus know, in my own mind at least, that I am afraid to face the truth.

I agree with historian Geoffrey Roberts when he says:

> In the last 15 years or so an enormous amount of new material on Stalin ... has become available from Russian archives. I should make clear that as a historian I have a strong orientation to telling the truth about the past, no matter how uncomfortable or unpalatable the conclusions may be. ... I don't think there is a dilemma: you just tell the truth as you see it.[5]

* * * * *

My research concludes that the Germans, not the Soviets, are guilty of the mass murders known as the Katyn massacre. This is the same conclusion as is drawn by a few Russian researchers, including the late Sergei Strygin, Vladislav Shved, Valentin Sakharov, Elena Prudnikova and Ivan Chigirin.

But I have not followed the method that these researchers use. Instead I have used the method that a detective would employ. A detective who did not care who was guilty, but whose aim was solely

---

[5] "Stalin's Wars," February 12, 2007. At http://hnn.us/roundup/entries/35305.html

to find out the truth and report that truth – and let the chips fall where they may!

To a person less familiar with the history of the scholarship on Katyn it might well appear that, in Konnikova's words, "there is too much information to begin with, too many details to be able to start making them into any sort of coherent whole, separating the crucial from the incidental." After all, just think about that library-full of books and articles on the subject!

But by that time I had been studying Katyn for years. I knew that there are only a few documents that constitute the primary-source evidence in this case. Once I began to systematically sort, categorize, and study this evidence, I came to the realization that there is really very little evidence to support either the "official" Soviets-did-it version or the opposite, Germans-did-it version. Upon even closer scrutiny I realized that *there is even less evidence than that – in fact, only a few bits of evidence – that* (for all practical purposes) *cannot possibly have been fabricated or falsified* in order to bias the case in favor of one or the other version.

Consequently, in this study I concentrate on these few bits of what I call "unimpeachable evidence" – meaning, evidence that it is impossible to discredit *as* evidence (the interpretation is something else again). You, the reader, will make up your own mind whether this evidence is as clear and unambiguous, and my interpretation of it as correct, as I believe it to be.

This book is written for the student of history who wants to know the truth, even when that truth is "dis-illusioning" in that it forces her to set aside her own illusions – her preconceived ideas – and actually *change her mind.* Researching and writing this book has changed *my* mind. I am no longer agnostic on the subject of Katyn.

I predict that those who have built their professional careers around the "official" version of Katyn will, as a matter of course, reject the conclusions of this research. They will reject it not because my method or my analysis of the evidence is faulty, but for *a priori* reasons – they are biased, unalterably prejudiced in favor of the view that the Soviets are guilty. No amount of evidence will change their minds. Obviously, this book is not written for them.

Before a juror can be seated on a jury in a criminal trial in the United States that juror is instructed that he or she must decide the guilt or innocence of the accused strictly on the basis of the evidence, not according to any preconceived idea, information learned outside of the courtroom, or bias. Historians too are professionally obliged to act in this way. Unfortunately, very few of those who have studied Katyn can honestly claim that they have adhered to this vital principle.

This book may not be pleasing to those students of history who are convinced that the Soviets were innocent of Katyn but think that this can be established by means that, in my judgment, are not valid – for example, by attempts to prove through internal analysis that the documents of Closed Packet No. 1 are forgeries. The defenders and detractors of Closed Packet No. 1 have argued back and forth for years. I think this is a sterile argument and explain my reasons for thinking so in these pages.

Another approach must be taken to solving the Katyn mystery. I believe it is the one I have taken here. This may seem arrogant to those historians and writers who have spent years following a quite different – and, to my way of thinking, incorrect – approach to the question.

In writing this book I do not expect praise from any side. I do expect sharper attacks from defenders of the "official" viewpoint. After all, they are not interested in the truth. In reality, they are not really interested in the Polish POWs who were killed at Katyn! If they were, they would welcome the discovery of who the real culprits, the real mass murderers, were.

Instead, they are interested only in how the notion of Soviet guilt at Katyn can be used today to justify their own political, historical, and cultural projects. Despite the hundreds of millions of dollars spent on memorials, conferences, books, articles, educational materials, and indoctrination of all kinds, neither the Polish nor the

Russian governments of today, nor their phalanxes of researchers, scholars, and politicians, really care about the Katyn victims. What they care about is their own political agendas.

I could claim that I do care about the men murdered at Katyn and that I demonstrate that in the only way it can be legitimately demonstrated: by solving the mystery and identifying the guilty party. But I do not make that claim. The mystery of Katyn has both intrigued and challenged me for years. That, and not concern for the victims as such, is the reason that I have done this research and written this book.

Of course, it does give appropriate respect to the victims of a murder to identify the guilty party after many years and "bring closure." However, in time the relatives and friends of the Katyn victims will pass from the scene, as all of us will. What will remain is the historical event. Now we know what happened, and what did not happen; who is guilty, and who is not. That will remain for posterity. It is that posterity, not the political purposes of yesterday or even of today, which will be served by discovering the truth about Katyn.

Introduction.

The "Official" Soviets-Did-It Version

The "official" version is the only version reflected in the Wikipedia article on Katyn, at http://en.wikipedia.org/wiki/Katyn_massacre. *This page is relentlessly anticommunist and anti-Stalinist. It makes no attempt to be objective or neutral, in that it has no serious discussion of the scholarly controversy about this question. It's useful only as a short and accurate summary of the "official" version.*

In April 1943 Nazi German authorities claimed that they had discovered thousands of bodies of Polish officers shot by Soviet officials in 1940. These bodies were said to have been discovered near the Katyn forest near Smolensk (in Western Russia), which is why the whole affair – including executions and alleged executions of Polish POWs elsewhere in the USSR – came to be called "the Katyn Massacre."

 The Nazi propaganda machine, headed by Joseph Goebbels, organized a huge campaign around this alleged discovery. After the Soviet victory at Stalingrad in February 1943, it was obvious to everyone that, unless something happened to split the Allies, Germany would inevitably lose the war. The Nazis' obvious aim was to drive a wedge between the western Allies and the USSR.

The Soviet government, headed by Joseph Stalin, vigorously denied the German charge. When the Polish government-in-exile, always ferociously anticommunist and anti-Russian, collaborated with the Nazi propaganda effort, the Soviet government broke off diplomatic relations with it, eventually setting up a pro-Soviet Polish authority and Polish army.

In September 1943 the Red Army drove the Germans from the Katyn area. In 1944 the Soviet Burdenko Commission carried out a study and issued a report that blamed the Germans for the mass shootings.

During the Cold War the Western capitalist countries supported the Nazi version which had become the version promoted by the anticommunist Polish government-in-exile. The Soviet Union and its allies continued to blame the Germans for the murders. In 1990 and 1991 Mikhail Gorbachev, General Secretary of the Communist Party of the Soviet Union and, after 1988, President of the USSR, stated that the Soviet Union under Joseph Stalin had indeed shot the Poles. According to this "official" version the Polish prisoners had been confined in three camps: at Kozel'sk, Starobel'sk, and Ostashkov and from there transferred to Smolensk, Kharkiv (Russian: Khar'kov), and Kalinin (now Tver'), where they were shot and buried at Katyn, Piatykhatky, and Mednoe respectively.

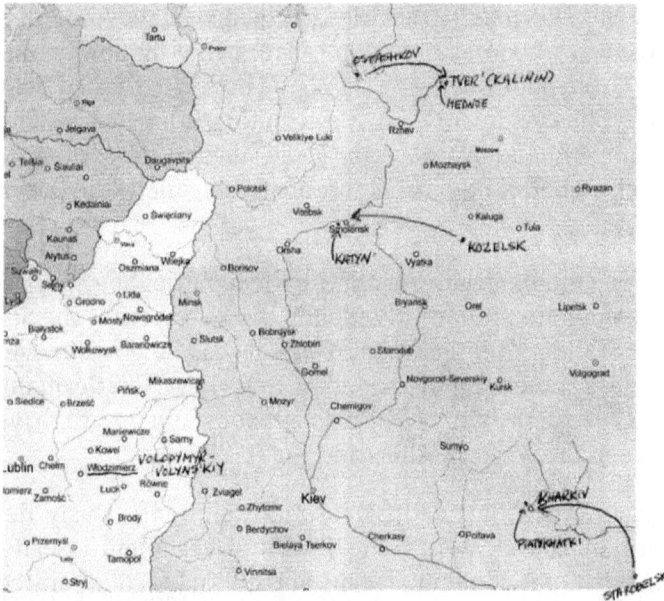

1939 map showing places mentioned in the "official" Katyn narrative. Arrows from the POW camps (Ostashkov, Starobel'sk, Kozel'sk) to cities (Kalinin/Tver', Kharkiv, Smolensk) show destinations on NKVD transit documents. Burial sites in the nearby countryside (Mednoe, Piatykhatky, Katyn) are also shown, as is Volodymyr-Volyns'kiy (Włodzimierz), which is about 700 miles (1200 Km) from Kalinin/Tver' - Mednoe.

In 1990, 1991, and 1992 three aged former NKVD men were identified and interviewed. They discussed what they *claimed* they
knew of executions of Poles in April and May of 1940. None of
these executions had taken place at the Katyn Forest, site of the
German exhumations.

In 1992 the Russian government under Boris Yeltsin handed over
to the Polish government documents supposedly signed by Stalin
and other Politburo members which, if genuine, would put Soviet
guilt beyond reasonable doubt. These documents are said to have
been found in "Closed Packet No. 1," where "closed" meant the
highest level of classification – secrecy. I call these the "smoking
gun documents," since they are conventionally assumed to be
"proof positive" of Soviet guilt. However, no evidence is ever uni-
vocal and definitive; all evidence, whether documentary or material, can be interpreted in multiple ways.

By 1992, therefore, the Soviet, and then the Russian, governments
had officially declared the Stalin-era Soviet leadership guilty of
shooting somewhere between 14,800 and 22,000 Polish prisoners
to death in April and May 1940.

The Soviet "Germans-did-it" Version

On April 13, 1943, the Germans charged the Soviets with murdering the Polish POWs at Katyn. On April 16, 1943, the Soviet government responded in a press release by Sovinformburo which
blamed the Germans. It explained the fate of the Poles:

> The German-Fascist reports on this subject leave no
> doubt as to the tragic fate of the former Polish POWs
> who in 1941 were engaged in construction work in
> areas west of Smolensk and who, along with many So-
> viet people, residents of the Smolensk region, fell into
> the hands of the German-Fascist hangmen in the

summer of 1941, after the withdrawal of Soviet troops from the Smolensk area.[1]

In September 1943 Smolensk was retaken by the Red Army. On November 2, 1943 the "Extraordinary State Commission for Ascertaining and Investigating Crimes Perpetrated by the German-Fascist Invaders and their Accomplices" had been formed, of which Dr. Nikolai N. Burdenko was a member. On January 12, 1944, Burdenko was appointed chairman of the "Special Commission for Ascertaining and Investigating the Circumstances of the Shooting in the Katyn Forest by the German-Fascist Occupiers."

Known as the "Burdenko Commission" this group researched the Katyn massacres from October 5, 1943 until January 10, 1944. Its report, first published in *Pravda* on January 26, 1944, blamed the Germans. It claimed:

> The Special Commission established that, before the capture of Smolensk by the Germans, Polish war prisoners, officers and men, worked in the western, district of the region, building and repairing roads. These war prisoners were quartered in three special camps named: Camp No. 1 O. N., Camp No. 2 O. N., and Camp No. 3 O. N. These camps were located 25 to 45 kilometers west of Smolensk.

> The testimony of witnesses and documentary evidence establish that after the outbreak of hostilities, in view of the situation that arose, the camps could not be evacuated in time and all the Polish war prisoners, as well as some members of the guard and staffs of the camps, fell prisoner to the Germans.

The Burdenko Commission claimed that the Germans murdered the Poles. In the spring of 1943 the Germans:

---

[1] Cienciala, Doc. 102 pp. 306.

...resolved to launch a provocation, using for this purpose the atrocities they had committed in the Katyn Forest, and ascribing them to the organs of the Soviet authorities. In this way they intended to set the Russians and Poles at loggerheads and to cover up the traces of their own crimes.[2]

The Two Versions Compared

Both the "official" version and the Soviet version agree that more than 10,000 Polish prisoners were held by the Soviets at three POW camps: Kozel'sk, in Eastern Russia; Starobel'sk, in Ukraine; and Ostashkov, near Kalinin (now renamed Tver'). In April and May, 1940, the Polish prisoners were shipped out of these three camps to the Directorates of the NKVD in Smolensk, Kharkiv and Kalinin respectively.

According to the "official" version the prisoners were executed there or at the burial sites, and buried at Koz'i Gory, near Katyn' (which is near Smolensk), Piatykhatky, near Kharkiv, and Mednoe, near Kalinin, respectively.

According to the Soviet version the prisoners were sent from the three NKVD centers to camps 1-ON, 2-ON, and 3-ON near Smolensk, and others were sent to the western Ukraine. All were to do road work. All were captured by the Germans and their Ukrainian Nationalist allies in June 1941, and subsequently murdered.

Both versions agree that small numbers of Polish prisoners were sent to other camps and were not killed.

---

[2] I use the translation in volume 3 of the Madden Commission hearings. *The Katyn Forest Massacre. Hearings before the Select Committee...Part 3 (Chicago, IL) March 13 and 14, 1952* (U.S. Government Printing Office, 1952), 228-247. (Henceforth BU + page number is to this edition). This translation is identical to the Soviet translation published as a Supplement to the "Soviet War News Weekly."

Crucial Points

The Soviet NKVD lists of prisoners shipped from the three camps to the NKVD at the three towns have been preserved and published. Everyone agrees that these lists are genuine.[3]

The "official" Soviets-did-it version relies on the *assumption* that the Polish prisoners were executed by the NKVD at the three towns named and then buried at the three burial places named. These shipments of prisoners are routinely stated to be "death transports."

The book *Katyn: A Crime Without Punishment* by Anna M. Cienciala, Natalia S. Lebedeva, and Wojciech Materski (Yale University Press 2007) is the definitive academic account of the "official" version. It refers to the shipments of prisoners this way (emphasis added):

> The final <u>death transport</u> left Kozielsk....

> The last <u>death transport</u> left Ostashkov for Kalinin (Tver) on 19 May...

> ...lists of those to be sent out of the camps <u>to be shot</u> (doc. 62)...

> ...and reporting on the number sent <u>to their death</u> (doc. 65).

Cienciala, who did the writing in this volume, added all the language about execution. Likewise in her discussion of the documents – none of which mentions executions, shootings, killing, death, etc., at all – Cienciala continuously adds language to remind the readers that, *in her interpretation*, these prisoners were being

---

[3] They are published in Jędrzej Tucholski. *Mord w Katyniu: Kozielsk, Ostaszków, Starobielsk. Lista ofiar.* Warszawa: Instztut Wydawniczy Pax, 1991. This is still the official and only edition of all the Soviet NKVD transit lists and the Polish lists of victims. The Soviet lists are reprinted in the original Russian.

transported to places where they would be executed. Here are a few examples (again, I have added the emphasis):

> They were transferred to NKVD prisons... <u>to be shot</u> there. (154)

> ... the same as the order in <u>the death transports</u>. (156)

> The first lists of victims to be <u>dispatched to their death</u>... (157)

> The delivery of lists for dispatching prisoners to their deaths... (159)

> Beria's directive of 4 April 1940 indicates the goal of <u>exterminating</u> not only the officers and police... (160)

> This is the first of many reports by the UNKVD head of Kalinin Oblast, Dmitry Tokarev, on the "<u>implementation," that is, the murder</u>... (162)

> Soprunenko's instruction to Korolev of 6 April 1940 was, in fact, <u>a death list</u>... (163)

> The dispatch of the prisoners of war <u>to their deaths</u>... (175)

> This 11 April 1940 report from Kozelsk shows that 1,643 officers were <u>murdered</u> in nine days. (175)

> ... the moods of the prisoners as they were being dispatched unwittingly <u>to their deaths</u>. (176-177)

> Most prisoners sent to Yukhnov camp... were exempted from <u>the death lists</u> for various reasons... (183)

> By 3 May, the UPV together with the 1st Special Department NKVD and with the personal help of Merkulov, had processed the cases of 14,908 prisoners and sent out dispatch lists – <u>death sentences</u> – for 13,682. (187)

> ...it is likely that they simply signed or stamped the "Kobulov Forms" (doc. 51) with the <u>death warrant</u> already filled in. (187)

> This report gives the number of lists of names received in the camp and the number of prisoners sent out from Kozelsk camp <u>to their deaths</u> for each date between 3 April and 11 May...(190)

> A report to Soprunenko shows the number of people <u>destined for execution</u> according to the lists received... (193)

> One of the last <u>executions</u> of POWs from the Ostashkov camp took place on 22 May 1940. (200)

> Ostashkov prisoners were still <u>being executed</u> that day... (200)

It is important to emphasize that not a single one of the transit documents themselves refers in any way to executions.

With very few exceptions, all the bodies identified – or supposedly identified – at Katyn' (Koz'i Gory) by both the Germans and the Soviets were identified by documents said to have been found on the corpses. No bodies identifiable as those of Katyn victims have been found at Mednoe or Piatykhatky.

The "official" version *assumes* that the corpses exhumed at Katyn were all from the Kozel'sk camp, having been sent there from Smolensk. If any bodies at Katyn are those of POWs who, according to the Soviet transit lists, were sent to Kalinin or Kharkiv, the "official" version would be undermined or disproven. Likewise, any bodies of POWs from any of these three camps found at other places would also undermine the "official" version.

Chapter 1. The Evidence That Can't Be Impugned

There is an enormous amount of writing about the Katyn massacre. The books about it would certainly fill a small library. At least one journal, „Zeszyty Katyńskie," is devoted entirely to Katyn. There are thousands of articles in historical journals, newspapers, and other periodical publications. The four-volume Polish document collection "Katyń. Dokumenty Zbrodni" (KDZ, "Katyn. Documents of the Crime") is more than 2000 pages long.

However, once I undertook to study Katyn I soon discovered that only a tiny amount of this material is primary source evidence of who killed the Polish POWs. The vast number of documents published in KDZ and a few other collections, however useful they may be for other purposes, obscure those few documents that do constitute real primary sources – the sole valid evidence – concerning the question: Who killed the Poles? All the rest concern peripheral issues. These side issues are important only for those who believe that they already know the guilty party and just want to "round out the story."

So in reality there is not much evidence. What's more, most of the evidence that does exist *could* have been fabricated in order to support one version or the other, either the "official" Soviets-did-it version, or the Soviet "Germans-did-it" version. Indeed, some of it *has* to be fabrication.

Both the Germans and the Soviets produced reports, each with its own exhumations, autopsies, expert testimony, and witnesses. The German report concluded that the Soviets had killed the Poles, while the later Soviet report concluded that the Germans had killed them. Clearly, they can't both be correct. Nor can they both be incorrect, for there was no third party aside from the Germans and the Soviets that could have killed the Poles.

In 1992 the Russian government produced documents which it claimed had been hidden in a top-secret Soviet archive and proved that the Soviets had murdered the Poles. The documents of "Closed Packet No. 1" – I call them the "smoking gun" documents – looked genuine. For a few years it seemed that the question of "Who killed the Poles" had been solved for once and for all.

In 1995 Iurii Mukhin, a Russian metallurgist, published "The Katyn Mystery" (*Katynskii detektiv*). In it Mukhin argued that the "smoking gun" documents are fabrications. Mukhin's book soon gathered supporters, mainly in Russia, and started a movement. In 2003 Mukhin followed up his first book with a 750+ page work titled "Anti-Russian Villainy" (*Antirossiiskaia podlost'*).

In October 2010 a credible case was made that the "smoking gun" documents are forgeries. This had been the position of many Russian communists and Left Russian nationalists since the publication of Mukhin's 1995 book. The materials adduced by Duma member Victor Iliukhin in October 2010 constitute the strongest evidence so far that these documents may well be forgeries.[1] The fullest account of these dramatic developments is on the late Sergei Strygin's web page. There is an English-language summary on the Swedish "Katynmassacern" page, and on the "Mythcracker" page.[2] A review of my posts in 2010 to the H-Russia list, in which I outline the discovery soon after it took place, is also available.[3]

Since Iliukhin's revelations no honest researcher can simply "accept" the validity of the documents in "Closed Packet No. 1" any longer. The fact that they were presented by Gorbachev, head of

---

[1] Links to Strygin's pages, with digital reproductions of the alleged forgery products, are on my page "The Katyn Forest Whodunnit" towards the top. See http://tinyurl.com/ktayn-the-truth

[2] "Katyn: Sensational new documents and Ilyukhin's letter to Gryzlov about the Katyn resolution in the Russian State Duma." At
https://mythcracker.wordpress.com/2010/11/27/katyn-sensational-new-documents-and-ilyukhins-letter-to-gryzlov-about-the-katyn-resolution-in-the-russian-state-duma/
"Katyn; Mysterious 'discoveries' of the Katyn documents."
https://mythcracker.wordpress.com/2011/01/03/katyn-mysterious-discoveries-of-the-katyn-documents/

[3] See "The Katyn Forest Whodunjnit" under November, 2010.

the CPSU at the time, and are accepted by anticommunists generally, is not evidence, but the well-known logical fallacy of "argument from authority."[4]

Some persons in the "Soviets-did-it" camp founded a website – http://katyn.codis.ru/ – devoted to promoting that position and to critiquing the opposing viewpoint. A little later some researchers adhering to the "Germans-did-it" viewpoint set up another website http://www.katyn.ru/. The researchers around this website, along with others, are convinced that the "smoking gun" documents are forgeries.

To sum up:

* Despite the vast amount of documentation there is in fact a very limited amount of primary source evidence.

* The evidence is contradictory. Some of it indicates the guilt of the Soviets, while other evidence supports the guilt of the Germans.

* Some of this evidence has certainly been faked – forged, fabricated.

The Document Collections

All the evidence relevant to establishing the guilty party is in one of the following four collections of documents:

A. The German Report, *Amtliches Material zum Massenmord von Katyn* (AM) of 1943 and related documents.

B. The Soviet Burdenko Commission Report (BU) of January 1944 and related documents.

---

[4] See, for example, https://en.wikipedia.org/wiki/Argument_from_authority

C. "Closed Packet No. 1" (CP), the existence of which was announced in 1992.

D. The archeological report on excavations at the mass murder site in Volodymyr-Volyns'kiy, Ukraine (VV) of November 2011 and related documents of 2010 – 2013.

The vast majority of studies of Katyn *assume* the validity of AM and CP, thereby also assuming that the Soviets were the guilty party at Katyn. This is the "official" viewpoint. It is the only one tolerated in academia and in the mass and semi-popular media. In this version BU is assumed to be a fabrication and receives no serious consideration. This "official" version is so hegemonic, and the contrary version so marginalized, that even informed researchers often do not know that any other version exists, or simply assume that anyone who doubts the "official" version is willfully ignoring the evidence.

The contrary position, that BU is honest and AM and CP are fabrications, is held by a few Russian researchers. This position has received some limited attention in Russia. Outside Russia it is virtually ignored. The VV discoveries are either ignored or denied by everyone except by those few Russian researchers.

The Need for Objectivity

The only way to arrive at the truth in any investigation is to proceed with objectivity. It is impermissible to allow one's own preferences or preconceived ideas to interfere with the search for the truth.

Therefore we must be determined from the start to treat Katyn like an unsolved mystery. We have to set side our own preconceived ideas, preferences, and prejudices. More than that: we have to recognize our own preconceived ideas and prejudices, and then take definite steps to prevent them from biasing our investigation.

We have to work out a method of looking with particular skepticism upon evidence that tends to support our own prejudices and preconceived ideas. We also need to give especially generous consideration to any evidence that tends to contradict our own prejudices and preconceived ideas.

If we fail to do this, we will do the opposite – give an especially generous reading to evidence that tends to support our preconceived ideas, and be quick to reject any evidence that tends to disprove our preconceived ideas. We will inevitably fall prey to confirmation bias.[5] Then we will have no chance at all of discovering the truth, for even if we stumble upon it we will not recognize it.

Virtually all the purported research on Katyn, including every one of the book-length academic studies in all languages, is guilty of exactly this failure. Their authors make no attempt to be objective. Instead, they misinterpret some evidence and ignore other evidence in an attempt to bolster their own preconceived idea: that the Soviets were the guilty party.

Method

There are many fascinating aspects to each of the document collections A through D. To discuss them all would require yet another voluminous work. But that would sidestep the question of primary importance: Who was guilty? The present book focuses narrowly on that question.

Therefore this book is not an attempt to review the history of the Katyn issue. We have set ourselves a more limited but much more important aim: to solve the Katyn mystery and to determine, on the basis of the evidence now available, who was the responsible party: the Soviets or the Germans.

What is the proper, objective method for approaching and, hopefully, solving the Katyn mystery – for determining which side, the

---

[5] "Confirmation bias, also called confirmatory bias or myside bias, is the tendency to search for, interpret, favor, and recall information in a way that confirms one's preexisting beliefs or hypotheses. It is a type of cognitive bias and a systematic error of inductive reasoning." (Wikipedia, accessed 11.25.17)

Germans or the Soviets, murdered the Poles? As far as I can tell, up till now no one has asked this question.

Our first task must be to decide whether, in all of the materials that constitute document collections A through D, there exists *any primary source evidence that cannot possibly have been fabricated, forged, or faked.*

The unique value of evidence that cannot have been fabricated should be obvious. Because we want to solve the mystery, to determine who murdered the Polish POWs, only evidence that cannot possibly have been faked is worthy of our attention. The rest of the mountain of Katyn information can be used only as a mine from which to extract that limited amount of evidence whose *bona fides* cannot be questioned, which is the only relevant evidence. If we focus on this evidence, and do not permit ourselves to be distracted by the enormous quantity of writing on Katyn, we should be able to solve the Katyn mystery and discover who murdered the Polish prisoners.

To determine whether any such evidence exists, all of the documents in collections A through D must be carefully studied. We must also study the voluminous scholarly works on Katyn in order to review the results of previous researchers.

Primary-source evidence that cannot have been faked does exist. This evidence is of two types:

* Evidence found in a source which the authors of that source would never have fabricated because the evidence appears to contradict their bias. Therefore, they must have included such evidence because they simply could not do otherwise.

* Evidence cited by a source before its authors recognized the significance of that evidence for its own position on the Katyn matter. In at least one case the authors never did recognize the significance of that bit of evidence and so never used it.

The Evidence

What follows is the list of the evidence that almost certainly cannot have been faked[6] and which therefore enables us to solve the Katyn mystery. We list this evidence according to the four document collections A through D.

A. The German Report, *Amtliches Material zum Massenmord von Katyn* (AM) of 1943 and related documents.

* The spent shells found at Katyn were German.

The Germans would never have fabricated or invented this detail. In his diary Joseph Goebbels expressed dismay at the discovery of this fact. The Germans went to some trouble to argue that the Soviets could have used German bullets. We will study their argument closely.

* A badge from the Ostashkov POW camp was discovered at Katyn.

The German report AM records this detail. It sets forth the explanation that it was associated with the remains of a Polish soldier who had received it from fellow prisoners who had been previously imprisoned at Ostashkov. AM presents no evidence that any such prisoners existed. As we will see, proponents of the "Soviets-did-it" camp have not succeeded in accounting for the presence of this badge in a way that supports their contention.

* The Polish POWs whose bodies were buried at Katyn were presumed to have been in the Soviet POW camp at Kozel'sk, near Smolensk. But many POWs listed among the bodies which the Germans claimed they exhumed at Katyn had in fact been in the Starobel'sk or Ostashkov POW camps. The Germans did not remove these

---

[6] I do not write "cannot possibly have been faked" because I believe absolute statements to be offputting and unwarranted. However, for all intents and purposes, the evidence here can be assumed to be genuine.

names. Perhaps, in a rush to complete and publish their report, they did not have time to do so. Or perhaps they could not do so because others, including the Polish observers, had already seen them; or because or they did not recognize the significance of the fact that POWs from Starobel'sk and Ostashkov were found at Katyn; or because they did not know that these men had been in Ostashkov and Starobel'sk; or for some combination of these reasons.

The main point is this: the Germans would never have "faked" – invented – these names. Today both sides recognize that their presence at Katyn undermines the "official" Soviets-did-it case.

B. The Soviet Burdenko Report (BU) of January 1944 and related documents.

Like the Germans the Soviets also exhumed bodies of murdered Poles and searched them for documents. Details concerning documents found on four bodies were published in BU. A list among the Burdenko Commission materials in a former Soviet archive gives details about materials found that were not included in the final report.

One document found among the bodies is from a prisoner who was shipped from the Ostashkov POW camp to Kalinin. The Soviet investigators were unable to identify him because the first part of his last name is illegible. Therefore they did not realize that he had been in Ostashkov. They did not recognize that his presence at Katyn undermines the German report and supports the Soviet case. So they made no use of this information. Therefore they would not have fabricated it.

C. "Closed Packet No. 1" (CP), the existence of which was announced in 1992.

This collection of documents contains one document that has been faked in a clumsy manner but for some reason not discarded. There is no plausible alternative explanation for it except that it was part of a broader forgery job. (For an account of the evidence set forth by Viktor Iliukhin that *all* of "Closed Packet No. 1" consists of forgeries see the preceding pages of this chapter.)

D. The archeological report on excavations at the mass murder site in Volodymyr-Volyns'kiy, Ukraine (VV) of November 2011 and related documents (VV) of 2010 – 2013.

* Badges of two Polish POWs were found in a mass grave in this town in Western Ukraine. These two men were from the Ostashkov POW camp. According to the "official" version they were shipped to Kalinin (now Tver'), Russia, where they were executed and buried at Mednoe. Their names are on memorial plaques in the Polish cemetery there.

No one, in particular the Polish-Ukrainian archeological team that uncovered these badges among the remains of many victims of execution, questions that the remains of these men must be among those murdered and buried at VV. (The Polish-Ukrainian team did not do DNA analysis of any remains.)

* Between 96% and 98% of the shell casings found at this mass execution site are of German make and are dated "1941."

* The execution method at VV was shown by the Polish archeologist to be characteristic of the *Einsatzkommando*, or German mass murder team, led by SS Obergruppenführer Friedrich Jeckeln, the so-called "Sardinenpackung."

* Independent research by another scholar has confirmed that German troops, aided by Ukrainian nationalist auxiliaries, shot many Soviet citizens and Jews at this place soon after the invasion in June 1941.

* Soon after the publication of the Polish archeologist's report of the findings at VV Polish and Ukrainian scholars recognized that the discoveries of these two badges endangers the "official" "the-Soviets-did-it" version of Katyn.

After the report on the discoveries at VV was published it was withdrawn. The excavation was closed and the mass murders are now attributed, without any evidence, to the NKVD.

Conclusion: The Germans Murdered the Poles

All the evidence that is of undoubted authenticity, that cannot have been faked, supports the conclusion that the Germans, not the Soviets, are guilty of the mass murders of Polish POWS that are known as the Katyn massacre. All of the unimpeachable evidence either points directly to German guilt, or contradicts the "official" and only version of Soviet guilt. None of it is compatible with Soviet guilt, provides support for the "official" version, or tends to disprove German guilt.

Therefore we must conclude that it was the Germans who murdered the Poles. The evidence simply does not permit any other solution to this mystery.

I predict that this conclusion will be rejected regardless of the evidence. It directly contradicts the "official" version which is accepted by the Polish and Russian governments, by every scholarly study since at least 1992 (except for a few studies by Russian scholars that have been largely ignored), and by a host of other influential bodies including the United States Congress and the International Court of Justice at The Hague.

The reader may wonder: "Doesn't the agreement of so many authorities carry some weight?" Indeed it does! The all-but-unanimous agreement that the Soviets were guilty at Katyn has served to make a "closed book" of the Katyn issue. The "official" version that the Soviets murdered the Poles dominates both expert and public opinion. Dissenting views are not tolerated. Such views, and their authors, are ostracized, ridiculed, and otherwise ignored in the sense of never cited or referred to in further writings.

But consensus is irrelevant to the question before us. That question is: What is the truth? This question cannot be decided by appeals to authority no matter how respectable or how numerous those authorities may be. It can only be decided on the basis of primary source evidence.

The evidence is unequivocal. *None of the evidence that cannot have been faked supports the hypothesis that the Soviets shot the Poles. All of it supports the contrary hypothesis.*

In this book we will carefully scrutinize each of the document collections A through D. In the conclusion we will address the question of why the approach employed in the present book has not been applied to Katyn before this.

Chapter 2. The German Report –

Amtliches Material (AM)

The German Report *Amtliches Material zum Massenmord von Katyn* (AM) contains many contradictions. Several local resident-witnesses whose testimony is included in it later repudiated their testimony. Its result were rejected by at least three members of the international scientific team which examined bodies at German request and who signed statements claiming Soviet guilt. Two of the separate team of Polish scientific experts also withdrew their support from it.

Each of these problems could be accounted for by assuming that the German report was faked. They might also be explained by other factors. Those local resident witnesses and scientific experts who later repudiated their statements might have done so in fear of Soviet reprisal. Or they might have made their initial statements to the Germans under threat from that side. The contradictions in the report might be due to haste and carelessness as the Germans rushed the report into print.

Various documents – diaries, calendars, notebooks, envelopes, letters, newspapers, inoculation certificates, and other kinds of documents – were found in the mass graves. According to AM none were dated after sometime in April 1940. Both the German and Polish teams falsely concluded that this meant the prisoners had been executed around this time. Of course, the Germans would not have reported, or allowed the Poles to see, any documents dated later than April or, at latest, early May 1940. The Germans, not the Polish observers, controlled this process.

And the German-Polish conclusion was false anyway. The latest date is only the *terminus post quem*, evidence that the victim in question was killed sometime *after* that date, perhaps long afterwards. Some, at least, of the Germans and Poles must have understood this elementary fact. Therefore, dishonesty was surely present from the beginning in the compiling of the report.

But the fact that AM was compiled tendentiously, with some lying, and in haste, does not in itself establish who shot the Poles. It does not establish that the Soviets were not guilty and therefore that the Germans were. The fact that AM is provably dishonest on many counts proves only that the report cannot be trusted. In a later chapter we will outline some of the more important contradictions and falsehoods in the German report.

However, our purpose is not to show that AM is a highly flawed document. Our aim is to "solve the mystery," to answer the question: Who murdered the Poles? Showing that the German report is flawed and dishonest cannot do that.

We might surmise that the Germans would not have had recourse to falsification if the Soviets really had killed the Polish POWs and all the Germans had to do was to tell the truth. But this reasoning, however suggestive, is not evidence.

The Evidence in AM That Cannot Have Been Faked and Therefore Is Genuine

1. The spent shells found at Katyn were German.

This is stated multiple times in AM:

> Außerhalb der Gräber wurden eine Anzahl beschossener Pistolenhälsen mit dem Bodenaufdruck „Geco DD 7.65" gefunden; desgleichen vereinzelt in den Gräbern zwischen den Leichen. (35)

> Translated:

> Outside the graves were found a number of pistol shells with the headstamp "Geco DD 7.65." Individual examples were also found in the in the graves among the corpses.

—————————

Im Grab 2 war nämlich beim Bergen der Leichen noch eine Originalpatrone auffindbar gewesen, bei der es sich um Pistolenmunition mit der Hülsenboden-prägung „Geco 7,65 D" handelte. (73)

Translated:

During the retrieval of the corpses there was found in grave 2 an original cartridge, pistol ammunition with the "Geco 7,65 D" headstamp.

—————————

Die Hülsenböden weisen übereinstimmend die Prägung „Geco 7,65 D" auf, entsprechen sonach dem an der aufgefundenen unversehrten Patrone erho-benen Befund. (74)

Translated:

The headstamps have the same stamp "Geco 7,65 D", which corresponds to that on the unused cartridge that was found.

—————————

Analoge äußere Befunde boten vier weitere Geco-Hülsen, die am südlichen Rande des Grabes 1 nahe an dessen Kniewinkel aus dem gewachsenen Erdreich leicht rechtsseitlich vor einer daselbst stehenden Kief-er freigelegt worden waren. (74)

Translated:

Analogous exterior findings were four more Geco shells which had been left on the southern edge of grave 1 near its knee angle to the undisturbed earth and slightly to the right of a jawbone.

Die in Katyn nachgewiesenermaßen benutzte Pistolenmunition Geco Kaliber 7,65 mm gleicht der Muni-
tion, wie sie seit vielen Jahren in der Munitionsfabrik
Gustav Genschow & Co. in Durlach bei Karlsruhe (Baden) hergestellt wird. (75)

Translated:

The Geco caliber 7.65 mm pistol ammunition used at
Katyn, is the same as the ammunition which has been
manufactured for many years in the ammunition factory of Gustav Genschow & Co. in Durlach near Karlsruhe (Baden).

Hieraus ergibt sich in Verbindung mit den früheren
Ausführungen über die Hülsenbodenprägung „Geco
7,65 D", daß die zu den Erschießungen im Walde von
Katyn verwendete Pistolenmunition 1930 oder 1931
hergestellt worden sein muß. (79)

Translated:

It follows from this, in connection with the earlier remarks on the headstamp "Geco 7,65 D", that the pistol
ammunition used for the executions by shooting in the
Katyn wood was produced in 1930 or 1931.

Im gleichen Untersuchungsgang wurde daselbst unter
einer Nachbarleiche der untersten Schicht auf der
Grabsohle auch eine Geschoßhülse (Geco 7,65 mm)
aufgefunden. (87)

> In the course of the same investigation, a bullet shell
> (Geco 7.65 mm) was found on the floor of the grave
> under an adjacent corpse of the lowest layer.

The Germans claimed that only German "Geco" cartridge shells were found at Katyn. They found no other shells there. The Germans would never have freely invented this fact. Had any Soviet cartridge shells been found among the corpses, the Germans would surely have reported this. Therefore we can be confident that only German shells were found at Katyn, though not necessarily only the kind of shells identified in AM.

The Germans claimed that German cartridges were exported to the USSR in the 1920s and early 1930s. The Soviets did not deny this. But, absent countervailing evidence, German shells suggest German guilt.

Neither the Soviets nor the pro-Soviet researchers have remarked on the following two curious facts about the German report of these shell casings.

First, the Germans claimed that *all* the shell casings bore exactly the same "headstamp" - "Geco 7.65 D" or "Geco 7.65 DD." No matter who did the shooting it would be unusual for a team of at least a half-dozen shooters, shooting several thousand individuals during a period of about 6 weeks, to all use exactly the same shells, with the identical markings, and all at least nine years old.

At the German mass murder site at Volodymyr-Volyns'kiy (VV) three different types of German shells were discovered. The two most common types of shells found there are dated 1941 on the headstamps. The number of victims at VV was about 1/10 of the number at Katyn.

Second, none of the photographs of the shell casings in AM are of the headstamps. The headstamps are the only way the shells can be identified. AM contains side photographs only, useless for identifying the shells.

Image 2.1 AM p. 304 Bild 34, bottom.

The Germans at Katyn knew this, of course. When they sent some shell casings to the Gustav Genschow firm, manufacturers of the 'Geco" ammunition, for identification the Genschow firm replied with a note showing the different headstamps that identify the ammunition produced during different years.[1]

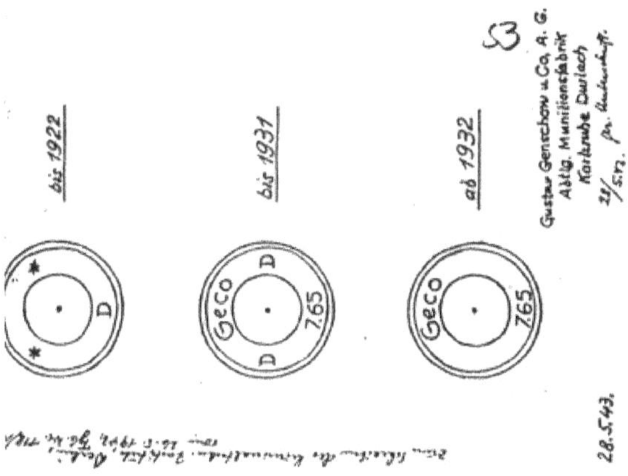

Image 2.2 Genschow firm drawing.

---

[1] This diagram raises another question. According to the Genschow firm – later, as we shall see, confirmed by Gustav Genschow himself to the U.S. Madden Commission – Genschow never manufactured any shells that said "Geco 7,65 D." Their shells either said "Geco 7.65 DD" (or "Geco DD 7.65", or "Geco D 7.65 D"). How could any German investigator have made this error if there were thousands of such shells lying in the graves?

Only photographs of the headstamps could provide evidence that it was precisely these shells that the Germans found in the Katyn burial pits. The Germans could have sent photographs of any shell casings they wanted and just claimed that they had been found at Katyn. But they did not. Instead the Germans took side views of the shells. They could easily have photographed the headstamps but they failed to do so.

The Germans were asking their readers to "believe" them. But then why bother with reproducing side views and views of bullets at all? It seems this can only be explained as an attempt to deceive the readers of the report.

Yet the Germans were right after all! Anticommunists have relied on the German report, which is the only evidence to support the "Soviets-did-it" version. And anticommunists have no incentive at all to be objective. To this day they have not questioned the fact that the Germans did not photograph the headstamps. We shall see that there are many more contradictions in the German report that have gone unremarked.

All accounts of Katyn accept the German claim that *only* these undated Geco shells were found at Katyn. This means that they accept the German AM as truthful – they *believe* the German report. This is an error, incompatible with a search for the truth, just as it would to "believe" the Soviet Burdenko Report (BU).

Joseph Goebbels, Hitler's minister of propaganda, clearly understood the problem that the finding of German shell casings *should* have posed for the German propaganda campaign around Katyn:

> Unfortunately German munitions were found in the graves of Katyn. The question of how they got there needs clarification. It is either a case of munitions sold by us during the period of our friendly arrangement with the Soviet Russians, or of the Soviets themselves throwing these munitions into the graves. In any case it is essential that this incident be kept top secret. If it

were to come to the knowledge of the enemy the
whole Katyn affair would have to be dropped.

- *The Goebbels Diaries, 1942-1943*. Praeger, 1970, p.
354.

Goebbels was correct. The use of German ammunition and *only*
German ammunition at Katyn is *prima facie* evidence of German
guilt. It is not evidence of Soviet guilt at all.

2. A badge from the Ostashkov POW camp was discovered at Katyn.

Bei einem weiteren Polen aus Grab 8 handelt es sich
um Wladislaw Czernuszewicz, geb. am 21. 10. 1898 in
Slonim, Zamkora 75, im Zivilleben Hilfsschreiber in
der Kanzlei des Kreishauptmannes im Kreis Slonim....

Abgesehen von einer mit dem Monogramm „WC"
versehenen Geldbörse, 190 Zloty in Banknoten und
einem Tabaksbeutel aus Leinenstoff fand sich letztlich
eine ovale Blechmarke unter den Asservaten vor, die
folgende Angaben enthält:

T. K. UNKWD K. O.

9 4 2 4

Stadt Ostaschkow. (AM 46)

Another Pole from grave 8 is Wladislaw Czernuszewicz, born on 21.10. 1898 in Slonim, Zamkora 75, in
the civilian life an auxiliary clerk in the office of the
district captain of the Slonim district....

In addition to a wallet with the monogram "WC", 190
zloty in bank notes and a tobacco pouch of linen cloth,
an oval sheet-metal marker was found among the ex-
hibits that contains the following information:

T. K. UNKWD K. O.

9 4 2 4

Ostashkov.

The finding of this badge caused some confusion in the German report. The report concludes that Czernuszewicz was brought from the Ostashkov POW camp to Kozel'sk by the Soviets for some purpose and then shot.

However, no one named "Czernuszewicz," "Czarnuszewicz", "Czernyszewicz", etc. is on the list of more than 4000 bodies in AM.

* A "Władysław Czarnuszewicz" – Чарнушевич Владислава Юльяновича – is on list 54/3 transported from the Kozel'sk POW camp on May 5, 1940 (Tucholski p. 716 #44).[2]

* A "Władysław Czernyszewicz" - ЧЕРНЫШЕВИЧ Владислав Леонардович – is on the list at the Starobel'sk POW camp (Tucholski p. 980 #3668).

The volume *Ubity v Katyni,* a recent attempt to shore up the official "Soviets-did-it" version, tries to solve this problem by claiming, *in brackets*, that "Czarnuszewicz" was first held at Ostashkov and then transferred to Kozel'sk in November 1939. (811) The brackets indicate that there is no evidence for this. "Ubity" assumes that the Russian "Charnushevich" (Чарнушевич) was really "Chernushevich" (Czernuszewicz).

Чарнушевич Владислав (Czarnuszewicz Władysław s. Juliana i Antoniny).... Чарнышевич Владислав Юльянович; DM-(30-33) Czernuszewicz Wladislaw

---

[2] Jędrzej Tucholski. *Mord w Katyniu: Kozielsk, Ostaszków, Starobielsk. Lista ofiar.* Warszawa: Instytut Wydawniczy Pax, 1991. This is still the official and only edition of all the Soviet NKVD transit lists and the Polish lists of victims. The Soviet lists are reprinted in the original Russian.

Among the "Kozel'sk" POWs Tucholski (90 col. 2) names Cher-nyshevich:

> Czernyszewicz Władysław Ur. 21.10.1898. Pchor. Pra-cownik Starostwa w Słonimiu.

This only confuses matters further since this is the spelling of the prisoner not in Kozel'sk or Ostashkov but in Starobel'sk.

Here is an individual named in the text of AM but not in the AM lists and about whom Tucholski and Gur'ianov (author of "Ubity") are also confused. Any honest and objective researcher should simply recognize this contradiction. But typical of dishonest schol-arship those who support the "official" version, rather than seek-ing the truth, want that version to be "seamless," without contra-dictions.

In reality, no historical or criminal investigations are "seamless," without contradictions and unexplained details. Honest investiga-tors recognize this fact. Falsifiers often strive to make their falsifi-cations appear to be "perfect."

This is a problem for the "official," "Soviets-did-it" version. A badge at Katyn from Ostashkov suggests that Polish POWs were shipped out of Ostashkov to Kalinin not to execution but for some other purpose. For if they were to be executed, why not execute them at Kalinin where, according to the "official" version, the Ostashkov POWs were murdered?

Rather than acknowledge this difficulty "Ubity" glosses over it without resolving it. In fact one must look very carefully to notice this sleight-of-hand at all. It appears to be a clumsy contradiction, unresolved because impossible to resolve, in order to get rid of the embarrassing presence of that badge from Ostashkov.

Why did the Germans mention it at all? Possibly they would have cut it out if they had had more time to produce a carefully edited version of AM.

3. Many POWs listed among the bodies exhumed by the Germans had been in the Starobel'sk or Ostashkov POW camps.

Through careful study of the primary sources we have established that a number of the bodies exhumed by the Germans at Katyn were of Poles imprisoned at and transported from the Ostashkov camp to Kalinin and from the Starobel'sk camp to Khar'kov.

The importance of the presence of these bodies at Katyn is well summarized by Andrei Pamiatnykh, a firm proponent of the "Soviets-did-it" version.

> "Посторонние" в Катыни очень важны для сторонников сталинской версии об ответственности немцев за катынское преступление. Их наличие означало бы, что в Катыни погребены узники не только Козельского лагеря, но и узники других лагерей, а значит, закрадываются сомнения в результатах немецкого следствия 1943 года и советско-российского следствия 1990-2004 годов – согласно этим результатам, в Катыни расстреляны и погребены узники Козельска, а узники Старобельска и Осташкова, по результатам советского-российского расследования, погребены в Харькове и Медном, соответственно. Вот что пишут поборники сталинской версии Владислав Швед и Сергей Стрыгин в своей главной статье по Катыни:
>
> > Но в катынских могилах были также обнаружены трупы поляков, содержавшихся в Старобельском и Осташковском лагерях. Эти поляки могли попасть из Харькова и Калинина в Смоленскую область только в одном случае — если их в 1940 г. перевезли в лагеря особого назначения под Смоленск. Расстрелять их в этом случае могли только немцы.

Translated:

"Outsiders" at Katyn are very important for supporters of the Stalin version of the responsibility of the Germans for the crime of Katyn. Their presence would mean that at Katyn were buried not only prisoners from the Kozel'sk camp, but also prisoners of other camps, and that would mean that doubts about the results of the German investigation of 1943 and the Soviet-Russian investigation of 1990-2004 are creeping in. According to the results [of these investigations] prisoners of Kozel'sk were shot and were buried at Katyn, and prisoners of Starobel'sk and Ostashkov, according to the results of the Soviet-Russian investigation, were buried at Kharkov and Mednoe respectively. Here is what Vladislav Shved and Sergei Strygin, proponents of the Stalin version, write in their main article on Katyn:

> But in the Katyn graves there were also found the corpses of Poles who had been held in the Starobel'sk and Ostashkov camps. These Poles could have arrived in Smolensk oblast' from Khar'kov and Kalinin only if in 1940 they were transported to the camps of special designation near Smolensk. In that case only the Germans could have shot them.

Pamiatnykh restates this a little later in the same article:

> Случай ШКУТЫ (или, в соответствии с моей гипотезой, ШКУТЫ-СЕКУЛЫ) представляется очень важным для сторонников сталинской версии об ответственности немцев за катынское преступление. А именно, если бы это был Шкута, и Шкута именно из Старобельска, это бы означало, что в Катыни погребены узники не только Козельска, но и «посторонние», а значит, закрадываются сомнения в результатах немецкого следствия 1943 года и советско-российского следствия 1990-2004 годов – согласно этим результатам, в Катыни рас-

стреляны погребены узники Козельска, а узники
Старобельска (по результатам советского след-
ствия) расстреляны и погребены в Харькове.
(Pamiatnykh, Problem)

Translated:

The case of SHKUTA (or, according to my hypothesis,
SHKUTA-SEKULA) is very important for the defenders
of the Stalin version that the Germans were responsible for the crime of Katyn. Namely, if this was Shkuta,
and Shkuta was from Starobel'sk, that would mean
that at Katyn there were buried prisoners not only
from Kozel'sk but also "outsiders," and that that would
mean that doubts were creeping in about the results
of the German investigation of 1943 and the Sovi-
et/Russian investigations of 1990-2004. According to
these results, at Katyn prisoners from Kozel'sk were
shot and buried, and prisoners from Starobel'sk (according to the results of the soviet investigation) were
shot and buried at Khar'kov.

The "Outsiders"

We begin by examining Pamiatnykh's attempt to resolve the question of the identity of one of the POWs on the AM list. Number
2398 in that list reads:

2398. Szkuta, Stanislaw, Ltn. Impfschein,
Mitgliedskarte d. Res.- Offiz.

No prisoner by that name is on any of the Soviet Kozel'sk (Smolensk – Katyn) transfer lists. The only Polish POW by that name in
the Soviet transfer lists was a Starobel'sk (Kharkiv – Piatykhatky)
prisoner.

#3729 - 3729. ШКУТА Станислав Францевич 1913
(Tucholski p.981)

The basic assumption of the "official" version of Katyn is that these prisoners were shot at Kalinin and Khar'kov and buried outside those cities at Mednoe and Piatykhatky respectively. The presence of Starobel'sk (or Ostashkov) POWs at Katyn would disprove that assumption and thereby would undermine the "official" version.

Accordingly Pamiatnykh attempts to show that Szkuta was actually someone else – Sekula – whose name was spelled incorrectly by the Germans. His hypothesis is that the Soviets misread the Polish barred "l" (ł) for a "t", then the ""e" for a "z" and so wrote «Шкута» - Shkuta – for "Sekuła". Pamiatnykh found a preliminary German list which appears to bear this out:

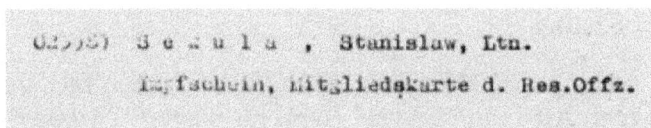

```
(02,,8)  S e ꞓ u l a  ,  Stanislaw, Ltn.
         Kriegschein, Mitgliedskarte d. Res.Offz.
```

A "Sekuła Stanisław" is named in Tucholski's Kozel'sk list:

> * Sekuła Stanisław
> Ur. 2.1 .1903, s. Szczepana i Antoniny.
> Ppor. piech. rez., 72. pp. Kierownik szkoły
> powszechnej w Sworzycach, pow. Radom,
> instruktor LOPP. (Tucholski p. 210 col. 2)

A "Sekula Stanislav" is #4 on Soviet transit list 040/3 dated April 20, 1940:

> 4. СЭКУЛА Станислава Степановича, (Tucholski p. 700)

A "Szkuta Stanisław" is also named in Tucholski's Kozel'sk list:

> Szkuta Stanisław Marian
> Ur. 7.5.1913. Ppor. art., dowódca 9. bat.
> 65. pal, od 7.9.1939 w III dyonie 21.
> pal. PCK (AM) Nr 01398. (Tucholski p. 226 col. 2)

Here Tucholski identifies this man as number 1398 in the AM list. But no such number exists in AM! The AM list skips directly from 1397 to 1399:

> 1397. Uniformierter.
> 1399. Leutnant.
> Verschiedene Zettel, Impfschein 2869

Tucholski does not explain why he states that "Szkuta" is number 01398 in the AM list when there is no such number in that list.

"Szkuta" is a problem for the "official" version because the presence at Katyn of a Starobel'sk prisoner is incompatible with the "official" version, according to which prisoners shipped from Starobel'sk to Khar'kov must have been shot there and buried nearby at Piatykhatky.

Pamiatnykh, writing in 2011, could not account for the fact that the draft German list read "Sekula" (with no barred "l") but the print version reads "Szkuta." Perhaps we can do so today.

In a later chapter we will see that the Germans captured the Soviet transit lists of POWs shipped from Kozel'sk to Smolensk, near Katyn. A "Sekula" – in Russian, "Сэкула" – is indeed on that list. The "Sekula" reading on the draft German list must have been the result of consulting the Soviet Kozel'sk transit lists. We discuss the fact that the Germans possessed these lists in a later chapter.

When the German list was revised the reading was changed to "Szkuta." The German editor must have thought that was a more accurate reading of the material before him than "Sekula." He did not realize that the only Polish POW named "Szkuta" on the Soviet transit lists was a Starobel'sk prisoner. The Germans had captured Soviet lists of POWs shipped from Kozel'sk to Smolensk but could not have known whether or not they were complete. They did not have the lists of POWs shipped from Ostashkov and Starobel'sk.

Tucholski's "Szkuta Stanisław Marian" to whom he gives the non-existent number AM 01398 must be an attempt to avoid the inconvenient presence of a Starobel'sk prisoner at Katyn – a fact that contradicts the "official" version. But Tucholski's entry has to be wrong. The Soviets had no "Szkuta" in Kozel'sk so they could not have transferred any "Szkuta" to Smolensk. "Szkuta" was transferred from Starobel'sk to Khar'kov. But he was not shot there. Instead he was transferred further to Smolensk, where he was eventually shot and buried.

But the "official" version of Katyn is wedded to the notion that the POWs were shot once they had arrived at the city to whose UNKVD they were shipped: Smolensk, Kalinin, or Khar'kov. According to the "official" version a Starobel'sk prisoner transferred to Khar'kov, as Szkuta was, but killed at Katyn, cannot have been shot by the Soviets.

Other "Outsiders"

In his article Pamiatnykh identifies two lists of "outsiders" – persons on the AM list who cannot be identified with a prisoner who, according to the Soviet transit lists, was at Kozel'sk. One list, that of IU. N. Zoria, is unpublished. The second list is the following:

> Tarczyński Marek, "Glossa do Księgi Cmentarnej Polskiego Cmentarza Wojennego w Katyniu", in "Zbrodnia Katyńska po 60 latach. Polityka, nauka, moralność." *Zeszyty Katyńskie* 12 (2000) pp. 191-198.

This article lists 231 "outsiders" or unidentified names in the German AM that are not on the Soviet Koz'elsk lists. I subtracted those that Pamiatnykh claims he has identified and searched for the rest in Tucholski. I succeeded in identifying 23 more Kozel'sk POWs who had not been identified by Tarczyński in 2000. These are not relevant to the present study.

I also identified four more POWs named in the AM list who are on the Soviet Starobel'sk lists and one who is on the Soviet Ostashkov lists.

Starobel'sk:

* Tarczyński 116   ŁAPIŃSKI Stanisław   AM #741

= ЛАПИНСКИЙ Станислав Томашевич   Starobel'sk (Tucholski p. 949, #2008)

AM 0741: 741.

Hauptmann.

Visitenkarte auf den Namen Lapinski Stanislawa, Gesangslehrer,
Fotos.

* Tarczyński 120   MAKOWSKI Janusz   WO – str. 3

= МАКОВСКИЙ Ян Юзефович Starobel'sk (Tucholski, p. 950,
#2082)

There is no Makowski in "Ubity"[3]

* Tarczyński 123   MICHALSKI Jan   AM #1536

= МИХАЛЬСКИЙ Ян Янович Starobel'sk (Tucholski p. 951,
#2114)

There is no Michałski in "Ubity." "Ubity" 512 reads "Possibly"
Michałowski Jan."

* Tarczyński 218 WRÓBEL, M. AM 161

= ВРУБЕЛЬ Марьян Войчехович   Starobel'sk (Tucholski p.
923, #483)

"Ubity" p. 242 claims this is "probably" Врубель Зыгмунт-
Миколай (Wróbel Zygmunt Mikołaj s. Edwarda i Anny). (Tucholski p. 611, #38) There is no other ВРУБЕЛЬ М. on the Soviet transit lists. Tucholski p. 252 col. 1, under Kozel'sk, reads as follows:

> Wróbel Zygmunt
> Ppor. Prawdop. jest to:
> Wróbel Zygmunt   Mikołaj

---

[3] This important volume is identified and discussed later in this chapter.

Ur. 19.11.1913. Ppor. piech. rez., baon
KOP .. Orany".

There was no prisoner named Wróbel M. at Kozel'sk.

Ostashkov:

* Tarczyński 211   WOJNOWSKI   AM 1948

= ВОЙНОВСКОГО Юзефа Францишека   Ostashkov (Tucholski p. 856, #88)

"Ubity" p. 884, #47 lists this person as still not identified. There
was no Wojnowski at Kozel'sk.

Ostashkov and Starobel'sk POWs at Katyn, from Gur'ianov

2015 saw the publication of a book that is at present the definitive
account of the Katyn victims from the "official" or "Soviets-did-it"
perspective. This is:

> Ubity v Katyni. Kniga pamiati pol'skikh voennoplen-
> nykh-uznikov kozel'skogo lageria NKVD, rasstreli-
> annykh po resheniiu Politbiuro VKP(b) 5 marta 1940
> goda. Moscow: Obshchestvo „Memorial" Izdatel'stvo
> „Zvenia" 2015. ISBN 978-5-78700-123-5

> (Translation of book title: "Men murdered at Katyn.
> Memorial book of Polish POW prisoners of the
> Kozel'sk NKVD camp shot according to the decision of
> the Politburo of the VKP(b) of March 5, 1940.")

The academic discussion is signed by Aleksandr Gur'ianov, a "Memorial Society" researcher. "Memorial" is a strongly anticommunist organization. As one might expect, "Memorial" and this
book support the "official", "Soviets-did-it" version of Katyn.

On pages 882-884 Gur'ianov names 41 persons in the AM list
whom he says no one has as yet identified. I have studied all these
names and have identified three POWs from the Ostashkov camp.
One, Wojnowski, is identified above.

The other two Ostashkov prisoners exhumed by the Germans at Katyn are:

("Ubity" p. 882):

* 6. Dudek (Дудек, имя не указано).

Военнослужащий.

V-209-0778 Dudek, имя не указано; AM-186-778 Dudek, имя

не указано (**в части тиража: Budek Karol**); PCK Dudek, имя не указано: APL3-22-0778, APL3-50-0778, APL3-77-0778, APL5-19-

0778, MUZ2-26-0778, MUZ6-17-0778.

[м.б., это Дудек Мечислав Яковлевич (список-предписание

№ 025/1 от 09.04.1940)?

The boldface text says that in part of the press run of AM "Dudek" is listed as "Budek Karol."

AM p. 186 # 778 reads:

778. **Budek, Karol**, Uniformierter,

Impfzettel, Zettel mit Namen des Obigen.

This must be the following person:

38. ЛАБУДЕК Кароль Яновича, 1895 г.р.   2568

Tucholski p. 896, #38   - Ostashkov.

This is the only POW whose name contains "Budek." Moreover, his first name was "Karol." Nine Dudeks are listed in Tucholski. None of them have "Karol" as the first name.

* 12. Jakowicz (Якович, имя не указано).
Военнослужащий, при останках найден членский билет Профсоюза работников умственного труда, выданный Главным-

правлением в г. Катовице.
V-61-02857; AM-242-2857; PCK перед фамилией
вопросительный знак в скобках: GARF-105-02857, APL7-18-
02857, APL7-152-02857, MUZ8-17-02857.

AM p. 242 #2857 reads:

2857. Jakowicz, ?, Uniformierter. Mitgliedskarte.
Tucholski p. 121 col. 1:
Jakowicz (?) ...
Z Katowic. PCK (AM) Nr 02857.

This must be:

64. ДЯКОВИЧ Микалая Гжегожа, 1892 г.р.   3224
Tucholski p. 766, #64 - Ostashkov.

Yet More "Outsiders"

The Burdenko Commission identified yet more corpses as belonging to Polish POWs from Ostashkov and Starobel'sk. Most are reported in BU. One, not used in the published report, is recorded
only in a working list of materials recovered from the corpses by
Burdenko Commission investigators. We will examine it in the
next chapter.

The mass grave of German victims at Volodymyr-Volyns'kiy,
Ukraine, contains the bodies of at least two and probably more
Polish POWs who had been Ostashkov prisoners who had been
transferred to Kalinin. But they had not been shot there, as the "official" version requires, but instead were killed at least 15 months
later and 700 miles distant from Kalinin. The "official" version
cannot accommodate this, so they must have been shot by the
Germans and their Ukrainian allies.

Another Piece of Unimpeachable Evidence

In Chapter 8 we examine the information about another "outsid-
er," a prisoner from Ostashkov whose corpse was tentatively identified by the Polish Red Cross at Katyn as that of "Krzesiński."

Conclusion

The unimpeachable evidence from the German AM is:

* the German shell casings;

* the badge from Ostashkov;

* the presence of corpses of Ostashkov and Starobel'sk prisoners found at Katyn.

All this evidence points towards German, not Soviet, guilt.

Chapter 3. The Burdenko Report

The Soviet Burdenko Report (BU) of January 1944 is the main document in which the Soviet version of Katyn is set forth. Proponents of the "official" version which blames the Soviets normally dismiss it without serious criticism.

BU contains one piece of evidence that cannot possibly have been faked and so is of prime importance for determining the guilty party. We will examine it here.

In 2007-2011 Andrei Pamiatnykh published an online article titled "From the unpublished materials of the Burdenko Commission."[1] In it Pamiatnykh, a firm adherent of the "official" Soviets-did-it version of Katyn, reproduces without comment 29 pages of a list or inventory of materials found by Burdenko Commission investigators among the bodies exhumed by the Soviet commission at Katyn in January 1944.

Among these materials are documents that the Soviet investigators found on the bodies. Some of those documents postdate the time that, according to the "official" version, the Polish POWs had been executed by the NKVD. They are "proof of life" later than the time that the "official" version insists the Polish POWs had been killed – in April and May, 1940. If they are valid, the "official" version of Katyn must be false, since the "official" version states that all the prisoners were shot by the NKVD during April and May, 1940.

But are these documents valid? Or are they fakes, forgeries created to exculpate the Soviets and planted on the bodies or in the graves by the NKVD or the Burdenko Commission? In this chapter we will:

---

[1] At http://katynfiles.com/content/pamyatnykh-burdenko-materials.html

A. summarize all the documents that purport to show that some of the prisoners whose bodies were found at Katyn lived until late 1940 and into 1941.

B. list the three identifiable Polish POWs who are associated with such documents.

C. identify and discuss the one primary source that cannot possibly have been faked.

A. Documents dated later than May 1940

Numbers at the left are to the 29 pages of investigators' notes reproduced as digital photographs in Pamiatnykh's article.

> 5. Date of April 4, 1941. Prayer book with signature Ядвиня (Jadwinia) and date "4.IV.41"

> 5. Dates of September and November, 1940. Tomasz Zigoń – dates 12.ix.40, 28.ix.40, 15.xi.40.

Zigoń's case is important. Tucholski p. 260 col 1 (Kozel'sk) reads:

> Zygoń Tomasz
> Ur. 7.3.1897, s. Tomasza i Urszuli. Podof.
> rez. Urzędnik Sekcji Prawnej Ubezpieczalni
> Społecznej w Warszawie, zam. Gołąbki
> k. Warszawy. **Wymieniony w komunikacie
> komisji Burdenki. Kozielsk lub
> Starobielsk. Porównaj listę starobielską.**

> (Translation of boldface text): Mentioned in the Burdenko commission report. Kozelsk or Starobel'sk. Compare the Starobe'lsk list.

On page 519 column 2 there is exactly the same entry, except the last sentence reads: "Porównaj listę kozielską" – "compare the Kozel'sk list."

Tucholski has no record of Zigoń in the Soviet transit lists. But Zigoń is on the "Ukrainian list"!

81. /1147/ ZIGOŃ Tomasz s. Tomasza ur. 1897

ZYGOŃ Tomasz s. Tomasza i Urszuli ur. 7.3.1897 w Soborzycach, podof. rez. zmobilizowany do Włodzimierza urzędnik sekcji prawnej Ubezpieczalni Społecznej w Warszawie, zam. Gołąbki, wymieniony w komunikacie Komisji Burdenki.

- Ukraiński Ślad Katynia 130.

Translated:

ZYGOŃ Tomasz son of Tomasz and Urszula born 7.3.1897 in Soborzyce, reserve under-officer mobilized to Włodzimierz direction of legal section of the Social Insurance Office in Warsaw, resident of Gołąbek, named in the report of the Burdenko Commission.

This means that Zigoń was arrested in the Ukraine – the list doesn't give us any more information than that. Logically, therefore, he would have been imprisoned in Starobel'sk camp. But he is not listed on the Soviet lists as one of those transferred out of Starobel'sk in April – May 1940.

Body #92 searched by the Burdenko Commission[2] must be Zigoń's because there is too much personal material on it to be anybody else's. Here is the complete entry from the Burdenko Commission's text:

> Letter from Warsaw, addressed to the Red Cross at the central bureau of POWs in Moscow, 12 Kuibyshev Street. The letter is written in Russian, in which Sof'ia

---

[2] I use the translation in volume 3 of the Madden Commission hearings. *The Katyn Forest Massacre. Hearings before the Select Committee...Part 3 (Chicago, IL) March 13 and 14, 1952* (U.S. Government Printing Office, 1952), 228-247. (Henceforth BU + page number is to this edition). This translation is identical to the Soviet translation published as a Supplement to the "Soviet War News Weekly."

ZIGON' asks to be informed of the location of her husband Tomash ZIGON', sergeant (*vakhmistr*) of cavalry. On the letter is the date September 12, 1940 (12.IX-40). On the envelope is a German postage stamp from Warsaw. IX-40 and the [cancellation?] stamp "Moscow. Post office 9, sent 28.IX-40 and a determination in red ink in Russian: "Find out which camp and send it for delivery. 15.IX-40. (signature unreadable)." (BU 246)

Since this letter was found on Zigoń's body, he must have received it. By this time he must have been in another camp. Eventually he ended up in a camp near Smolensk, probably in one of the three camps 1-ON, 2-ON, or 3-ON.[3] As we shall see, the existence of these three camps is documented in other materials found by Burdenko Commission investigators on other bodies.

So Zigoń was alive sometime after September 28, 1940, the latest date in Moscow. His body, along with many others, was exhumed at Katyn. *This means that these men were also alive at that time, or Zygoń could not have been buried among them. Therefore they were not shot by the Soviets in April-May 1940.*

That means that they were shot by the Germans and their Ukrainian Nationalist allies. This fact dismantles the "official" version of Katyn.

7. Date of June 29, 1940. Body #95 – 2 postcards dated 13.I.1940 and 29.VI. 1940.

18. Dates of April 6 and May 5, 1941.

(See more discussion below of Vladimir Araszkiewicz, under "identifiable Polish POWs.")

---

[3] "ON" is short for особого назначения, "osobogo naznachenia", "Of Special Purpose."

25. Date of November 1940. Postcard no. 0112 from Tarnopol' with postage cancellation "Тарнополь 12.Х1-40 года."

27. Dates of March 14, 1941 and May 18, 1941. See discussion below of Eduard Levandowski.

B. The three identifiable Polish POWs associated with documents placing them at other POW camps or dating from later than May 1940.

9. Receipt from Starobel'sk camp dated 26.xi.1929 [this must be 1939] in the name of "Дзевоньского Мечислава Якубовича."

Tucholski p. 896 #24: Ostashkov list 054/2 of May 5, 1940:

24. ДЗЕВОНЬСКОГО Мечислава Якубовича, 1895 г.р.

On p. 285 col. 1, in his Ostashkov list, Tucholski lists the only person of this surname among the prisoners:

Dziewięcki ...
Funkcj. PP, posterunek Ząbkowice, pow.
Będzin.

This must mean that Dziewięcki was in Starobel'sk before he went to Ostashkov. Tucholski does not mention the fact that this receipt was found at Katyn. Most of the four thousand or so bodies exhumed by the Germans at Katyn were identified by documents only. Only a few had names on clothing. None, of course, could be identified by appearance; the bodies were far too decomposed to permit facial identification.

18. Body #46 – АРАШКЕВИЧА Владимира Рудольфовича / Araszkiewicz, – note dated **25 March 1941**; receipt from camp 1-ON (1-OH) from **6 April 1941**.

Receipt from camp 1 – ON from **5 May 1941**.

Araszkiewicz appears on Ostashkov transit list 062/2 of May 19, 1940 (Tucholski 908 #7):

> 7. АРАШКЕВИЧ Владимира Рудольфовича, 1896 г.р.

Tucholski lists Araszkiewicz under Kozel'sk:

> Araszkiewicz Włodzimierz Marian Jan
> Ur. 13.9.1896, s. Rudolfa. Por. łącz.
> rez., CWŁącz. Mgr prawa, adwokat, radca
> prawny w Chodakawskich Zakładach Jedwabiu,
> zam. Łódź.
> (Tucholski p. 68 col. 2)

Tucholski does not inform his readers that Araszkiewicz was an Ostashkov prisoner shipped from there to Kalinin in May 1940 but obviously not killed there. Tucholski must have realized that this one fact would cast doubt upon the whole "official" version of Katyn.

> 27. Body #101 – ЛЕВАНДОВСКОГО Эдуарда Адамо-вича [Lewandowski]

> Receipt from Kozel'sk camp dated 19.XII. 1939. On reverse, date of **14 March 1941**;

> Receipt from camp 1-ON dated **18 May 1941**.

On page 891 #35 Tucholski lists Lewandowski in Ostashkov list 051/2, of some date in April 1940:

> 35. ЛЕВАНДОВСКОГО Эдуарда Адамовича 1893 г.р.

On page 317 col. 2 Tucholski lists him again as an Ostashkov prisoner:

> Lewandowski Edward
> Ur. 21.2.1893, s. Adama i Walerii. Kpt.
> piech. sł. st., KOP.

Tucholski does not mention that BU lists his body as having been found at Katyn. That would cast doubt on the "official" Soviets-did-it version.

Despite the fact that the Burdenko Commission claims to have identified the bodies of Araszkiewicz and Lewandowski at Katyn, both are listed in the official Polish Mednoe Cemetery book. That means that the official Polish story is that they were both shipped from Ostashkov to Kalinin – true enough, as we have seen – and then were executed there. That means that Tucholski is tacitly claiming that the BU is a fabrication.

But we have good evidence that these findings of the BU are genuine, not fabrications.

C. One Primary Source That Cannot Have Been Faked

On page 22 of the 29-page inventory of materials found by the Burdenko Commission investigators at Katyn we read the following:

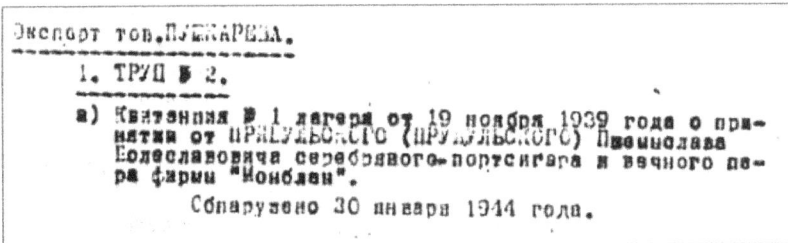

Image 3.1 Burdenko Commission inventory report

Expert com. PUSHKAREVA.

1. Body #2.

a) Receipt of camp "1" of November 19 1939 for a silver cigar case and "Montblanc" ballpoint pen from PRIAPUL'SKOGO (PRUTSUL'CKOGO) Pshemyslava

Boleslavovicha (ПРЯПУЛЬСКОГО (ПРУЦУЛЬСКОГО)
- Пшемислава Болеславовича)

The Burdenko investigator could not read the first part of the surname. He believed the surname ended in –ПУЛЬСКИЙ / -pulski or –ЦУЛЬСКИЙ / -culski. The name and patronymic are clear: in Polish, Przemysław s. Bolesław – in Russian "Пшемислав Болеславович."

No Katyn POW from any of the camps has a surname that ends in "-pulski." There is only one POW whose surname ends in "-ulski" (Russian: –УЛЬСКИЙ) and whose name is Przemysław and whose father was named Bolesław. He is in Ostashkov list 050/3 of sometime in April 1940 (Tucholski p. 886 #36):

36. КОЗЕТУЛЬСКОГО Пшемислава Болеславича

In fact, no other Katyn POW in any of the POW camps had the Christian name Przemysław and a father named Bolesław. This is the only one. So this has to be the man.

Tucholski identifies the only "Kozietulski," a "Jan," at all three camps!

At Kozel'sk: Tucholski p. 143 col. 2 – 144 col. 1:

Kozietulski Jan
Ur. 22.1 0.1899. Por. art. st. sp., oficerska
kadra OK l. Porównaj listy ostaszkowską
i starobielską.

At Ostashkov, Tucholski p. 310 col. 2:

Kozietulski Jan
Ur. 22.10.1899. Por. art. st. sp., oficerska
kadra OK l. Porównaj listy kozielską
i starobielską.

At Starobel'sk, Tucholski p. 435 col. 2:

Kozietulski Jan
Ur. 22.10.1899. Por. art. st. sp., oficerska
kadra OK l. Porównaj listy kozielską
i ostaszkowską.

Nevertheless, Volume I, page 425 of the "Mednoe Cemetery Book" – *Miednoje. Księga Cmentarna Polskiego Cmentarza Wojennego.* (Warsaw: Rada Ochrony Pamięci Walk i Męczeństwa, 2005) – does have an entry (though no photograph) for Przemysław Kozietulski, son of Bolesław.

Por. piech. **Przemysław Piotr KOZIETULSKI** s. Bolesława i Heleny, ur. 22 II 1911 w Żyrardowie. Ppor. Ze starszeństem 15 VIII 1933, por.- 1 1 1936. W 1939 służył w baonie KOP „Stołpce".

L. 050/3 (36), 123.

Cemetery book entry recreated based upon original entry.

The editors of this book probably took this entry from the Ostashkov transit list. But in reality Kozietulski is buried not at Mednoe but at Katyn.

Despite the fact that Tucholski mentions this Kozietulski three times Gur'ianov, in "Ubity," fails to mention anyone named Kozietulski. Tucholski himself does not mention Przemysław Kozietulski, son of Bolesław, at all, despite the fact that he is in the Soviet transit list and the Mednoe cemetery book.

Together with other prisoners from the Ostashkov camp Kozietulski was shipped to Kalinin. But he – and, no doubt many or even all of his fellow Ostashkov POWs – was not executed at Kalinin (or buried at Mednoe) but was sent on to Smolensk. This fact dismantles the "official" version.

Interpretation

The most important thing about the Kozietulski receipt is that BU fails to mention it. The Burdenko Commission investigator was unable to identify the person because the Burdenko Commission did not have the transit lists from the three POW camps.

Even if they had realized that this was an Ostashkov POW they probably would not have mentioned in in the report. Judging from what was included in BU the investigators were looking for documents dated later than May 1940. As we have seen, they found some. But this receipt is dated November 19, 1939. It would probably not have attracted their interest.

It is this lack of interest by the Burdenko Commission that makes it such a valuable piece of evidence.

* It cannot have been fabricated. Therefore the Burdenko Commission "expert" (investigator) really found this receipt.

* The fact that Kozietulski was in the Ostashkov POW camp and that the Burdenko Commission did not recognize this fact suggests that the other Ostashkov prisoners they identified – Dziewięcki, Araszkiewicz, and Lewandowski – are probably also genuine.

BU did not use Dziewięcki either. Once again, either they did not know that he was an Ostashkov prisoner, or they were looking only for documents dated after May 1940. This is good evidence that the Dziewięcki receipt is genuine too.

If the Kozietulski receipt were the only evidence we had of Ostashkov POWs killed and buried at Katyn we might strain for some exotic explanation to account for its presence. But in fact the opposite is the case. We have a lot of evidence, much of it independent of BU, that Ostashkov and Starobel'sk prisoners were killed and buried at Katyn.

The Kozietulski receipt supports the hypothesis that Polish prisoners from Ostashkov and Starobel'sk were killed at Katyn. They were indeed transferred to Kalinin and Kharkiv, as the Soviet transit lists show. But they were not shot there. Instead, they were further transferred to some camp or camps – again, probably the three camps 1-ON, 2-ON, or 3-ON named by the Soviets – where they did road work, were captured by the Germans, and shot.

Therefore, we have these results:

* We have a good deal of solid evidence that at least some prisoners lived after May 1940, the *terminus ante quem* that the "official" version states they must have been killed.

* We also have unimpeachable evidence that prisoners from Ostashkov and Starobel'sk camps were indeed transferred in April and May 1940 to Kalinin and Khar'kov but not to execution and burial at Mednoe and Piatykhatky Instead, they were transferred onward to Smolensk.

There is no alternative "official" version that would allow the Polish prisoners to have been killed after May 1940 or as late as 1941. Accordingly, the Kozietulski receipt constitutes further proof that the "official" version of Katyn is false.

Chapter 4. Closed Packet No. 1

The documents in this folder or "packet" are said to have been giv-
en to President Mikhail Gorbachev of the USSR and then by him to
Boris Yeltsin in December, 1991. On October 14, 1992 Yeltsin's
representative gave them to Polish President Lech Walesa.

"Closed Packet No. 1" contains the following documents:

> 1. An NKVD memorandum dated March 5, 1940 and
> numbered No.794/Б, signed by Lavrentii Beria, Peo-
> ple's Commissar of the NKVD, and recommending that
> Polish prisoners be shot.
>
> 2. Excerpt from Protocol No. 13 of the Politburo ses-
> sion of March 5, 1940 titled "A Question of the NKVD
> of the USSR."
>
> 3. Pages excerpted from Protocol No. 13 of the Polit-
> buro session of March 5, 1940, point n. 144.
>
> 4. A handwritten letter No. 632-SH signed by Ale-
> ksandr Shelepin proposing to destroy all files on the
> operation carried out by the NKVD in connection with
> the Politburo resolution of March 5, 1940 with an at-
> tached draft of a resolution of the Presidium of the
> Central Committee of the CPSU. Shelepin was Chair-
> man of the KGB between December 25, 1958 and No-
> vember 13, 1961.

For a few years after their publication these documents were accepted as the "smoking gun," as close to definitive proof of Soviet
guilt as one could wish for. Along with the German AM report they
constitute the backbone of the "official" version of Katyn.

Since 1995, and especially since 2010, there have been challenges
to the authenticity of these documents. These challenges are either

ignored or dismissed with derision by proponents of the "official" version. We have discussed this matter briefly in Chapter One.

We will take a closer look at the controversy over these documents in a later chapter. In this chapter we will discuss the one document in "Closed Packet No. 1" that has obviously been faked yet is usually ignored.

The Two Versions of "Excerpt from Protocol No. 13 of the Politburo session of March 5, 1940 titled 'A Question of the NKVD of the USSR'"

Excellent photographic copies of this document may be seen at the bottom of this page at the katyn.ru site:

http://www.katyn.ru/index.php?go=Pages&in=view&id=26

For ease of access I have created the following shortcut to this page:

http://tinyurl.com/shelepin

With the death of Sergei Strygin, this page may be removed from the Internet. If this happens the reader should copy and paste the original URL:

http://www.katyn.ru/index.php?go=Pages&in=view&id=26

...into the top search window, labeled "Wayback Machine," at the Internet Archive:

https://archive.org/

In fact it is already there, saved at multiple dates.[1] I will also put it on my Home Page.

---

[1] For example, at
https://web.archive.org/web/20160304112701/http://www.katyn.ru/index.php?go=Pages&in=view&id=26

The first document is the "excerpt." It is addressed at the top to «Тов. Б е р и я.» – "Tov[arishch] Beria" or "To Tov[arishch] Beria." At the bottom are the typed words «СЕКРЕТАРЬ ЦК» – "Secretary of the CC [Central Committee]."

It is the second document that interests us here. This appears to be a carbon copy of the first document on which a few changed have been made so crudely that anyone can notice them immediately.

> * The words «Тов. Б е р и я.» have been removed and replaced by the words «Тов. Шелепину" meaning "To Tov[arishch] Shelepin."

> * The date at the upper left has been changed from «5 . м а р т а 1940 г.» (March 5, 1940) to «27 . февраля 1959 г.» (February 27, 1959), without double spacing between the letters of the word «февраля» (of February).

> * At the bottom of the document the words «И. СТА-ЛИН» (= J. Stalin) have been typed in capital letters that stand clearly out from the much darker and heavier type of the carbon copy.

> * At the bottom of the carbon copy but not of the original is the seal of the Central Committee of the Communist Party of the Soviet Union. The name of the Party was official changed from "All-Union Communist Party (bolshevik)" at the 19th Party Congress in October, 1952. The earlier name for the Party is on the letterhead. The form itself is from the 1930s, with "193" preprinted where the date should go.

> * On the Shelepin document but not on the Beria document there is a faint stamp in the upper left corner, above the first word in the letterhead, «Всесоюзная», in the middle of which are the words «НЕ СЖИГАТЬ» - "Ne szhigat'," "Do not burn." See the figure below.

Image 4.1 The Shelepin document (detail)

No one has come up with a satisfactory explanation for this document.

* It is not mentioned at all by either Cienciala or Sanford. Sanford's book is an important study in English[2], while Cienciala and Materski is the definitive one-volume study in any language.

* In the official Polish government publication *Katyn. Documents of Genocide. Documents and Materials from the Soviet archives turned over to Poland on October 14, 1992*. Edited by Wojciech Materski, introduction by Janusz I. Zawodny (Institute of Political Studies, Polish Academy of Sciences, 1992), it is published on pages 12-13 but without any comment whatever.

Despite the fact that the documents of "Closed Packet No. 1 are the only evidence that the Soviet government ever planned to shoot the Polish POWs, this document is passed over in silence by defenders of the "official" version of Katyn. It is easy to understand this as the silence of embarrassment. This document undermines the case for the bona fides of all the "Closed Packet No. 1" documents.

Shved (384) and Prudnikova and Chigirin (518) cite Shelepin's friend Valerii I. Kharazov as saying that Shelepin did in fact learn

---

[2] George Sanford. *Katyn and the Soviet Massacre of 1940: Truth, Justice and Memory* (BASEES / Routledge Series on Russian and East European Studies). London, UK: Routledge, 2009.

about the Katyn documents early in his tenure as head of the KGB. Document number 4 of "Closed Packet No. 1" contains a proposal from Shelepin that all the files relating to Katyn be destroyed. According to Kharazov Khrushchev did not agree with this proposal.

So either Kharazov was mistaken and the files were destroyed, or they were not destroyed at all. At any rate it appears that this destruction, actual or only contemplated, had something to do with the stamp "Do not burn" on the Shelepin version of Document 2.

It is hard to imagine archivists giving permission to alter archival documents in the way that the Shelepin version of Document 2 has been altered. But if the Beria version of Document 2 were a forgery and carbon copies were made, then the Shelepin version might be understood as an experiment to see what further forgery was possible. But whatever the motive, the "Shelepin" document has been falsified.

The addition of Stalin's name at the bottom also suggests an attempt at forgery. Khrushchev organized an attack on Stalin over a number of years. A genuine document of 1940 signed "Secretary of the C.C." would not need to carry Stalin's name. There were a number of secretaries, any one of whom could sign a document as "secretary." In 1940 there was no longer a post of General Secretary. But by Khrushchev's day the office of General Secretary had been revived for Khrushchev himself.

An attempt to implicate Stalin in the Katyn massacres might be less persuasive if Stalin's name were not on the letter.

Conclusions

> * The Shelepin version of Document 2 was certainly created during Khrushchev's time.

> * The manipulation of the "Beria version" of Document 2 suggests that it may have been created at the same time and so may also be a forgery.

        * The "do not burn" stamp on the Shelepin version
        suggests that there was a plan to burn at least some
        documents.

        * The addition of Stalin's name suggests that this was
        an aborted attempt to produce false evidence in order
        to accuse Stalin of guilt in the Katyn massacre.

That, in turn, suggests that such documents did not already exist. For if the "Beria Letter" with Stalin's bold and readable signature had been available in 1959 there would have been no need to contemplate adding "J. STALIN" to Document 2, as the Shelepin letter does.

Kharazov's testimony, and remarks made by an aged Shelepin to investigators in the early 1990s, are good evidence that some kind of Katyn forgery was contemplated during Khrushchev's day. It is no wonder that Khrushchev did not go through with it. He himself was in the Politburo in March 1940. Khrushchev was in the Ukraine but visited Stalin's office during these months, for example on March 1, April 3, 4, and 5, and May 21 and 22, 1940.[3] If Khrushchev decided to blame Stalin for the Katyn massacre he would have also implicated himself.

We do not know what process led to the fabrication of the Shelepin version of Document 2 or why it was not destroyed. We are fortunate that it wasn't destroyed, since it provides solid evidence that the other documents in "Closed Packet No.1" may also have been forged. It provides additional evidence, together with the purported forgery documents adduced by Viktor Iliukhin in 2010. Therefore, at the very least, we cannot accept the CP documents at face value as primary source evidence.

There is a lot of other evidence that these documents are forgeries. We will examine some of the most important points of this evi-

---

[3] "Posetitlei kremlevskogo kabineta I.V. Stalin." *Istoricheskii Arkhiv* 2, 1996. ("Visitors to the Kremlin office of J.V. Stalin.")

dence in a later chapter. But in my opinion none of the internal problems in these documents are in themselves conclusive evidence of forgery.

And – it is important to recognize this also – it is likewise impossible to prove from internal evidence that the documents in "Closed Packet No. 1" are genuine. They are of questionable validity. As such, they are useless as evidence.

On the basis of a study of the documents alone we cannot say that *all* the documents in "Closed Packet No. 1" are forgeries. But we *can* make that statement about the Shelepin version of Document 2. It is definitely a forgery. The presence of a glaring forgery in "Closed Packet No. 1" casts a shadow of suspicion over the other documents in that packet.

Chapter 5. The Excavations at Volodymyr-Volyns'kiy

In 2011 and 2012 a joint Polish-Ukrainian archeological team partially excavated a mass execution site at the town of Volodymyr-Volyns'kiy, Ukraine. Shell cases found in the burial pit prove that the executions there took place no earlier than 1941. In the burial pit were found the badges of two Polish policemen previously thought to have been murdered hundreds of miles away by the Soviets in April-May 1940 during the Katyn massacre.

The Badges

1. Jósef Kuligowski

In May 2011 Polish news media reported that in the Western Ukrainian town of Volodymyr-Volyns'kiy a numbered metal badge had been unearthed which had been identified as that of a Polish policeman, Jósef Kuligowski. According to the "official" or "the Soviets did it" version of Katyn it had been assumed that Kuligowski, along with thousands of other Polish POWs, had been executed by the Soviet NKVD at Kalinin (now Tver'), Russia, and buried with other such victims at Mednoe, outside of the town.[1]

> Czy osoby z Listy Katyńskiej mordowano również na Grodzisku we Włodzimierzu Wołyńskim?! Odnaleziona przez ukraińskich archeologów odznaka Policji

---

[1] A photograph of Kuligowski's badge may be viewed at
http://katyn.ru/images/news/2012-12-29-zheton-1441.jpg and a somewhat lighter, more legible copy at http://msuweb.montclair.edu/~furrg/research/kuligowski_badge_1441.jpg
Most of the images and graphics mentioned in this book will be found on the "Images" page at https://tinyurl.com/furr-katyn-images .

Państwowej o numerze 1441 / II na to wskazuje. Jak nas poinformował pan Piotr Zawilski, dyrektor Archiwum Państwowego w Łodzi odznaka o tym numerze należała do posterunkowego Józefa Kuligowskiego z IV komisariatu w Łodzi. Informacja o przydziale i numerze służbowym pochodzi z maja 1939 roku. Nazwisko posterunkowego figuruje na jednej z list dyspozycyjnych dla obozu w Ostaszkowie. Dotychczas uważano, że został zamordowany w Kalininie i spoczywa w Miednoje. Jak wytłumaczyć fakt, że odznaka Józefa Kuligowskiego znaleziona we Włodzimierzu Wołyńskim? Czy zginął w Kalininie, czy we Włodzimierzu?[2]

My translation:[3]

Were persons from the Katyn List also murdered at Grodzisk in Włodzimierz Wołyński?! This is indicated by the National Police badge number 1441 / II found by Ukrainian archaeologists. As Mr Piotr Zawilski, director of the National Archive in Łódź has informed us, the badge with this number belonged to constable Jósef Kuligowski of the IV commissariat in Łódź. Information concerning the issuance and service number is from May 1939. The surname of the constable figures on one of the dispositional lists for the camp at Ostashkov. Up to now it was believed that he had been murdered in Kalinin and lies in Mednoe. How to explain the fact that Jósef Kuligowski's badge has been found at Włodzimierz Wołyński? Was he killed at Kalinin or at Włodzimierz?

---

[2] "Osoby z Listy Katyńskiej mordowano we Włodzimierzu Wołyńskim?!" (Persons from the Katyn List murdered at Włodzimierz Wołyński?!), ITVL May 25, 2011. At http://www.itvl.pl/news/osoby-z-listy-katynskiej-mordowano-we-wlodzimierzu-wolynskim--

[3] All translations are mine.

This account continues by identifying Kuligowski as one of the men who, according to the "official" version, were killed as a part of the Katyn massacre.

The discovery occasioned considerable discussion in the Polish press about the relationship between the Katyn Massacre and this site near the Ukrainian town of Volodymyr-Volyns'kiy (Polish: Włodzimierz Wołyński; Russian: Vladimir-Volynskii).[4] At that time no one doubted that this was a site of Soviet NKVD killings.[5]

The Ukrainian media also reported the excavations under the assumption that the Soviet NKVD was responsible for the killings, as in the following account in the Ukraine-wide online newspaper *Tyzhden.ua* of October 4 2011.[6]

> І хоча офіційної версії щодо того, хто ці люди й чому були розстріляні, ще немає, науковці схиляються до думки, що замордовані – жертви НКВС 1941 року. Польські піддані, військові й цивільні, заможний клас. Про це свідчать знайдені на місці страти артефакти.

---

[4] The surrounding region of Volhynia was part of Austria-Hungary until the end of World War I; then part of Poland; then part of the Soviet Ukraine; then occupied by the Germans; then again part of Soviet Ukraine, and is now part of Ukraine.

[5] See "Tropem zbrodni NKWD pod Włodzimierzem Wołyńskim" (Trail of NKVD crime near Włodzimierz Wołyński) at http://wolyn.btx.pl/index.php/component/content/article/1-historia/168-tropem-zbrodni-nkwd-pod-wodzimierzem-woyskim.html ; Włodzimierz Wołyński - groby polskich ofiar NKWD" (graves of Polish victims of the NKVD) at http://www.nawolyniu.pl/artykuly/ofiarynkwd.htm ; "Czyje mogiły odnaleziono we Włodzimierzu Wołyńskim?" (Whose graves found at Włodzimierz Wołyński?) http://wpolityce.pl/depesze/10407-czyje-mogily-odnaleziono-we-wlodzimierzu-wolynskim This last article speaks of „ofiar pomordowanych przez NKWD w latach 1940-1941 w sowieckiej katowni na zamku we Włodzimierzu Wołyńskim" (victims murdered by the NKVD in 1940-1941 in the Soviet execution chamber in the castle at Włodzimierz Wołyński). Many more similar articles could be cited.

[6] "Волинська Катинь. У Володимирі-Волинському знайдено масове поховання жертв НКВС 1939–1941 років." Tyzhden'.ua October 4, 2011. At http://tyzhden.ua/Society/31329

Ось два жетони офіцерів польської поліції, і
оскільки на них є номери, то ми вже знаємо, кому
вони належали: Йозефу Куліговському та Людвігу
Маловєйському. Обидва з Лодзя. За документами
НКВС, одного з них розстріляно в Калініні (Твер),
другого – в Осташкові біля Харкова.

Translated:

And although there is as yet no official version of who
these people were and why they were shot, scientists
are inclined to think that the murdered people were
victims of the NKVD in 1941. Polish citizens, military
and civilians, the wealthy class. This is what the arti-
facts found at the execution site suggest.

Here are two badges of officers of the Polish police,
and since there are numbers on them we already
know to whom they belonged: to Josef Kuligovs'kiy
and Liudvig Maloveis'kiy. Both were from Lodz. According to NKVD documents one of them was shot at
Kalinin (Tver'), the other at Ostashkov [sic] near
Kharkiv.[7]

In November 2012 the Polish members of a joint Polish-Ukrainian
archaeological group published a report on the excavation of this
mass murder site. In mass grave No.1, 367 sets of human remains
were exhumed and examined during 2011, and 232 more sets in
2012. The locations of more mass graves were also determined.
Concerning the finding of Kuligowski's badge this report reads as
follows:

Była to odznaka Polskiej Policji Państwowej z nume-
rem 1441, która należała do: Post. PP Józef KULIGOW-
SKI s. Szczepana i Józefy z Sadurskich, ur. 12 III 1898 w
m. Strych. WWP od 20 VI 1919. 10 pap. Uczestnik woj-

---

[7] The journalist has made several errors here. No NKVD documents mention any shooting.

ny 1920, sczególnie odznaczył się w bitwie pod Mariampolem 24 V 1920. W policji od l921. Początkowo
służbę pelnił w woj. tarnopolskim. Następnie od 1924
przez wiele lat w Łodzi – w 1939 w V Komis. W sierpniu 1939 zmobilizowany do l0 pal. Odzn. VM V kl.
nr679.L. 026/l (15), 35[.]6.; za: red. Z. Gajowniczek, B.
Gronek „Księga cmentarna Miednoje," t. l, Warszawa
2005, s. 465. Odznaka została przekazana do
miejscowego muzeum.[8]

It was a Polish National Police badge number 1441,
which belonged to: Constable of the National Police
Jósef Kuligowski son of Stephen and of Josepha née
Sadurska, b. 12 March l898 in the village of Strych. In
the Polish army on 20 June 1919. 10 pap. Participant
in the 1920 war, particularly distinguished himself at
the Battle of Mariampol 24 May 1920. In the police
from l921. Initially served in the Tarnopol region.
Then from 1924 for many years in Lodz – in 1939 in
the V Komis. In August 1939 mobilized to l0 pal. as
Nr679.L class V VM. [NKVD transfer list] 026 / l ([po-
sition]15), 35 [.] 6, according to: ed. Z. Gajowniczek, B.
Gronek,, "Mednoye Cemetery Book," Vol. l, Warsaw
2005, p. 465. The badge has been transferred to the
local museum.

---

[8] Sprawozdanie z Nadzoru Nad Badaniami Archeologiczno-Ekshumacyjnymi na Terenie
Rezerwatu Historyczno-Kulturowego Miasta Włodzimierza Wołyńskiego (Ukraina). Opra-
cowanie zespołowe pod kierunkiem dr Dominiki Siemińskiej. Rada Ochrony Pamięci Walk i
Męczeństwa. (Report of the Supervision on the Archaeological-Exhumation Investigation in
the Area of the Reservation of the Historical-Cultural Town of Volodymyr-Volyns'kiy
(Ukraine). A Team Description under the Direction of Dr. Dominika Siemińska. Council for
the Commemoration of Struggle and Martyrdom). Toruń, 2012, Note, pp. 1-2. At
http://www.kresykedzierzynkozle.home.pl/attachments/File/Rap.pdf

Image 5.1 Artist's rendering of badge of Constable Police Constable Jósef Kuligowski unearthed at Volodymyr-Volyns'kiy

Here is the entry for Kuligowski from Volume One of the "Mednoe Cemetery Book":[9]

Post. PP **Józef KULIGOWSKI** s. Szczepana i Józefy z Sadurskich, ur. 12 III 1898 wm. Strych. W WP od 20 VI 1919, 10 pap. Uczestnik wojny 1920, szczególnie od-znaczył się w bitwie pod Mariampolem 24 V 1920. W policji od 1921. Początkowo służbę pełnił 2 w woj. tarnopolskim. Następnie od 1924 przez wiele lat w Łodzi –w 1939 w V Komis. W sierpniu 1939 zmobilizowany do 10 pal.   Odzn. VM V kl. nr 679.

L. 026/1 (15), 35[.]6.

Cemetery book entry recreated based upon original entry.

Kuligowski was taken prisoner by the Red Army sometime after September 17, 1939, when Soviet troops entered Eastern Poland to prevent the German Army from establishing itself hundreds of miles further east at the USSR's pre-September 1939 border. He was held in the Ostashkov prisoner-of-war camp in Kalinin oblast' (province), now renamed Tver' oblast'. In April 1940 along with other prisoners he was transferred from Ostashkov to the town of Kalinin (now Tver'). After that there is no further information about him.

---

[9] *Miednoje. Księga Cmentarna Polskiego Cmentarza Wojennego.* Warsaw: Rada Ochrony Pamiêci Walk i Mêczeństwa 2005. Tom 1, 465.

Kuligowski is counted as one of the victims of the "Katyn Massacre." What purports to be a record of his transfer, with the word "Mord" (Murder) added, is on one of the official Polish websites about Katyn.[10]

Nazwisko: **Kuligowski**

Imię: **Józef**

Imię ojca **Szczepana**

Data urodzenia: **1898**

LP	Opis losów	Początek r	m	d	Koniec r	m	d	Kraj	Woj/Oblast	Pow.	Miej.
1	Mord				1940	04		Rosyjska FSRR	Kalinińska (Twerska)		Twer
2	Obóz				1940	04		Rosyjska FSRR	Kalinińska (Twerska)		Ostaszków

LP	opis źródła	sygnatura
1.	Ankiety personalne wypełniane przez samych represjonowanych bądź ich rodziny, zbiory Ośrodka KARTA, sygnatura IR/ numer ankiety.	IR -/11707
2.	Listy wywozowe NKWD (kwiecień-maj 1940) z Ostaszkowa, kopia w zbiorach Ośrodka KARTA - strona, pozycja.	OST/ -148-152/15

As stated in the Polish media account of May 25, 2011, Kuligowski's name is on the transfer lists of Ostashkov prisoners reproduced in the official account by Jędrzej Tucholski published in 1991.[11] Kuligowski is also listed in other recent Polish lists of

---

[10] http://www.indeks.karta.org.pl/pl/szczegoly.jsp?id=11036 According to the Home Page „Indeks Represjonowanych" (http://www.indeks.karta.org.pl/pl/index.html) this online record is a digital version of the contents of the official volume: Maria Skrzyńska-Pławińska, ed. *Rozstrzelani w Twerze : alfabetyczny spis 6314 jeńców polskich z Ostaszkowa rozstrzelanych w kwietniu-maju 1940 i pogrzebanych w Miednoje, według źródeł sowieckich i polskich.* Warszawa : Ośrodek KARTA, 1997.

[11] Jędrzej Tucholski. *Mord w Katyniu: Kozielsk, Ostaszków, Starobielsk. Lista ofiar.* Warszawa: Instytut Wydawniczy Pax, 1991, p. 810. No. 15: NKVD list No. 026/1 of 13 April 1940, position 15. In spite of the presence of Kuligowski's name on this NKVD list, for some reason the alphabetical section of Tucholski (p. 314 col. 2) lists Kuligowski on its "victims list" (lista ofiar) as "probably Ostashkov" (Prawdop. Ostaszków).

Katyn victims.[12] Naturally the original Russian record of prisoner transfer reprinted in Tucholski's *Mord w Katyniu* does not contain the word "Mord" (=murder).

The Polish archaeologist in charge of the excavations and author of the report, Dr. Dominika Siemińska, has determined that the victims buried in the mass grave in which this badge was found were killed no earlier than 1941:[13]

> Z pewnością stwierdzono, że zbrodnia została dokonana nie wcześniej niż w 1941 roku. (p. 4)

> *Translated:*

> It can be confirmed with certainty that the crime did not take place earlier than 1941.

The time period of execution was determined from the shell casings found in the graves. All but a very few were of German manufacture and are datable to 1941.

Some of the bodies were arranged in the "sardine-packing" (*Sardinenpackung*) formation[14] favored by Obergruppenführer[15] Friedrich Jeckeln, commander of one of the *Einsatzgruppen*, extermination teams whose task it was to carry out mass executions. A

---

[12] See "INDEKS NAZWISK - Katyń - zamordowani przez NKWD w 1940 r."
http://www.ornatowski.com/index/katyn.htm

[13] See above, note 14.

[14] A description of this method of execution may be found on the English-language Wikipedia page on Jeckeln at
http://en.wikipedia.org/wiki/Friedrich_Jeckeln#World_War_II_mass_murderer

[15] Equivalent to full or four-star General, the highest SS rank aside from that of Heinrich Himmler, whose rank was Reichsführer-SS.

photograph of the bodies in grave no. 1 shows this arrangement of bodies.[16]

Also, a large percentage of the bodies in the mass graves are of children. There has never been any evidence that he Soviets executed children. There is a great deal of evidence that the Germans did. So the evidence is strong that this is a site of German, not Soviet, mass executions.

This conclusion is confirmed by the recent research of other Ukrainian scholars concerning this very burial site. Relying on evidence from German war crimes trials, eyewitness testimony of Jewish survivors, and research by Polish historians on the large-scale massacres of Poles by Ukrainian Nationalists, Professor Ivan Katchanovski and Volodymyr Musychenko have established that the victims buried at this site were mainly Jews but also Poles and "Soviet activists."

Katchanovski concludes that Ukrainian authorities have tried to throw the blame onto the Soviet NKVD in order to conceal the guilt of the Ukrainian Nationalist forces who are celebrated as "heroes" in today's Ukraine, including in Volodymyr-Volyns'kiy itself.[17]

---

[16] Photograph at http://katyn.ru/images/news/2012-12-29-gruppa4.jpg (accessed March 5 2018). It is taken from page 8 of the Polish archeological report cited above. A description of this method of execution may be found on the English-languageWikipedia page on Jeckeln at http://en.wikipedia.org/wiki/Friedrich_Jeckeln#World_War_II_mass_murderer

[17] Volodymyr Musychenko. "Закатованними Жертвами Були Євреї?" *Slovo Pravdy* (Volodymyr-Volyns'kiy) March 29, 2011. At http://spr.net.ua/index.php?option=com_content&view=article&id=919:2011-09-29-07-41-57&catid=1:newsukraine ; Ivan Katchanovski, "Katyn in Reverse in Ukraine: Nazi-led Massacres turned into Soviet Massacres." *OpEd News*, December 13, 2012, at http://www.opednews.com/articles/Katyn-in-Reverse-in-Ukrain-by-Ivan-Katchanovski-121212-435.html ; I. Katchanovski, "Сучасна політика пам'яті на Волині щодо ОУН(б) та нацистських масових вбистств," Ukraina Moderna No. 19 (April 30 2013). At http://www.uamoderna.com/md/199

Images 5.2 and 5.3 Jeckeln during the war (L.); in Soviet captivity (R.) He was tried and executed for war crimes in Riga, Latvian SSR, in 1946.

Kuligowski was indeed transported from Ostashkov POW camp to Kalinin in April 1940. But he was not shot until 1941 at the earliest. This means that the transportation lists, which the "official" Soviets-did-it version of Katyn assumes to be lists of victims being shipped off to be shot, are not that at all. Kuligowski was transported to Kalinin in April 1940 by the Soviets not in order to be shot but for some other reason. He remained alive, to be captured and executed by the Germans, most likely in the second half of 1941. Moreover, Volodymyr-Volyns'kiy is more than 700 miles (1200 km) from Kalinin (Tver').

This is the major deduction from this discovery that is relevant to our understanding of the Katyn Massacre case: The fact that a Polish POW's name is on one of the Soviet transportation lists can no longer be assumed to be evidence that he was on his way to execution, and therefore that he was executed by the Soviets.

2. Ludwik Małowiejski

There is evidence that more Polish POWs are buried in these same mass graves, and therefore were executed at the same time, by the

Germans in 1941 or 1942. The epaulette of a Polish policeman's uniform and Polish military buttons were found in grave No. 2.[18]

In September 2011 Polish media reported that police badge number 1099/II belonging to Senior Police Constable (*starszy posterunkowy*) Ludwik Małowiejski had been found in the Volodymyr-Volyns'kiy mass graves.[19] It had been claimed that, like Kuligowski, Małowiejski was a Katyn massacre victim whose body was buried in a mass grave at Mednoe near Kalinin, where, according to the "official" version, other Katyn victims shot by the NKVD in 1940 are buried.

Małowiejski's name is also on the recent Polish lists of Katyn victims.[20] Like Kuligowski he is memorialized in the "Mednoe Cemetery Book" – in this case, Volume 2, page 541:

St. post. PP **Ludwik MAŁOWIEJSKI** s. Jakuba i Marinnny z Jagiełłów, ur. 22 VIII 1890 W Żychlinie. Żołnierz I Korpusu Polskiego, plut. W policji od 1919. Od 14 I 1930 przeniesiony do Rez. Konnej m. Łodzi i tam nadal pełnił służbę we wrześniu 1939. Do Ostaszkowa przniesiony ze szpitala w Szepietówce. Odzn. MN, MPzaW, MDzON.

L. 050/3 (76), 7783.

Cemetery book entry recreated based upon original entry.

---

[18] Photos available at
http://msuweb.montclair.edu/~furrg/research/polskie_guziki_pagon_VV2012.jpg from the Polish archaeological report.

[19] "Kolejny policjant z Listy Katyńskiej odnaleziony we Włodzimierzu Wołyńskim.." [Another policeman on the Katyn List is found in Volodymyr-Volynsky]. At
http://www.itvl.pl/news/kolejny-policjant-z-listy-katynskiej-odnaleziony-we-wlodzimierzu-wolynskim I have not been able to find any photograph of Małowiejski's badge.

[20] "INDEKS NAZWISK - Katyń - zamordowani przez NKWD w 1940 r." At
http://www.ornatowski.com/index/katyn.htm

His transfer record with the word "Mord" (murder) added, like Kuligowski's, is also on the same official Polish Katyn website:[21]

Nazwisko: **Małowiejski**

Imię: **Ludwik**

Imię ojca: **Jakuba**

Data urodzenia: **1890**

:

LP	Opis losów	Początek			Koniec			Kraj	Woj/Oblast	Pow.	Miej.
		r	m	d	r	m	d				
1	Obóz				1940	04		Rosyjska FSRR	Kalinińska (Twerska,		Ostaszków
2	Mord				1940	04		Rosyjska FSRR	Kalinińska (Twerska)		Twer

LP	opis źródła	sygnatura
1.	Ankiety personalne wypełniane przez samych represjonowanych bądź ich rodziny, zbiory Ośrodka KARTA, sygnatura IR/ numer ankiety.	IR -/11591
2.		*OSTA -/290-297/76

Table recreated based on original.

Like Kuligowski's, Małowiejski's name is also on the Russian lists of prisoners shipped out of the Ostashkov camp.[22]

In 2011 it was still claimed that the mass graves at Volodymyr-Volyns'kiy were those of victims of the Soviet NKVD. Therefore this apparent discrepancy about the place of burial of one victim received little publicity. Since then the Polish archaeological team has definitively dated the site as 1941 at the earliest and argues that it is an SS *Einsatzgruppe* mass murder site. This in turn means that Kuligowski and Małowiejski were killed by the Germans in 1941, not by the Soviets in 1940. Other Polish POWs – perhaps

---

[21] The following text is from http://www.indeks.karta.org.pl/pl/szczegoly.jsp?id=11445

[22] Tucholski p. 887 No. 76. Małowiejski was in a transport of 100 Polish prisoners sent to the Kalinin NKVD on April 27, 1940. His name is also on Tucholski's alphabetical list (p. 322, col. 2) as is Kuligowski's, and on other official lists of Katyn victims.

many others – claimed to have been Katyn victims may well have been shot along with Kuligowski and Małowiejski, and be buried in the mass graves at Volodymyr-Volyns'kiy or elsewhere in the Ukraine.

An article by Sergei Strygin contains photographs of the memorial tablets of both Kuligowski and Małowiejski at the special Polish memorial cemetery at Mednoe. These and the thousands of other memorial tablets at this site reflect the assumption that the "transit lists" were really "execution lists" – an assumption that the discoveries at Volodymyr-Volyns'kiy prove is false.

It is clear today that neither man's body is buried at Mednoe. *The question now is: Are any of the Polish POWs whose memorial tablets are at Mednoe alongside those of Kuligowski and Małowiejski really buried there? At present there is no reason to think so.*

Images 5.4 and 5.5 The memorial plaques of Kuligowski and Małowiejski at Mednoe Cemetery. They are not buried there.
(Thanks to Aleksandr Zenin of Tver' and his colleagues)

The Cover-Up

Kuligowski's name, the discovery of his badge, and the information that ties him to Katyn, are only mentioned in a footnote in the Polish archeologist report. The Katyn information is cited in such an abbreviated manner that only those expert in the Katyn issue will even recognize the connection.

For example, this is how the footnote in the Polish archeologists' report refers to the entry for Kuligowski on the Soviet transit list in Tucholski's book:

026/l (15), 35[.]6

Here is the actual citation of Kuligowski's name in Tucholski, p. 810:

15. КУЛИГОВСКОГО Юзефа Степановича, 1898 г.р. 35.6

The number of the transit list, 026/1, is at the top of Tucholski, page 810. Kuligowski's name is number 15 on this list. The entry "35[.6]" refers to the "delo" or case file in the NKVD list – information that is irrelevant since this file has not been found and was probably destroyed long ago.

One might assume that this, by far the most significant discovery of the whole Volodymyr-Volyns'kiy dig, would be highlighted. Instead it is "buried" in this footnote and virtually disguised with obscure words. There can be little doubt that this was done for fear that this discovery would undermine the claim that the Soviets committed the massacre at Katyn – a claim which Polish authorities want not only to keep alive, but to continue maintain is unquestionably true.

No doubt that is why, Małowiejski's name is omitted altogether from the Polish archeologist report. *This* important discovery is completely ignored!

These two facts: the "burying" of the reference to Kuligowski and the complete omission of the discovery of Małowiejski's badge, are good evidence that the Polish archeologists wanted to play down the Katyn connection at Volodymyr-Volyns'kiy. But in the *Ukraini-*

an archeologists' report on the Volodymyr-Volyns'kiy dig neither man's name is even mentioned!

The Shell Casings

Details of the shell casings, 150 in all, found in grave No. 1 are given in footnote 3, page 8 of the Polish report but are absent from the Ukrainian report:

> 1. "kam, 67, 19, 41"- 137 szt; 2. "dnh, *, l , 41" - 7 szt; 3. Geco, 9 mm - l szt; 4. łuski bez oznaczeń, 7,62 x 25, wz. 30, produkcja ZSRR - 5 szt.
>
> *Translated:*
>
> 1. "kam, 67, 19, 41" – 137 units; 2. "dnh, *, 1, 41" – 7 units; 3. Geco, 9 mm. – 1 unit; 4. Shells without markings, 7.62 x 25 caliber, USSR production of 1930s type – 5 units.

One hundred forty-four, or 96% of the 150 shells found, were of German make and can be dated to 1941. These identifying marks on shell casings are known as "headstamps." According to the analysis by Sergei Strygin "kam, 67, 19, 41" signifies the Hasag factory in Skarżysko-Kamienna, "67" the percentage of copper in the bullet, "19" the lot number, and "41" the year of production. "dnh *, 1, 41" signifies the Dürlach factory, "*" means the shell was jacketed in brass; "1" is the lot number, and "41" the year of production.

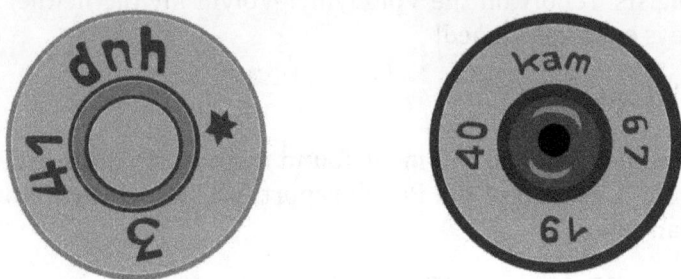

Images 5.6 and 5.7 Artist's rendering of shells of the type found in graves
No. 1 and 2
(From Strygin)

The Polish report, but not the Ukrainian report, also specifies the
shells found in grave No. 2:

> l. "kam, 67. 19, 41"- 205 szt; 2. „dnh, .*, l, 41" - 17 szt;
> 3. łuski bez oznaczeń. 7.62 x 25. wz. 30, produkcja
> ZSRR – 2 szt; 4. łuska „B , 1906"

> *Translated:*

> 1. "Kam, 67, 19, 41" – 205 units; 2. "dnh, *, 1, 41" – 17
> units; 3. Shells without markings, 7.62x25 caliber –
> USSR production of 1930s – 2 units; (one) shell "B ,
> 1906."

Of 225 shells found in this grave, 205 are the German 1941
"Hasag" type, 17 are the German 1941 "Dürlach" type, 2 are of the
unmarked 1930s Soviet type; and one is marked "B 1906."[23] Hence
98.67% of the shells are of 1941 German manufacture.

---

[23] "B 1906" appears to be Austrian rifle ordnance made for the Tsarist Army during the
Russo-Japanese War. See the drawing at
http://7.62x54r.net/MosinID/MosinAmmoID02.htm#Austria and the photograph obtained
by Sergei Strygin at http://katyn.ru/images/news/2012-12-29-gilza_B_1906.jpg

By contrast neither of the two Ukrainian reports cites the numbers of each type of shell or the fact that German shells made in 1941 constitute the overwhelming majority of those found. The following paragraph appears word-for-word in each of the Ukrainian reports:

> У поховальних ямах виявлено ідентичні гільзи , головним чином калібру 9 мм. Більшість з них мають позначки dnh (виробництво заводу Верк Дурлах в Карлсрує, Німеччина) та kam (виробництво фабрики Hasag у Скаржиці Кам'яній, Польща) 1941 р. Проте виявлені і декілька гільз радянського зразка. Все це потребує додаткових досліджень, оскільки стверджувати про те, що розстріли проводилися гітлерівцями при наявності в поховальних ямах гільз радянського зразка– не є об'єктивним. Відомі факти (**зокрема дані розстрілів польських військових у Катині**), що радянські органи НКВС використовували при розстрілах німецьку зброю.[24]

Translated:

> In the burial pits were found identical shells, mainly of caliber 9 mm. Most of them have the mark "dnh" (Werk Dürlach production plant in Karlsruhe, Germany), and "kam" (production factory in Hasag Skarżysko Kamienna, Poland) in 1941. However, several shell casings of Soviet model were also found. All this requires more research inasmuch that it is not objective

---

[24] Doslizhdennia (online); Звіт про результати археологічно-ексгумаційних рятівних досліджень на городищі "вали" у м. володимирі-волинському 2012 р. (Report on the results of the archaeological exhumation recovery investigations at the "Vali" ["shafts"] site in the town of Volodymyr-Volyns'kiy in 2012.). Luts'k, 2012. (Zvit) Available at http://www.formuseum.info/uploads/files/Звіт 2012_Володимир-Волинський.pdf These are two versions of the same report. The much fuller PDF version contains many pages of photographs, graphs, tables, and drawings, but no clear accounting of the cartridge shells as the Polish report has.

> to assert that the shootings were carried out by the
> Hitlerites even though shells of Soviet model were
> found in the burial pits. Examples are known (**includ-
> ing data of shootings of Polish soldiers in Katyn**[25])
> that the Soviet organs of the NKVD used German
> weapons in executions.

There are some problems with the conclusion in the Ukrainian report. First, it is an example of circular reasoning. It assumes that
the mass killings at Katyn, which even the Germans admitted were
carried out with German ammunition, was a Soviet crime. But that
is the very assumption that the discoveries at Volodymyr-
Volyns'kiy call into question.

Second, it assumes that even the overwhelming preponderance of
German ordnance is not enough to establish that the killings were
done by the Germans, since the Soviets could also use German
ammunition. No doubt this is the reason the Ukrainian report does
not give the numbers of shells or the percentage of them that are
German and of 1941 manufacture. (The Ukrainian reports should
have added that Germans could also use Soviet ammunition. The
Germans captured immense amounts of Soviet arms and ammunition in 1941.)

The Ukrainian report does note that women clutching children to
their breasts were also found in the mass graves.

> Відмічено також, що вбиті часто прикривали об-
> личчя руками, або обіймали іншу жертву (жінки
> тулили до себе і прикривали дітей). (Doslizhdennia;
> Zvit 15)

> *Translated:*

---

[25] Emphasis added.

> It is also noted that those killed often covered their
> faces with their hands, or embraced another victim
> (women hugged to themselves and covered children).

There are no examples anywhere of the Soviet NKVD shooting children.

Ukrainian archaeologist Oleksei Zlatohors'kiy (Russian: Aleksei Zlatogorskii) has pointed out the political problems raised by the Polish archaeologist's identification of the Germans as the murderers:

> Неосторожные высказывания польских археоло-
> гов о принадлежности останков, найденных на
> территории замка Казимира Великого во Влади-
> мире-Волынском, **могут поставить под сомнение
> уже известные преступления НКВД по отноше-
> нию к польским офицерам**, сообщил директор
> ГП "Волынские древности" Алексей Златогорский
> в комментарии Gazeta.ua.

Translated:

> Incautious statements by Polish archaeologists about
> the belongings of the remains found on the land of the
> castle of Kazimir Velikii in Vladimir-Volynskii **could
> cast doubt upon the already known crimes of the
> NKVD in relation to Polish officers**, said the direc-
> tion of the state enterprise "Volyn antiquities" Aleksei
> Zlatogorskii in a commentary to Gazeta.ua.[26]

---

[26] Скороход, Ольга. "Польские археологи нагнетают ситуацию вокруг жертв, расстрелянных в 1941-м." (Ol'ga Skorokhkod. Polish archeologists stir up the situation around the
victims shot in 1941). Gazeta.ru February 20, 2013,
http://gazeta.ua/ru/articles/history/_polskie-arheologi-nagnetayut-situaciyu-vokrug-
zhertv-rasstrelyannyh-v-1941-m/483525 Gazeta.ru is a Russian-language Ukrainian newspaper. Roughly half the population of today's Ukraine use Russian as their first language.

The only "already known crimes of the NKVD in relation to Polish officers" is the Katyn massacre – or, to be more precise, the "official" version of the Katyn Massacre. Prof. Zlatohors'kiy does not explain how the Polish report "casts doubt" upon the "official" version of Katyn.

The Ukrainian report cited above appears to be a shorter, perhaps Internet version of a longer report written by Zlatohors'kiy and two other Ukrainian archaeologists, S.D. Panishko and M.P. Vasheta. This report (Zvit) omits any mention of Kuligowski, Małowiejski, or their badges. Its appendix does include some photographs also found in the Polish report. Among them are a photo of the Polish policeman's epaulette and of the "sardine-packing" arrangement of bodies in Grave No. 2. (Zvit pp. 91, 92, 97).

The opening of an exhibition concerning this site at the Volodymyr-Volyns'kiy Historical Museum on March 5, 2013, was announced. The accompanying article states only that in 1997 researchers assumed that the victims buried there were Poles shot by the NKVD in 1939-1940, and suggests that this is still their conclusion.[27]

Katchanovski and Musychenko cited evidence that the Germans killed the victims at Volodymyr-Volyns'kiy. More than 96% of the ammunition found in the mass graves is German and was manufactured in 1941. The "transit" or "shipment" lists from Kozel'sk, Ostashkov, and Starobel'sk are from April and May 1940. Kuligowski and Małowiejski could not have been killed earlier than 1941. No one has suggested that they were killed in Kalinin and Kharkiv in April-May 1940 and then their badges brought to a

---

[27] Запрошуємо на відкриття Виставки "Прихована історія: археологічні дослідження на городищі Володимира-Волинського 2010-2012 років" (We invite you to the opening of the exhibition: "Hidden history: archaeological investigations at a site in Volodymyr-Volyns'kiy in the years 2010-2012"), http://volyn-muse-um.com.ua/news/zaproshuemo_na_vidkrittja_vistavki_prikhovana_istorija_arkheologichni_doslidzhennja_na_gorodishhi_volodimira_volinskogo_2010_2012_rokiv/2013-02-27-655

mass grave in Volodymyr-Volyns'kiy, hundreds of miles away, and there thrown into the burial pit.

Kuligowski and Małowiejski were indeed shipped out of their POW camps in April 1940, as recorded in the Soviet transit lists published by Tucholski in 1991. But neither of them was being sent to execution. They were killed in 1941 in Volodymyr-Volyns'kiy, Ukrainian SSR. According to the evidence now available they were killed by the Germans.

The badges and the shell casings are primary source evidence that cannot have been forged or faked in any way. The Polish archeologist would never have fabricated the badges or invented the identities of their owners. Nor would she have fabricated the fact that the shell casings found in the mass graves were not only German but were manufactured in 1941, long after the Katyn killings.

On the contrary: the Polish authorities are now denying the report of the Polish archaeologist. Funding has been withdrawn; the mass graves have been filled in. A small number of victims, unidentified, have been reburied and are now officially called "victims of the NKVD." We will discuss this in more detail in a later chapter and point out that this constitutes a tacit admission by Polish authorities that the "official" version of Katyn has been disproven.

The *material* evidence discovered at Volodymyr-Volyns'kiy – the badges and the German shells dated 1941 – are the most important kind of evidence we could ask for. They could not have been "planted" or otherwise faked. In this they are unlike documentary evidence and personal testimony.

If we had no other unimpeachable primary evidence indicating that the "official" version of the Katyn massacre is false, these discoveries would be sufficient to establish that fact. On the basis of the badges and shell casings at Volodymyr-Volyns'kiy alone we can conclude that the prisoners shipped out of the Soviet POW camps in April-May 1940 were not being sent to their deaths. This in itself disproves the "official" version of the Katyn massacre.

Chapter 6. What the Unimpeachable Evidence Shows

In chapters 2 through 5 we have examined all of the unimpeachable evidence that we have been able to identify:

Document Collection A: The German Report (AM):

> * The German spent shell casings;
>
> * The badge from Ostashkov;
>
> * A considerable number of bodies found at Katyn of POWs from the Ostashkov and Starobel'sk POW camps.

Document Collection B: The Soviet Burdenko Report (BU)

> * The receipt from Przemysław Kozietulski, son of Bolesław.

Document Collection C: "Closed Packet No.1" (CP)

> * The "Excerpt from Protocol No. 13 of the Politburo" that has been altered, probably in 1959.

Document Collection D: The Archeological Report from Volodymyr-Volyns'kiy (VV).

> * The badges of Jósef Kuligowski and Ludwik Małowiejski;
>
> * The hundreds of German shell casings dated 1941.

According to the "official" version of Katyn the Polish POWs were transferred from Kozel'sk, Ostashkov, and Starobel'sk POW camps to the Smolensk, Kalinin, and Khar'kov NKVD, who oversaw their murder, and then buried them at Katyn (in fact Koz'i Gory near

Katyn), Mednoe, and Piatykhatky respectively. The executions took place within a short period after the POWs arrived at the cities in question.

There has never been any *evidence* that the Polish POWs were shot in this way. Gur'ianov of "Memorial," a fervent defender of the "official" version, admits this in several places in his lengthy analysis in 'Ubity."

* He admits that Soviet transfer lists are the only official source containing almost the full list of POWs from Kozel'sk, but that they say nothing about any shooting or Politburo decision:

> Исключительное значение списков-предписаний как доказательств обусловлено тем, что это единственный официальный источник, содержащий практически полный поименный список расстрелянных военнопленных Козельского лагеря[20]. **Однако списки-предписания не содержат каких-либо упоминаний о том, что перечисленные в них лица подлежат расстрелу на основании решения Политбюро ЦК ВКП(б)**. (66)

Translated:

> The exceptional importance of the prescription lists as evidence is due to the fact that this is the only official source containing a practically complete list of names of the executed POWs of the Kozel'sk camp. **However, the prescription lists do not contain any reference to the fact that the persons listed in them are to be shot on the basis of a decision of the Politburo of the C[entral] C[ommittee] of the VKP (b).**

Therefore there is no formal connection between the (supposed) Politburo document of March 5 – the "Beria letter" – and the shooting of the POWs:

> Следовательно, если ограничиться только перечисленными советскими источниками, с фор-

мальной точки зрения связь между решением По-
литбюро от 5 марта 1940 г. о расстреле польских
военнопленных и списками-предписаниями НКВД
установить невозможно. (66-7)

Translated:

Consequently, if we restrict ourselves to only the Soviet sources listed, from a formal point of view it is
impossible to establish any connection between the
decision of the Politburo of March 5, 1940 on the
shooting of Polish prisoners of war and the NKVD pre-
scription lists.

Gur'ianov recognizes that the lack of evidence of life after spring
1940 is the "weakest link" in "official" version:

Необходимость сослаться на отсутствие призна-
ков жизни после весны 1940 г. и общность судьбы
опознанных и неопознанных по результатам экс-
гумации для того, чтобы считать списки-
предписания НКВД списками отправки на рас-
стрел, - **самое тонкое звено** в нашей формально-
юридической доказательной цепочке. (67)

Translated:

The need to refer to the absence of signs of life after
the spring of 1940 and the commonality of the fate of
the identified and the unidentified by the results of the
exhumation, in order to consider the NKVD prescrip-
tion lists as lists of dispatching for execution by shooting – this is **the weakest link** in our formal legal evidence chain.

This is a deceptive statement – in plain language, a lie. As we have
seen, there is plenty of "evidence of life" for Polish POWs after May
1940. Gur'ianov is only able to claim there isn't by deliberately ignoring the Burdenko report, the exhumation records of the BU

that were published by Pamiatnykh, and the Volodymyr-Volyns'kiy discoveries. He is busy "ignoring the elephant in the living room."

If Gur'ianov were an honest historian whose purpose was to discover the truth he would acknowledge these issues and present his readers with an examination of them. That is what we have done in the present book. But Gur'ianov is not an honest historian. What he is writing is not history but "propaganda with footnotes."

Gur'ianov *assumes* – or, more accurately, *pretends* to assume – that all the remains exhumed in 1943 at Katyn by the Germans, including the unidentified remains, are of POWs from Kozel'sk.

> Мы исходим из того, что все останки, эксгумированные в 1943 г. в Катынском лесу, включая перечисленные в списке «посторонних» в Приложении, - это останки значащихся в документах НКВД военнопленных из Козельского лагеря. (77)

> *Translated:*

> We proceed from the premise that all the remains exhumed in 1943 in the Katyn forest, including those listed in the list of "outsiders" in the Appendix [Gur'ianov means the appendix to his own analysis], are the remains of prisoners of war from the Kozel'sk camp mentioned in the documents of the NKVD.

Gur'ianov points out that Aleksei Pamiatnykh makes the same assumption:

> Алексей Памятных еще в 2005 г. пришел к выводу, что «В польских могилах в Катыни находятся останки офицеров ТОЛЬКО из Козельского лагеря» (Pamiatnych A. O identyfikacji nazwisk ... S. 142).

>> Dlatego uważam, że w polskich mogiłach w Katyniu znajdują się szczątki oficerów TYLKO z obozu Kozielskiego. **Hipoteza ta jest głównym wynikiem mojej pracy.**

Already in 2005 Alexei Pamiatnykh came to the conclusion that "In the Polish graves in Katyn there are
remains of officers ONLY from the Kozel'sk camp."

Therefore, I believe that in Polish graves at Katyn
there are remains ONLY of officers from the
Kozel'sk camp. **This hypothesis is the main result of my work.**

This "hypothesis" – really, a pretense – is false. I suspect that
Gur'ianov and Pamiatnykh know it is false. Evidently, they hope
that their readers will not know it. Their omission of these facts,
which dismantle the "official" version of Katyn, is essential if they
wish to continue to uphold the "official" Soviets-did-it version.

Gur'ianov admits that no "shooting lists" have been discovered,
though he insists that they did exist.

Как показала Н.С. Лебедева, одновременно со
списками-предписаниями, которые высылались в
три лагеря начальником УПВ или его заместите-
лем, списки с теми же фамилиями военнопленных,
но подписанные зам. наркома НКВД Меркуловым
и содержащие распоряжение привести в исполне-
ние ВМН в отношении перечисленных в них лиц,
должны были высылаться начальникам соответ-
ствующих областных УНКВД[85] . **Ни один из таких
списков (назовем их расстрельными) до сих
пор не обнаружен...** (80)

Translated:

As N.S. Lebedeva has shown, along with the instruc-
tion list that were sent to the three camps by the head
of the division of Polish POWs or his deputy, lists with
the same names of prisoners of war, but signed by
deputy People's Commissar of the NKVD Merkulov
and containing an order to carry out the executions of
the persons listed in them, were to be sent to the
heads of the relevant regional NKVD Directorate. **Not**

a single one of these lists (let us call them execution lists) has yet been found...

What Lebedeva and Gur'ianov really mean is that, *if the "official" version is to be saved*, such lists *must have* existed. For Gur'ianov, "Memorial," and anticommunist researchers and writers generally, the "official" version is to be considered "true beyond any legitimate doubt" – meaning, questioned only by biased, pro-communist, and therefore "immoral" people.

This is not history. It is anticommunist ideology masquerading as history, disguised as history to fool the majority of people who rely on "experts" like these.

The Conspiracy to Defend the "Official" Version of Katyn

You, the reader, should be wondering: "If the solution to the Katyn murders is as obvious as this book makes it seem, why haven't I heard about it? What can account for the fact that the only version of Katyn that we ever hear about is the one that blames Stalin and the NKVD for murdering the Poles?"

The answer is that there is a worldwide *anti*communist conspiracy to ignore the truth about Katyn, as about many other alleged "crimes of Stalin."

* The Russian researchers who have been critiquing the "official" version for more than two decades are completely ignored. None of their work is available in any language other than Russian. They are seldom mentioned even in the Russian media, and almost never mentioned outside Russia.

+ The recent 470-page book by German research Claudia Weber *Krieg der Täter: Die Massenerschießungen von Katyn.* Hamburg: Hamburger Edition, HIS Verlaggesellschaft, 2015. ISBN 978-3868542868 does not mention any of them.

+ Neither does the authoritative English-language study by Wojciech Materski and Anna Cienciala, *Katyn: A Crime without*

Punishment (Annals of Communism Series). Yale University Press, 2008. ISBN 978-0300195477

+ In *Katyn and the Soviet Massacre of 1940: Truth, Justice and Memory* (BASEES / Routledge Series on Russian and East European Studies). London, UK: Routledge, 2009) British professor George Sanford does devote a single paragraph to the Russian researchers who deny Soviet guilt. But he dismisses their arguments as "a method associated with Holocaust revisionist David Irving" and claims that to question Soviet guilt after Gorbachev's admission and Yeltsin's release of the NKVD evidence was a wholly perverse, and politically motivated, attempt to cloud and mitigate the issue of Stalinist guilt. (204)

Sanford is referring to Document Collection C, "Closed Packet No. 1".

It should be obvious to the reader that Sanford's position here is bankrupt and dishonest. *In principle* there cannot be anything wrong, much less "perverse," in subjecting any and all evidence to critical scrutiny. But the "official" version of Katyn cannot withstand such scrutiny. Therefore it must be defended by lies, insults, and threats.

There is a policy of suppression, repression, and – when that proves inadequate – slander and dismissal, of any study of Katyn that questions the "official" version. This, and not any evidentiary considerations, is the reason that criticisms of the "official" version are excluded from public and even from academic discussion.

Since 1943 anticommunist Polish nationalism has been based on the claim that the Soviet Union committed the Katyn murders. So vital is Katyn to them that the Volodymyr-Volyns'kiy exhumations are now falsified by Polish authorities because the discoveries there disprove the "official" version of Katyn.

A few Russian researchers have been investigating Katyn, reassessing the evidence already available, and discovering new evidence. We will consider some of their research in the chapters that follow. Their work has been marginalized within Russia and, when not slandered, as Sanford does, has been ignored elsewhere. This is both "politically motivated" (to use Sanford's phrase) and intellectually irresponsible.

All *honest* scholars know that it is never legitimate to ridicule, dismiss, or ignore evidence (as opposed to mere unsupported opinion) that tends to call one's own preconceived ideas and prejudices into question. After all, why not just refute such evidence and arguments, as historians of the Jewish Holocaust have done to Holocaust deniers? These vituperative attacks suggest that the defenders of the "official" Soviets-did-it version are unable to refute the critiques of the "official" version.

* * * * *

In the preceding chapters we have examined all the evidence that cannot have been fabricated. Consequently, this is the evidence that any honest researcher is duty bound to accept as evidence, and account for. As we have seen, the evidence permits only one conclusion: that the "official" version of Katyn is false. Therefore that version must be discarded by any honest, objective student.

Our analysis has not only proven that the "official" version of Katyn is false. It has also provided the evidence to prove German guilt in the Katyn murders.

> * We have "evidence of life" of some of the Poles long after May 1940.

> * Only German bullets were used at Katyn and at Volodymyr-Volyns'kiy.

> * Kuligowski, Małowiejski, and possibly many more Polish POWs were shot by the Germans in 1941.

> * There was no other party besides the Soviets and the Germans that could have killed the Poles. If the evidence excludes the Soviets then the Germans were guilty.

In the following chapters we will examine the other evidence in Document Collections A through D.

>   * We will see that there are so many problems, con-
>   tradictions, and inconsistencies in Document A, the
>   German Report that all *objective* researchers, regard-
>   less of political viewpoint, must agree that it must be
>   disqualified as evidence.

>   * We will examine the objections that have been
>   raised against Document Collection B, the Burdenko
>   Report. We shall see that those objections are not only
>   groundless but dishonest.

>   * We will see that Document Collection C, "Closed
>   Packet No. 1," is a fabrication – a forgery.

>   * We will see that Polish authorities now deny all the
>   findings of the Polish archeologist report of the VV ex-
>   cavations. In fact they have tacitly withdrawn the re-
>   port itself! Now they claim that the killings at VV were
>   by the NKVD. We will show that the reason for this
>   brazen denial lies in the implications that the VV re-
>   port has for disproving the "official" version of Katyn.

The Unimpeachable Evidence Is Decisive

Ours is the first study to identify the evidence which cannot have been faked and to point out that this unimpeachable evidence should be considered decisive in determining who murdered the Polish POWs. As far as I can determine, it is also the very first study of Katyn to approach the question objectively and, therefore, as not solved prior to the present study.

Most researchers who are at all concerned with the Katyn issue make no attempt at all to be objective or to consider that their pre-conceived notions about Katyn might be incorrect. These persons have never approached Katyn through a study of all the available evidence. This is true of the major and supposedly "definitive" studies by Cienciala / Materski, by Sanford, and of many others as well.

In fact the situation with respect to research on Katyn is even worse than the paragraph above may suggest. For the proponents of Soviet guilt have tried their best to declare Katyn a subject that is "settled" forever. By this they mean, and sometimes explicitly state, as Sanford does, that any attempt to study Katyn objectively – an effort which necessarily means subjecting all conclusions about Katyn, including the "official" Soviets-did-it position, to doubt – is perverse and even immoral.

Because Katyn has seldom if ever been studied according to the evidence, and never by the method used in this book, I think it is inevitable that some partisans of the "official," Soviets-did-it version, will ask:

> "Why should the unimpeachable evidence be decisive? After all, you cannot prove that the evidence supporting Soviet guilt is false. The most you can say is that it, like a great deal of other evidence, *might be* false.
>
> But suppose that at least some of it is *not* false? Suppose, for example, that the other documents in CP, like the "Beria Letter," are genuine? Wouldn't the genuineness of the CP documents, once established, equal or even outweigh the so-called 'unimpeachable' evidence you have cited? Wouldn't it, at the very least, leave open the possibility that the Soviets shot the Polish POWs?"

The answer to such questions is, briefly: No. In fact, the unimpeachable evidence is also additional evidence that CP and AM are invalid as evidence.

The "official" version of Katyn is a *narrative*, a hypothesis concerning a supposed sequence of events:

* First the three POW camps were emptied in April
and May, 1940. No one contests this fact so we may
take it as true.

* Then the Polish POWs were shot by the Soviets at
Smolensk or at Katyn (Koz'i Gory) or at both places; at
Kalinin (or there and also at Mednoe); and at Khar'kov
(or there and at Piatykhatky). But the unimpeachable
evidence shows that this did not happen. Therefore,
AM and CP are false.

The evidence compels us to conclude that AM was a fabrication by
the Germans. We shall study AM in more detail in the following
chapters and show that the evidence it supposedly contains that
the Soviets shot the Polish POWs is all specious and falls apart
when scrutinized. As for CP, it is a complex of documents that cannot be genuine because it contradicts all the valid evidence we
have. In addition, there is much other evidence that the CP documents are forgeries.

The unimpeachable evidence firmly establishes that the "official"
version of Katyn could not have taken place. But there is no other
version of Katyn compatible with Soviet guilt. The Polish POWs
must have been killed either by the Soviets or by the Germans because there was no third force that could have committed these
mass murders. We also have evidence of German guilt in AM, BU,
and VV. Therefore, on the evidence we are forced to conclude that
the Germans killed the Polish POWs.

If there are any readers of this book who only want to know the
solution to the Katyn "Whodunnit" – Who really murdered the
Polish POWS? – they can stop reading at this point. "Whodunnit"
has been determined beyond the shadow of any reasonable doubt:
the Germans "did it."

But I suspect and hope that most readers will want a more detailed
examination of the evidence. The remaining chapters present that
more detailed study.

Chapter 7. The German Report

More research has been done on the German Report (AM) and on the documents of Closed Packet No. 1 than on the other two document collections. We'll begin with AM.

Lies and Contradictions in the German Report

> Unter den übrigen Opfern findet sich unter anderem eine ganze Reihe von Geistlichen. (AM 10)

> *Translated:*

> Among the other victims there is also a number of [lit. a whole series of] clergymen.

In reality, only one ecclesiastic is listed.

> Unter den identifizierten Ermordeten befinden sich 2 Brigade-Generale, 12 Oberste, 50 Oberstleutnante, ... und 10 Veterinäre **sowie ein Feldgeistlicher**. (AM 47)

> *Translated:*

> Among the murder victims that have been identified there are two Brigadier Generals, 12 colonels, 50 lieutenant colonels .. and 10 veterinarians as well as one military clergyman.

> 2. Neben zwei Brigadegenerälen wurden unter den Mordopfern 2250 Offiziere verschiedenster Ränge, 156 Aerzte und Veterinäre, 406 Offiziere ohne erkennbaren Rang, Fähnriche und Mannschaften **sowie ein Feldgeistlicher** sofort an Ort und Stelle identifiziert. (AM 92)

Translated:

In addition to two brigadier generals, among the murder victims 2250 officers of various ranks, 156 doctors and veterinarians, 406 officers whose rank could not be determined, ensigns and personnel as well as one military clergyman were immediately identified on the spot.

Several witnesses testified that the woods around the mass graves were closed off by the NKVD in 1931.

Das Waldgelände Kosi-Gory durfte bis 1931, wenn nicht gerade Erschießungen stattfanden, von jedermann betreten werden. Kinder, welche dort Pilze suchten, erzählten immer von frischen Grabhügeln. (AM 19, testimony of Kuzma Godonov)

Translated:

Until 1931 the forest area of Kozy Gory was accessible to anyone, as long as executions were not taking place. Children who were looking for mushrooms there always talks about fresh grave mounds.

Bis zum Jahre 1931 konnten wir, d. h die Dorfbewohner, in dieses Gelände gehen, um dort Pilze und Beeren zu sammeln, und auch ich habe als Junge in Kosi-Gory Pilze gesucht. ... Im Jahre 1931 wurde das Gelände von Kosi-Gory eingezäunt, das Betreten durch Warntafeln, die von der OGPU. unterschrieben waren, verboten. (AM 19, testimony of Ivan Krivozertsev)

Translated:

Until 1931 we, the villagers, were able to go to this area to gather mushrooms and berries, and I too, as a boy, collected mushrooms in Kozy-Gory. ... In 1931 the area of Kozy-Gory was fenced off and entry was prohibited by warning sign issued by the OGPU.

Seit ungefähr 10 Jahren wurde das Schloß im Wald als Sanatorium für höhere NKWD.-Beamte benutzt. Das ganze Waldgelände war durch einen 2 Meter hohen Stacheldraht eingezäunt. (AM 25, testimony of Parfeon Kisselev)

Translated:

For about 10 years, the castle in the forest has been used as a sanatorium for higher NKVD officials. The whole forest area was fenced off by barbed wire two meters in height.

This was contradicted by the testimony of witness Gregor Silvestrov.

Die einen behaupteten, es wären Polen; manche aber, es wären Finnen gewesen. Ebenfalls nur gerüchtweise hörte man, die Gefangenen seien zu dem etwa 4 km von hier entfernten sogenannten „Ruhehaus der Kollektiven" geschafft und dort erschossen worden. Dies nahm auch ich an, da **zur Zeit dieser Transporte das in der Umgebung des Hauses übliche Pilzesammeln verboten war**. (AM 24)

Translated:

Some said it was Poles. But many said it had been Finns. It was also rumored that the prisoners had been taken to the so-called "rest house of the collectives," some 4 km from here, and shot there. I too assumed this, because at the time of these transports the usual mushroom gathering in the vicinity of the house was forbidden.

Kisselev testified that the local people thought there were about 10,000 Poles killed by the NKVD at Koz'i Gory.

> Die Leute der Ortschaften erzählten, daß es sich um zirka 10 000 Polen gehandelt haben soll. (AM 25)

Translated:

> The local people used to say that it was a matter of about 10,000 Poles.

This is the same wildly inaccurate figure that the German report (AM) gives.

> Für die Gesamtzahl können die endgültigen Ergebnisse der schaurigen Untersuchung und Zählung abgewartet werden; eine vorsichtige Schätzung läßt aber mit mindestens 10 000—12 000 Opfern der bolschewistischen Mordgier rechnen. (AM 10)

Translated:

> For the total number we must await the final results of the gruesome investigation and census. However, a cautious estimate would be that of at least 10,000-12,000 victims of Bolshevik murder.

The only place the local people could have gotten this figure is from the Germans.

Former Polish officer Glaeser told the Germans that the Kozel'sk transits began on March 20, 1940, and ended May 9, 1940. (AM 31) This is false. According to Tucholski's book, which prints all the Soviet transit lists, there is no list earlier than April 1.

The report claims that some Starobel'sk POWs were transferred to Katyn via Kozel'sk:

> Bekannt ist, daß eine geringe Anzahl von Starobielsk
> über Kozielsk nach Katyn gebracht worden ist. (AM
> 34)

> It is known that a small number of Starobel'sk prison-
> ers were brought to Katyn via Kozel'sk.

This is an interesting remark! The Germans did not identify any bodies as being of men who had been transferred from Starobel'sk. Evidently the Germans must have known that some POWs had been in Starobel'sk. There is no evidence for any "small number" having been transported from Starobel'sk to Kozel'sk before April-May 1940. The Soviet NKVD transit lists, reproduced in Tucholski, record nothing like this.

As we have seen, a number of Starobel'sk and Ostashkov POWs were indeed killed at Katyn. But these men had first been trans-ferred to Khar'kov and Kalinin and only then to Kozel'sk.

> In einem Falle, und zwar am 4. 4. 1940, wurden 2402
> Offiziere abtransportiert. (AM 34)

> *Translated:*

> In one case, on April 4, 1940, 2402 officers were
> shipped out.

Not all the Soviet transfer lists in Tucholski are dated. But it ap-pears that there was never anything like 2400 prisoners sent on a single day.

The Insect Question

The German Report, and proponents of the "official" version since then, have emphasized that the Germans found no insects in the mass graves "from the time of burial" (*aus der Zeit der Einschar-rung*). They have used this fact to allege that the murders musts have taken place in the spring – April and May – and so must have been committed by the Soviets. They assert that, had the murders

taken place in the fall, and been committed by the Germans, there
would have been insects.

> Nirgends fanden sich an den Leichen oder deren Klei-
> dung Spuren von Insektenfraß oder ihrer Ablagerung,
> die aus der Zeit der Einscharrung stammen könnten.
> Die nach der Auflegung der Leichen relativ häufig an-
> getroffenen Lederlaufkäfer, die von Insektenmaden
> leben, sind erst nach der Bergung der Leichen, also
> sekundär, angewandert.

Translated:

Nowhere on the corpses or their garments were there
any signs of insect-feeding or their deposits which
might have come from the time of burial. The leather
beetles, which are found frequently after the laying
out of the corpses, and which live on maggots, have
only arrived after the bodies have been salvaged, that
is, secondarily.

> Hieraus ergibt sich, daß die Erschießungen und die
> Einscharrungen in einer kalten, insektenfreien
> Jahreszeit stattgefunden haben müssen, ... (AM 52)

Translated:

From this it follows that the shootings and the burials
must have taken place in a cold, insect-free season ...

> Es fehlen gänzlich an den Leichen Insekten und In-
> sektenreste, die aus der Zeit der Einscharrung stam-
> men könnten. Hieraus ergibt sich, daß die
> Erschießungen und die Einscharrungen in einer kal-
> ten, insektenfreien Jahreszeit geschehen sein müssen.
> (AM 117)

Translated:

> Insects and insect remains on the corpses that could
> have come from the time of burial are entirely lacking.
> From this it follows that the shootings and the burials
> must have taken place in a cold, insect-free season.

AM admits that beetles (Lederlaufkäfer) were found that live off
maggots (Insektenmaden). Maggots hatch from eggs which are laid
by flies. Dr. Orsós, the openly pro-German medical expert, wrote
that he found no evidence of insects in one of the corpses he examined.

> Insekten oder Insektenteile wie auch andere niedere
> Tiere ließen sich weder an der Leiche selbst noch an
> der Kleidung nachweisen. (AM 123)

Translated:

> Insects, insect parts, and other lower animals, could
> not be detected either on the corpses themselves or
> on the clothing.

But Dr. Palmieri, an Italian member of the medical team brought to
Katyn by the Germans, did find evidence of insects.

> In der Kleidung eine ganze Menge toter Larven. (126)

Translated:

> In the clothing a large number of dead larvae.

> Die Zunge ist flach. Im Rachen eine große Menge toter
> Larven. (126)

Translated:

> The tongue is flat. In the throat a large number of dead
> larvae.

Larvae develop from maggots, which hatch from eggs laid by flies. So there had been flies after all! During this testimony at Nuremberg Dr. Markov noted this contradiction in the AM:

> As to the insects and their larvae, the assertion of the general report that none were discovered is in flagrant contradiction to the conclusions of Professor Palmieri, which are recorded in his personal minutes concerning the corpse which he himself dissected. In this protocol, which is published in the same German White Book[1], it is said that there were traces of remains of insects and their larvae in the mouths of the corpses. (Nuremberg Trials Vol. XVII, 354)

Failure to recognize the *terminus post quem*

Dr. Miloslavich, a member of the expert team called to Katyn by the Germans, wrote:

> Der Tod des Obengenannten erfolgte im Frühjahr 1940, wie dies aus den an der Leiche und an vielen umliegenden Leichen vorgefundenen Privat-Dokumenten ersichtlich ist. (133)

> The death of the above-mentioned person occurred in the spring of 1940, as can be seen from the private documents found on the body and on many surrounding corpses.

The Polish Red Cross team made the same logical error in their telegram to the International Red Cross of April 21, 1943:

> 4. jugeant d'après les papiers et documents trouvés sur les cadavres, l'assassinat a du avoir lieu environ aux mois mars — avril 1940. (AM 137)

---

[1] This is AM.

Translated:

4. judging from the papers and documents found on
the corpses the murder must have taken place around
the months March – April 1940.

In reality the latest date of documents found in the mass graves
could only establish that the victims were shot *after* that date. This
apparent error in logic – ignorance of the elementary concept of
"terminus post quem" – is made multiple times in the German report. It defies credulity to believe that *all* the Germans, *all* the foreign experts, and *all* the Poles, could have made this error. Therefore this must be a deliberate effort to deceive – or, at least, to deceive those who *wanted* to be deceived, who wanted to believe
that the Soviets shot the Poles.

Denial of Polish Collaboration with the Germans – While the Poles Were Collaborating

The German Report quotes the Soviet charge that some of the
Poles were working hand in glove with the Germans in this propaganda campaign. It also quotes the response of the Polish government –in-exile in London to the Soviet charges.

Jede Zusammenarbeit mit den Deutschen ist
verschmäht worden. Im Lichte dieser in der gesamten
Welt bekannten Tatsachen haben die polnische Re-
gierung und die polnische Nation es nicht nötig, sich
gegen irgendeine Vermutung hinsichtlich einer Füh-
lungnahme oder einer Verständigung mit Hitler zu
verteidigen. (AM 147)

Translated:

All collaboration with the Germans has been scorned.
In the light of this fact, known throughout the world,
the Polish government and the Polish nation have no
need to defend themselves against any presumption
regarding a meeting or an understanding with Hitler.

This statement was made while the Polish Red Cross team was in fact working as closely as possible with the Germans at Katyn!

In fact we know that, after Stalingrad made it obvious that Germany would almost certainly lose the war, the Polish Home Army began to collaborate with the Germans against their mutual enemy, the Soviet Union. One well-documented example of this collaboration is discussed in a recent German collection.[2] We will return briefly to this important point in the Conclusion.

---

[2] Bernhard Chiari, "Kriegslist oder Bündnis mit dem Feind? Deutsch-Polnische Kontakte 1943-44." In *Die Polnische Heimatarmee. Geschichte und Mythos der Armia Krajowa seit dem Zweiten Weltkrieg.* Munich: R. Oldenbourg Vlg, 2003, 497-527.

Chapter 8. The German Report, continued. Sakharov's Article 'Secrets of Katyn'

The Research of Valentin A. Sakharov

Since 2010 Professor Valentin Sakharov of Moscow State University has published several very important research articles on the subject of the German Report at Katyn. I have never seen any of them acknowledged, much less studied or critiqued, by any of the advocates of the "official" version of Katyn. The reason for this silence about Sakharov's research appears to be that it deals yet another serious blow to the credibility of AM.

We will examine two of his articles here:

> * "Tainy Katyni." ("Secrets of Katyn") *Svobodnaia mysl'* 1 (2013), 133-146. Online: http://svom.info/entry/319-tajny-katyni/

> * "Germanskie dokumenty ob eksgumatsii i identifikatsii zhertv Katyni (1943 g.)." ("German documents concerning the exhumation and identification of the victims of Katyn") Online at https://kprf.ru/rus_law/79589.html

In this chapter we will examine Sakharov's first article. We will study his second article in the chapter that follows.

"Secrets of Katyn"

In this article Sakharov examines some of the documents allegedly found in the mass graves by the Germans. He provides evidence that the Germans falsified some of these documents.

In a number of cases I do not agree with Sakharov's determination that a document was falsified. Here I will only discuss those cases where I believe that falsification can be reliably established.

1. "Lemberg"

Lemberg was the German name of the city of Lwów, in Russian L'vov, Ukrainian Lv'iv. L'vov was taken by Poland from Soviet Russia in the Polish-Soviet war of 1919-1921 and ceded to Poland in the Treaty of Riga of March 1921. It was occupied by the Red Army on September 22, 1939 and reverted to the Ukrainian SSR in October 1939 as a result of the Treaty of Nonaggression between Germany and the USSR, commonly called the Molotov-Ribbentrop Pact.

It was renamed "Lemberg" by the Germans after they captured it in June 1941 during their invasion of the Soviet Union. According to the "official" version and the German Report (AM) the Polish POWs were murdered by the Soviet NKVD more than a year earlier, in April and May 1940. Therefore there should not have been any documents found in the mass graves with the name "Lemberg" on them. But according to AM such documents were found.

Here we will examine some examples of these documents. The number represents the number assigned in AM to the corpse exhumed by the Germans in April-June 1943.

892. Uniformierter.

1 Foto mit Anschrift: Hanina Gajowska, Lemberg, Zyzyinska 24. (?) 1 Medaillon. (AM 189)

«Anschrift" – "inscription" – means that these were the actual words on the photo. If genuine, this proves that the body and document were from after June, 1941, and therefore that the victim was murdered by the Germans.

If the inscription really read "Lwów" and some German, in an excess of patriotism or political correctness, changed the name to "Lemberg," the name in use at the time of the exhumations in

1943, then that would mean that the Germans were altering the documents they found. And that would compromise the *bona fides* of the German AM.

One entry in AM does contain the word "Lwow."

> 1824. Gondek, Zdzisław, Hptm., geb. 26. 9. 08, Lwow.

> 1 Offz.-Ausweis, 1 Rgt-Abzeichen, Postsparbuch, Post-karten. (AM 216)

If this one mention of "Lwow" was an oversight and the Germans were changing "Lwow" to "Lemberg" wherever they found it that would mean that the Germans were altering the documents whenever they saw fit to do. If that were the case it would mean that we cannot trust any of these documents in AM, because the Germans might have altered or even invented them.

At first glance it appears that the Germans did change "Lwow" to "Lemberg in at least one case:

> 867. Terpiac, Josef, Hptm.

> Diplom des Kadettenkorps Lemberg, 1 Offiziersaus-weis, 4 Postkarten, 1 Tagebuch. (AM 189)

This man could not have graduated from the Cadet Corps after the German occupation. But this example is different from the others. The German entry does not claim that these are the words on the diploma. Rather, they are a translation into German of the words on the diploma.

> 1776. Chmielewski, Kazimierz, Fliegerhptm. Offz.-Ausweis, Waffenschein, Gestellungsbefehl, versch. milit. Befehle,

> 2 Fliegerabzeichen, 2 Briefe a. Namen: Irena Schmidt, Lemberg, ul. Bulwarska 1, adressiert an: Eward [presumably this should be "Edward"] Schmidt, Kozielsk. (AM 215)

The letter could not have been sent from "Lemberg" before June 1941 at the earliest.

> 781. K......, Boleslaw, Sohn des Zygmunt.

> 1 Foto mit Anschrift: Deine sich sehnende Frau, Lemberg, den 13. 2. 1940, Impfschein, Brief, Briefumschlag. (AM 186)

Once again, "Anschrift" means "inscription," the actual words on the photo. But here the inscription is in German rather than Polish, the date given is February 13, 1940, and the name of the city is "Lemberg." This cannot be accurate. Therefore, the Germans translated – that is, lied about – the inscription on the photograph, which in 1940 would have either "L'vov", the Russian name, or "Lwów," the Polish name, or conceivably "L'viv," the Ukrainian name, but never "Lemberg." In addition, it would have been written in Polish.

Conclusion about "Lemberg"

Either the documents cited above really read "Lwów", L'viv", or "L'vov" and the Germans altered them to read "Lemberg" even in those cases where they said these were the "Anschriften", the inscriptions on photographs; or the documents really did read "Lemberg" as stated in AM.

In the first case the *bona fides* of the German AM are destroyed because the Germans were making changes on the materials they found. Who knows what other changes, inventions, forgeries, etc., they may have been making that have gone undetected?

In the second case the Germans have provided "proof of life" for a number of Polish POWs who lived after the German occupation in June-July 1941, and also provided evidence that these men were murdered by the Germans, not by the Soviets. Since these men were buried among all the rest of the prisoners, this is also evidence that the Germans shot the other Polish POWs at Katyn too.

Whichever is the case, the appearance of the word "Lemberg" in AM proves that it cannot be considered any kind of honest report.

2. German-Language Materials

> 3708. Pufahl, Roman, Kapitän, geb. 26.1. 1894,
> wohnh.: Warschau, Straße des 6. August 58 m 2.
>
> Offiz.-Ausweis, Führerschein, 3 Briefe, 1 Postkarte, 1
> Taschenmesser, Bescheinigung über Militärdienstzeit
> in deutscher Sprache. (AM 262)

Why would a Polish captain be carrying a certificate of military service written in the German language? According to the "Katyn Cemetery Book" (page 509) Pufahl had fought in the First World War. But he would have fought in the Russian army, since Poland was part of Tsarist Russia at that time. If by some chance he had served with the Austro-Hungarian or the German army in WW1 he might have had German-language papers. But why would he carry them when fighting against Germany in 1939?

It is possible that he was given this certificate in a German POW camp after the German occupation of 1941 (but see below).

> 4120. — — Josef, Hptm., Liebenau, Schloßstraße 6.
> 1 Lebenslauf in deutscher Sprache, 3 Briefe (AM 272)

There were a number of towns named Liebenau. None were in prewar Poland. One of them is in Lower Silesia, which between 1919 and 1945 was in Germany, not Poland. Why would a Polish captain, a resident of Germany, have a "curriculum vitae" in German on his person while fighting against Germany in the Polish army? Such documentation would leave him vulnerable to being charged with treason against Germany, where his residence was.

It seems likely that these papers were taken from a dead German. This may be the case with the certificate of military service under Pufahl's name too. In the next chapter we will see that the Germans mixed up a lot of documents, including many documents not found associated with any specific corpse.

"Krzesiński": Another Piece of Evidence That Cannot Be Impugned

> 439. Leutnant.
> Brief in deutscher Sprache an den Kommandanten des
> Lagers, Dat. vom 4. 2. 1940. (AM 177)

Tucholski says this is the following person:

> Krzesiński ...
> Ppor. z Warszawy. PCK (AM) Nr 0439. (Tucholski p.
> 148 col. 1)

"PCK" means the Polish Red Cross (Polski Czerwony Krzyż). Its members at Katyn made this identification. There is no other information about this person.

It is not credible that a Polish POW would write the commandant of a Soviet POW camp in German, or have in his possession a letter in German from another prisoner to the commandant of a Soviet POW camp.

So this prisoner must almost certainly have written to the commandant of a *German* POW camp. That means that this soldier was taken prisoner by the Germans. It would also mean that the Germans falsified the date on the letter. We have already shown that the Germans falsified documents in AM.

I have not found any evidence that the Soviets accepted prisoners captured by the Germans in 1939. Certainly there was no reason for the Soviets to accept from the Germans any POWs whose homes were in the part of Poland occupied by Germany, as Warsaw was. Therefore this soldier must have been captured by the Germans after the German invasion of the USSR in June 1941. And that means that he was shot by the Germans.

Another important and ignored fact: the only "Krzesiński" (КШЕСИНСКОГО) in the Soviet transit lists was an Ostashkov prisoner (Tucholski p. 889 # 43). This man is listed on volume 1 page 449 of the Polish Mednoe Cemetery Book (*Księga Cmentarna Miednoje*):

Komis. PP Mieczysław **Justyn KRZESIŃSKI** s.Hieronima i Justyny z Agopso-wiczów, ur. 15 III 1878 w Czortkowie. Emerytowany (w 1934) Kmdt Pow. Kołomyja. W 1939 zamieszkały w Kołomyi.

L. 051/1 (43), 2630.

Cemetery book entry recreated based upon original entry.

In the latest study of the Katyn victims, *Ubity v Katyni*, no prisoner named either "Krzesiński" or (Russian) Кшесинский is mentioned at all. If the Polish Red Cross was correct in identifying this corpse he would be the sixteenth POW from either Ostashkov or Starobel'sk that we have identified.

I think that Entry No. 439 should be considered to be another piece of unimpeachable evidence. The Germans would hardly have fabricated a false claim that a Polish POW had written to the commander of a Soviet POW camp in German! As such, it would be evidence of life after May 1940 of another Katyn POW. However, I have thought it simpler to consider this evidence here, where it may be studied in the context of other doubtful statements in the German AM, rather than trying to deal with it in Chapters 1 and 2.

3. Litzmannstadt

The Polish city of Lodz (Łódz) was renamed "Litzmannstadt" by the Germans on April 11, 1940.[1] "Lodz" – we will use the English

---

[1] The Germans named it after General Karl Litzmann, whose troops captured Lodz during the First World War and who later joined the Nazi party.

spelling – occurs 19 times in the German Report, including the letter mentioned in this entry:

> 3294. Oberleutnant.
> Brief aus Lodz v. 24. 1. 1940 „Lieber Jurku", 1 Kruzifix.
> (AM 253)

Here the salutation is translated into German but not the name of the city.

"Litzmannstadt" occurs three times in AM:

> 678. Schreer, Joachim, Ltn., Litzmannstadt, Narotowicza 48 m 2.
> 1 Ausweis, Mobilmachungskarte, Impfschein, 3 Briefe, Fotos. (AM 183)
> 1300. Frelkewicz, Józef, Ltn.
> 2 Briefe, 1 Karte, Absender: Frelkewicz, Litzmannstadt, Adolf-Hitler- Str. 104a. (AM 201)
> 2870. Krochmalski, Jan, Uniformiert, wohnh. Litzmannstadt, Allee uni 18 m 32. Notizbuch, Medaillon.
> (AM 242)

Checking these names in Tucholski we find the following:

> Schreer:
> Tucholski p. 650 #100 - 100. ШРЕЕРА Еахима Юльюшевича,
> Tucholski p. 646 – List 025/1 9 April 1940
>
> Tucholski p. 210 col. 1:
> Schreer Joachim
> Ur. 27.11.1913. Ppor. art. rez., 10. pal.
> Zam. Łódź. PCK (AM) Nr 0678.

Schreer was transferred from Kozel'sk on April 9, 1940. Lodz, in the German-occupied area of Poland, was not renamed Litzmannstadt until April 11, 1940.

Schreer could only have had identification with the name "Litzmannstadt" on his person if he had been in German captivity after April 11, 1940. That means he was captured by the Germans, not by the Soviets.

> Krochmalski:
> Tucholski p. 676 #67 - 67. КРОХМАЛЬСКОГО Яна
> Александровича, 1900 г.р.
> Tucholski p. 675: List 032/4 14 April 1940

Krochmalski was transferred from the Kozel'sk camp three days after Lodz was renamed Litzmannstadt. His place of residence ("Wohnhaft" = "residing in") would be listed as Litzmannstadt only if it had been issued by the Germans. Therefore he too was imprisoned and shot by the Germans in 1941.

The Germans Possessed the Soviet List of Kozel'sk Prisoners

The third of the "Litzmannstadt" entries is the following:

> 1300. Frelkewicz, Józef, Ltn.
> 2 Briefe, 1 Karte, Absender: Frelkewicz, Litzmannstadt, Adolf-Hitler- Str. 104a. (AM 201)

Here are his entries in Tucholski:

> Tucholski p. 677 #7 - ФРЕЛЬКЕВИЧА Юзефа Феликсовича, 1915 г.р.

> Tucholski p. 102 col. 2 – Frelkiewicz Józef;

When we examine Sakharov's second article we shall see that the Germans had captured the Soviet NKVD transit lists of Polish POWs shipped from Kozel'sk to Smolensk – the same lists that are reproduced in Tucholski. This soldier's name was spelled with –kie-. But the entry on AM 201 has "-ke." This could not have been on any postcard ("Karte") to him. No Pole would make this error.

Therefore the Germans must have transliterated this from the Russian list. The Russian letter "е" is a palatalized "ye" and corresponds to the Polish "ie." In transliterating the name from Russian, the Germans got the soft "l" correct: the Russian "ль" makes the "l" soft (the Polish hard "l" is the "barred l", written Ł ł). But the Germans did not know that the correct Polish spelling was –kie- , not –ke- , because they had only the Russian transit list.

According to the Soviet transit list in Tucholski, Frelkiewicz was transferred in convoy 035/1 on April 16, 1940. (Tucholski 677) He could not have received a card from a sender in "Litzmannstadt" in the 4 days between the renaming of the town and the departure of his convoy.

In fact the Polish POWs had been forbidden to receive mail after sometime in March, 1940. Their mail privileges were not restored until sometime in September, 1940. Therefore Frelkiewicz could not have received a letter from a sender in "Litzmannstadt."

Therefore Frelkiewicz received the letters and card after the Polish POWs' mailing privileges had been restored sometime in September, 1940. Therefore, this document is "proof of life" of a Kozel'sk POW. Frelkiewicz was alive long after May 1940. He had not been shipped out of Kozel'sk on April 16, 1940 in order to be shot. Instead, he had been sent to some other camp where he received these letters and card in September 1940 or afterwards. That means he murdered by the Germans, not by the Soviets.

But it is also possible that the Germans fabricated all of this information about Frelkiewicz. If genuine, the two letters and the one card would have used the –kie- Polish spelling. Since the Germans transliterated his name from the Soviet NKVD transit list, they may well have fabricated all the information under number 1300. And if they did so in this case they could have done likewise in many other cases as well. This would further undermine the validity of the German AM as evidence.

Conclusion

We have studied Sakharov's article, looked a little more carefully into his results, and identified nine entries in the AM list that are can demonstrate were either partially falsified or entirely faked: AM numbers 892, 1776, 781, 4120, 439, 3294, 678, 1300, 2870.

Either we have here a lot of evidence in the German AM that these men were alive months after the "official" version claims they had been killed and buried by the Soviets – which would prove that the "official" Soviets-did-it version of Katyn is incorrect. Or we have a lot of evidence that the Germans were falsifying the documents that they were supposedly recording as they took them from the mass graves.

In either case the German report (AM) is dishonest and the "evidence" it supposedly contains is invalid and cannot not be used in any *honest* effort to prove that the Soviets murdered the Polish prisoners.

Chapter 9. The German Report, continued: Sakharov's Article 'German Documents'

In the present chapter we review the results of Valentin A. Sakharov's second article "Germanskie dokumenty ob eksgumatsii i identifikatsii zhertv Katyni (1943 g.)."[1] In it Professor Sakharov makes and examines a number of important discoveries relevant to the Katyn issue and the German Report. Most of them are supported by archival documents, some of which Sakharov publishes here for the first time. We will take them up in turn. They are:

1. Reports of Soviet partisans giving details about German falsification of the Katyn exhumation site.

2. Evidence supporting the testimony of local residents that they were forced by the Germans to sign statements written in the German language that they did not understand.

3. Evidence that the Polish prisoners who were transferred from Kozel'sk to Smolensk were sentenced to various prison terms, not sentenced to execution.

4. The statement of the German tree expert that he did not personally collect the treelings sent to him by the Germans at Katyn, but only reported on what had been sent to him.

---

[1] "German documents concerning the exhumation and identification of Katyn victims (1943)."

5. Evidence that the Germans captured and possessed the Soviet transfer lists of POWs.

6. Unpublished documents which show that both the Poles and the Germans at Katyn acknowledge that the identifications made there were falsified because the documents were often not found associated with individual corpses.

7. Evidence that the names assigned to bodies in the German list are not based on real identifications but on the haphazard association of unidentified corpses with documents not necessarily found on those corpses.

1. Reports of Soviet partisans giving details about German falsifications at the Katyn exhumation site.

Soviet partisans testified that the Germans had dug up bodies from the Smolensk civilian cemetery and bodies of Red Army officers and men killed during the 1941 defense of Smolensk against the German invasion, and transported them to Katyn.

Sakharov publishes excerpts from five such reports. We have obtained a copy of one of them from GANISO, the State Archive of Contemporary History of the Smolensk Oblast.[2]

> Информация Западного штаба партизанского движения в Центральный штаб партизанского движения начальнику.
>
> 27 июля 1943 г.
>
> Раздел: «Как немцы сфабриковали Катынскую авантюру».
>
> «Военнопленные, сбежавшие из Смоленского лагеря 20.7.1943 года, как очевидцы – рассказали:

---

[2] Государственный архив новейшей истории Смоленской области (ГАНИСО).

Немцы, чтобы создать могилы в Катынском лесу, якобы, расстрелянных советской властью польских граждан, отрыли массу трупов на Смоленском гражданском кладбище и перевезли эти трупы в Катынский лес, чем очень возмущалось местное население. Кроме того, были отрыты и перевезены в Катынский лес трупы красноармейцев и командиров, погибших при защите подступов гор. Смоленск от немецких захватчиков в 1941 году, и погибших при вероломном нападении фашистской авиации на Смоленск в первые дни Отечественной войны. Доказательством этому служат вырытые при раскопках комсоставские ремни, знаки отличия, плащи и другие виды обмундирования Красной Армии.

Эту провокационную стряпню фашистских жуликов не отрицают даже и сами фашистские врачи, входящие в состав этой комиссии по расследованию.

Врачи, входящие в состав экспертизы по исследованию трупов, говорили среди военнопленных, работающих при госпитале, что при любом их старании они, по существу, не могли установить времени похорон трупов, их принадлежности и национальности – вследствие их разложения».

ГАНИСО. Ф.8. Оп. 2. Д.160. Л.38.

English translation:

Information of the Western staff of the partisan movement to the Central staff of the partisan movement – to the chief.

July 27 1943

Section "How the Germans fabricated the Katyn escapade

"Prisoners of war who fled the Smolensk camp on July 20, 1943 recounted as eyewitnesses:

In order to create graves in the Katyn woods supposedly of Polish citizens shot by Soviet authorities the Germans disinterred a large number of bodies at the Smolensk civilian cemetery and transferred these bodies to the Katyn woods, which enraged the local population very much. In addition there were disinterred and transferred to the Katyn woods bodies of Red Army soldiers and commanders who had perished in defense of the approaches of the city against the German invaders in 1941, and of those who had been killed during the first days of the Patriotic war by the treacherous attack on Smolensk of the fascist aviation. The military belts, insignia, raincoats and other items of the uniform of the Red Army serve as evidence of this.

This provocative concoction of the fascist crooks is not denied even by the fascist doctors who are part of this commission of inquiry.

The doctors, who are part of the group of experts in the examination of the corpses, said in the presence of the prisoners of war who were working at the hospital that, despite all their efforts, they could not in fact determine the time of burial of the corpses, where they came from or their nationality – because of their decomposition.

Below we reproduce a photocopy of the original, obtained from this archive by my colleague Vladimir L. Bobrov.

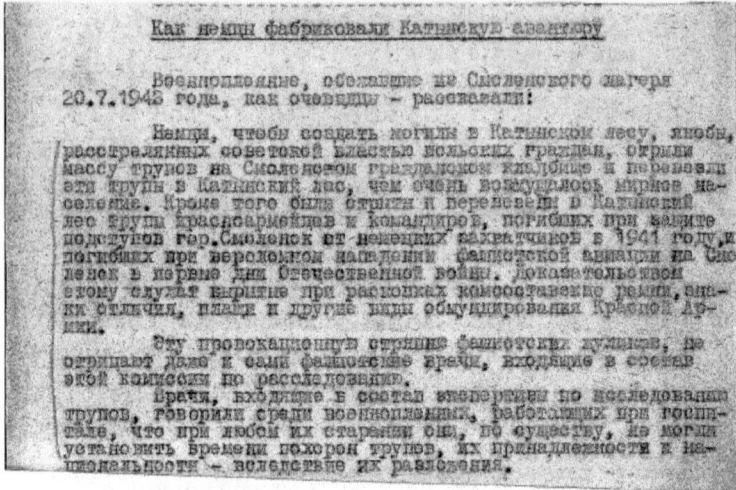

Image 9.1 "How the Germans fabricated the Katyn escapade" photocopy.

The other four documents from partisan reports tell a similar story.

These documents might be considered among the unimpeachable evidence. It seems to be almost impossible that they were fabricated in order to support the Soviet version. On July 20, 1943, the German Report (AM) had not yet been published. The partisans could not have known that the Soviet leadership would take the German allegations seriously enough to mount a full-scale Soviet investigation commission.

Moreover, the partisan documents about the Germans bringing other bodies to Katyn and so falsifying their whole investigation occur in the middle of much longer written reports about the partisans' activity. The Katyn materials, like the one above, are mentioned almost incidentally, rather than being featured as part of any effort to advocate Soviet innocence in the murders.

2. Evidence supporting the testimony of local residents that they were forced by the Germans to sign statements written in the German language that they did not understand.

Sakharov reproduces photographic copies of longer statements from five local residents who gave testimony to the Germans that the Soviets had killed the Poles, and short affidavits from 11 other similar witnesses in which they certify that their statements previously given were truthful.

Ivanov, one of the witnesses testified to the Burdenko Commission that the Germans had forced him to sign a statement in German and would not give him that statement in Russian.

> ... I again refused to give false testimony to the German officer. He started shouting at me, threatened me with beating and shooting, and said I did not understand what was good for me. However, I stood my ground. **The interpreter then drew up a short protocol in German** on one page, and gave me a free translation of its contents. This protocol recorded, as the interpreter told me, only the fact of the arrival of the Polish war prisoners at Gnezdovo station. **When I asked that my testimony be recorded not only in German but also in Russian, the officer finally went beside himself with fury, beat me up with a rubber club and drove me off the premises** ... (BU 238)

Another witness, Savvateev, said something similar:

> After threatening and cajoling me for a long time, the officer consulted with the interpreter about some-

thing in German, and then **the interpreter wrote a short protocol and gave it to me to sign. He explained that it was a record of my testimony. I asked the interpreter to let me read the· protocol myself, but he interrupted me with abuse**, ordering me to sign it immediately and get out. I hesitated a minute. **The interpreter seized a rubber club hanging on the wall and made to strike me. After that I signed the protocol shoved at me.** The interpreter told me to get out and go home, and not to talk to anyone or I would be shot. (BU 238-9)

The documents published by Sakharov confirm that *all* the witnesses signed statements in German, which none of them could read.

Sakharov also notes that none of the witnesses in the German Report who testified that the Soviets had shot the Poles in April – May 1940 remarked on the smell. Sakharov logically suggests that there would have been a considerable odor of decaying flesh, as the graves would have been left open for many days. This argument is consistent with the contradictions in the witnesses' statements that we noted in a previous chapter. It is negative evidence, however. It confirms other evidence but it cannot stand as evidence by itself because it is indirect and therefore weak.

3. Evidence that the Polish prisoners that were transferred from Kozel'sk to Smolensk were sentenced not to execution but to various prison terms

In his 1991 book *Katynskii labirint* Vladimir K. Abarinov, a proponent of the "official" Soviets-did-it version, noted that he found records indicating that it was the 136th battalion that had convoyed the prisoners from Kozel'sk to Smolensk. (10-11, 27 ff.)

In the Russian State Military Archive – RGVA in Russian – Sakharov found the schedule of transfers carried out by convoy units of the NKVD for the second quarter of 1940. The document is titled:

Сведения о характере и сроках осуждения заклю-
ченных, отконвоированных эшелонными, сквоз-
ными и плановыми конвоями частей и соедине-
ний конвойных войск НКВД СССР за 2-й квартал
1940 г.

Translated:

Information on the nature and length of sentence of
convicted prisoners transferred by escorted trains and
by direct and planned convoy escort units and for-
mations of convoy troops of the NKVD for the 2nd
quarter of 1940.

This schedule includes the information about the 136th battalion of
the 22nd division of convoy troops, commanded by Major Mezhov.
According to Sakharov and Abarinov this was the unit that transferred ("convoyed") the Polish officer POWs from the Kozel'sk
camp to the Smolensk oblast' NKVD.

Here is the information from this schedule about this specific battalion's activity for the 2nd quarter of 1940:

Наименование соединение и частей	Осуждено на сроки							Подследственных	Ссыльных и спец переселенцев	Всего отконвоировано
	До 3-х лет	От 3-х до 5 лет	От 5-ти до 8 лет	От 8-ми до 10 лет	От 10-ти до 15 лет	Свыше 15 лет	Всего осужденных			
11-я бригада В т.ч.	22456	10593	4720	1505	660	40	39974	7333	7785	55092
236 полк	14877	8712	3584	1079	523	36	28811	4382	6224	39417
127 б-н	1972	577	408	48	72	-	3077	418	-	3495
134 б-н	616	305	162	53	-	-	1136	150	1561	2847
147 б-н	4991	999	566	325	65	4	6950	2383	-	9333
15 бригада В т.ч.	9877	3431	2044	535	529	130	16546	16377	34314	67237
136 б-н	4300	858	443	134	34	-	5769	2512	2635	10916

Table recreated based on original.
(hi-res available at: https://tinyurl.com/furr-katyn-images)

According to this schedule, in the second quarter of 1940 this battalion convoyed 10, 916 persons. Of these, 5769 had been sentenc-

es to various terms of imprisonment («Всего осужденных»): 1 – 3 year, 4300; 3 – 5 years, 858; 5 – 8 years, 443; 8 – 10 years, 134; 10 – 15 years, 34; more than 15 years, 0. In addition, this NKVD unit convoyed 2512 persons under investigation and 2635 persons sentenced to exile and special settlements. The whole schedule may be seen as Appendix No. 13 ("Prilozhenie No.13") at the end of Sakharov's article.

This evidence too is confirmatory only. It is not unimpeachable itself. It might be argued that the convoy troops had not been informed of the true fates of the prisoners they were transferring from Kozel'sk to Smolensk and Gnezdovo. But it is consistent with the unimpeachable evidence we have analyzed previously.

4. The statement of the German tree expert that he did not collect the treelings sent to him by the Germans at Katyn, but only reported on what had been sent to him.

The German Report stated that small pine treelings had been planted over the mass graves.[3]

> An der Bodenbewachsung war ersichtlich, daß diese Hügel von Menschenhand aufgeworfen und mit jungen Kiefern bepflanzt worden waren. (AM 15)

> *Translated:*

> It was evident from the ground cover that these hills had been raised by human hands and planted with young pines.

> Diese Gräber befanden sich nahe beieinander in größeren, mit einem auffällig jungen Kiefernbestand

---

[3] Perhaps in order to conceal them, in time.

bepflanzten, nach Südwesten zu abfallenden Waldlichtungen (s. Lageskizze). (AM 39)

Translated:

These graves were located near each other in larger
forest clearings planted with a conspicuously young
pine grove and falling away towards the southwest.

The German Report states that the treelings were submitted to a
master forester, von Herff, who concluded that they were at least 5
years old that had been transplanted to their present location
three years previously – that is, in 1940, before the German invasion of the USSR..

Die Massengräber befinden sich in Waldlichtungen.
Sie sind vollkommen geebnet und mit jungen Kiefern-
bäumchen bepflanzt. Nach dem eigenen Augenschein
der Kommissionsmitglieder und der Aussage des als
Sachverständigen zugezogenen Forstmeisters von
Herff handelt es sich um wenigstens fünfjährige, im
Schatten großer Bäume schlecht entwickelte Kiefernpflanzen, die vor drei Jahren an diese Stelle gepflanzt
wurden. (AM 116)

Translated:

The mass graves are located in forest clearings. They
are completely levelled and planted with young pine
trees. According to the Commission members' own
opinion and the statement by the forestry master von
Herff, who had been brought as an expert, they were
pine plantings poorly developed from the shade of
larger trees that had been planted at this place three
years earlier.

Sakharov located a transcription of von Herff's report in which he
states that he did not collect the six treeling samples himself but
received them from Dr. Birkle and Dr. Buhtz. This transcription is
photographically reproduced as Appendix 14 of Sakharov's article.

This means that there is no chain of evidence here. The treelings could have been collected somewhere else before being given to von Herff. Unless we are going to simply "believe" the Germans, von Herff's conclusions concerning the treelings are no good as evidence.

In the fourth week of August 1943 Dr. Burdenko wrote a letter to Nikolai Shvernik, the Chairman of the Extraordinary State Commission on Establishing and Investigating the Crimes of the German and Fascist Occupiers.[4] In his letter Burdenko described something of what he had learned in investigating a number of German mass murder sites, most recently in Orel, Russia. Burdenko described a "German signature" in their practice of mass murder that included the planting of little trees:

> Но зато есть такое обстоятельство: в протоколе сказано: «На могиле с целью скрыть следы расстрела русские насадили деревца». Мое внимание было привлечено к следующему факту: у общей могилы в укромном углу — в застенке тюремного двора — место общей могилы тоже засажено «деревцами». Эти факты, начиная со способа расстрела и кончая засаживанием «деревцами», свидетельствуют о «немецкой системе». Из приводимых описаний является несомненным факт расстрела польских офицеров. Это — дело рук немецких фашистов, ...

Translated:

But consider this matter. In the German report [AM] it says: "On the grave the Russians planted treelings with the aim of hiding the traces of the executions." My attention was drawn to the following fact: at a

---

[4] See the Russian-language Wikipedia page on Shvernik at
https://ru.wikipedia.org/wiki/Шверник,_Николай_Михайлович This information is not on the corresponding English language Wikipedia page.

common grave in a secluded corner – in the wall of the courtyard of a prison – a site of a common grave is also planted with "treelings." These facts, beginning with the method of shooting and ending with the planting of "treelings," are evidence of a "German system." From the cited descriptions it appears as an unquestionable fact that the massacre of Polish officers is the work of the German fascists ... (Sorokina, at note 57; Lebedeva, at note 8)

In his July 1945 talk to the Czech Medical Society Frantisek Hájek, one of the medical team that the Germans had brought to Katyn to certify their claims that the bodies had been buried for about three years and thus had been killed by the Soviets, testified that the German forester had told him, Hájek, that the treelings might not have been transplanted at all.

6. Dukaz petiletými borovickami.

Jako dukaz uvádí Nemci také mladé petileté borovicky, které byly nasázeny na nasypaných pahorcích. My jsme jich sami nevideli …Zjišteno. že je nejméne petiletá a na rezu blíže stredu bylo lze videti málo znatelný temnejší pruh. Zavolaný lesmistr von Herff prohlásil, že takový pruh vzniká, když je rust borovicky necím zabrzden, na pr. presazením a soudil, že borovická byla presazena pred 3 lety. Sám však uznal, že borovicky jsou špatne vyvinuté, rostoucí ve stínu velkých stromu — mohl tedy býti tento pruh zavinen také vlivem jiným a ne jen presazením.

Translated:

6. The Evidence of the Five-Year-Old Pines.

As evidence, the Germans also pointed to the five-year-old young pines that were planted on the mounds. We did not see them, because the graves were already opened, they showed us only one of the pines. … It was established that it was at least five

years old and that in the cut closer to the center there
was visible a scarcely noticeable little dark band. The
master forester von Herff said that such a dark stripe
occurs when something stops the growth of the
treeling, for example as a result of a transplant, and
believed that the pine was transplanted 3 years ago.
**However, he conceded that the little pine was
poorly developed from growing in the shade of
other trees, and this band could thus be the result
of other influences, not only as a result of a transplant.**

Von Herff also stated that he was given the treelings and did not
collect them himself from the graves.

Mir wurden von der Delegation ausländischer
Gerichtsme[dikern] 6 Kiefernpflanzen zur Unter-
suchung vorgelegt, die von Her[rn] Birkle aus Bu-
karest und Herrn Prof. Buhtz aus Breslau in [der]
nächsten Umgebung der Massengräber von Katyn
persönlich [ge] nommen worden sind.

Translated:

I was presented with 6 pine plants by the delegation
of foreign forensic medical doctors for the purpose of
examination. They had been taken from the area close
to the mass graves at Katyn by Dr. Birkle of Bucharest
and Dr. Buhtz of Breslau personally.

5. Evidence that the Germans captured and possessed the Soviet transfer lists of POWs.

German possession of these lists explains the occasional agreement between the order of bodies listed as found and identified at
Katyn and the Soviet transfer lists.

Defenders of the "official" version have assumed that this agreement – occasional, not consistent, but still striking when encoun-
tered – was evidence that the prisoners were shot convoy by con-

voy as they arrived from Kozel'sk. Vladislav Shved, among others, has set transfer lists side by side with the lists of disinterred bodies in AM, presumably given in the order in which they were exhumed. He has shown that, at least in the case that he examined, there is no consistent pattern of agreement between the two lists.

However, Sakharov's article has made this line of inquiry moot. He discovered documents that prove that the Germans had the lists of POWs sent from Kozel'sk to the Smolensk NKVD. These are the same lists that are reproduced in Tucholski's book. We have confirmed this by obtaining from the Russian State Military Archive the documents cited by Sakharov here and from which he quotes some passages in Russian translation. The original documents are, of course, in German. Facsimiles of these documents may be found on the "Images" web page of this volume. They are:

* ГАРФ. Ф.7021. ОП.114. Д.23. Л.109. (GARF. Fond. 7021. Opis. 114. Delo. 23. List 109.)

* ГАРФ. Ф.7021. ОП.114. Д.23. Л.108.

* ГАРФ. Ф.7021. ОП.114. Д.23. Л.102.

We saw in Chapter 8 that Jósef Frelkiewicz's name was copied from the Soviet list of Kozel'sk POWs. There is at least one more entry in AM that shows that the Germans were using the Soviet list rather than documents from the graves:

3733. Liachowski, Boleslaw, (Vater Antoni), Uniformierter.

Impfzettel, 1 Brief mit Stempel, New York, Brooklyn, 1 Zettel mit Notizen.

In Tucholski, p. 153 col. 1, we read: "Lakowski-Brzuszek" But on the Soviet transit list we read:

ЛЯХОВСКОГО Болеслава Антоновича, 1909 г.р. (Tucholski p. 682 #19)

The Soviet list transliterates the name ЛЯ – "L + ya". But the name in Polish begins with "La", not "Lia." The Germans could not have obtained this name from any letter or other document on this body, or found in a grave or anywhere else. Therefore the Germans transliterated this name from the Russian-language Soviet list.

So we have the documentary evidence that the Germans had the Russian list of Kozel'sk prisoners. But if we did not have it, the examples of Frelkiewicz and Lachowski would be sufficient proof of it.

6. Unpublished documents show that both the Poles and the Germans at Katyn acknowledge that the identifications made there were falsified because the documents were often not found on individual bodies.

Sakharov quotes from a meeting in Kraków of June 10, 1943 in which the main directorate of propaganda of the German *Generalgouvernement* (the Government of German-occupied Poland during the war) stated that the identifications of bodies at Katyn that had been published in Polish newspapers were unreliable since they were accurate in only a few instances.

> Например, на совещании, проведенном 10 июня 1943 г. в Кракове главным управлением пропаганды правительства генерал-губернаторства было констатировано: «до сих пор предоставленные и в польской прессе опубликованные списки трупов, идентифицированных в Катыни, недостоверны, так как только в немногих случаях соответствуют действительности»
>
> [16 to ГАРФ. Ф.7021. Оп.114. Д.23. Л.118.]
>
> For example, at a meeting that took place on July 10 1943 in Krakow it was affirmed by the main directorate of propaganda of the government of the Generalgouvernement: "The lists of bodies identified at Katyn that have been presented up to this point and

published in the Polish press are unreliable, since they correspond to reality in only a few cases.

According to Sakharov representatives of the Polish Red Cross also participated in this meeting.

В одном из писем ПКК, в частности, говорилось: «Из до сих пор поступавших списков мы лишь в немногих случаях можем считать данные доста- точным основанием для информирования родных, так как при таком большом количестве имен от- сутствуют личные данные, допускающие несо- мненное опознание умерших (выделено нами. – В.С.)»[17 to ГАРФ. Ф.7021. Оп.114. Д.38. Л.9.]

Translated:

In particular, one of the letters of the PRC states: "Of the lists available to this point we can only in a few cases consider the data a sufficient basis for informing relatives, since for a large number of names we lack personal data that would permit us to identify the dead with certainty."

7. Evidence that the names assigned to bodies in the German list are not based on real identifications but on the haphazard association of unidentified corpses with documents not necessarily found on those corpses.

In a letter of July 27, 1943 to the German Red Cross the Propagan- da Section of the German *Generalgouvernement* admitted that the documents from different bodies were often mixed up and the documents of a single person were scattered among 12 different envelopes.

Andererseits wurden durch die verschiedenen Bes- chichtigungen der Dokumente die Papiere durchei- nander gebracht und zudem die zu einer Leiche gehö- rigen Dokumente bei Verpacken auf verschiedene

Umschläge verteilt. So fanden sich z.B. die Papiere
eines Offiziers in 12 verschidenen Umschlägen.

Translated:

Also through the different layerings of the documents
the papers have been mixed up and in addition the
documents belonging to one corpse have been divided
in the packing-up process among different envelopes.
So for example the papers of a single officer were located in 12 different envelopes.

Sakharov reproduces a photographic copy of this document as Appendix 16. It is also attached as an appendix to the present chapter. The documents were all mixed up, names either false or "ent-
stellt geschrieben" – written in a disfigured, inaccurate manner.

The Polish Red Cross agreed. On October 12, 1943 the Technical
Commission of the Polish Red Cross sent a lengthy letter to the International Committee of the Red Cross in Geneva in which they
reported, among other things, the following:

Andererseits selbst wenn das PRK sämtliche
Ergebnisse der Exhumation und Identifikationsarbeit-
en einschließen der Dokumente und Andenken
besäße könnte es offiziell und in endgültiger Form
nicht bescheinigen daß der betreffende Offiziere in
Katyn gestorben ist. Der unerkennbare Zustand der
Leichen, die Tatsache, daß in vielen Fällen bei 2
Leichen Dokumente vorgefunden worden sind, die
zweifellos einer einziger Person angehörten, die min-
imale Zahl der Kennmarken, der einzig einwandfreien
Beweisstücke, die auf den Leichen gefunden wurden,
endlich der der Mordtat vorangegangene Zustand, das
die in Katyn ermorderten Militärpersonen nicht auf
dem Schlachtfelde, sondern nach einer Zeitraum
fielen, in welcher der Wechsel der Uniform, das Verk-
leiden und die Fluchtversuche an der Tagesordnung
waren, alle diese Urstände berechtigen das DRK nur

bescheinigen zu können, daß die betreffenden
Leichen, gewisse Dokumente getragen hat.

Translated:

On the other hand, even if the PRC were in possession
of all the results of the exhumation and identification
work of the documents and memorabilia, it could not
officially and definitively certify that the officer in
question died in Katyn. The unrecognizable state of
the corpses, **the fact that, in many cases, documents
were found on two corpses that doubtless belonged to a single person**, the very few [literally,
minimal number of] distinguishing marks, the only
flawless evidence, found on the corpses, and finally
the state of affairs preceding the murder, that the soldiers killed at Katyn did not fall on the battlefield, but
after a period of time during which changes of uniform, dress, and attempts at escape were the order of
the day, **all these circumstances entitle the PRC only to certify that the corpses in question carried
certain documents.**

- ГАРФ. Ф.7021. ОП.114. Д.23. Л.31 – 38 at l. 38.

The entire document is also reproduced in the original German in
the volume *Nemtsy v Katyni. Dokumenty o rasstrele pol'skikh voen-
noplennykh osen'iu 1941 goda.* (The Germans in Katyn. Documents
concerning the shooting of Polish POWs in the Autumn of 1941.)
Moscow: Izdatel'stvo ITRK, 2010, 106 – 117.

In a previous letter of August 16, 1943, to the International Committee of the Red Cross the leadership of the Polish Red Cross admitted that:

a part of the documents found which belonged to a
single individual were found in the pockets of the uniform of one corpse, and others either in the sand of
the grave or on other corpses.

Therefore, the PRC leadership considered that the list of names of Polish victims "should be regarded as provisional" subject to follow-up activity "in connection with the official results of the forensic medical expert examination under way in Cracow." (Sakharov, at note 27)

The report of the Technical Commission of the Polish Red Cross was published long ago. But it does not mention either of these letters at all. Nor are they mentioned in the four-volume official Polish collection *Katyń. Dokumenty Zbrodni*. They are simply omitted.

This omission conceals the unreliable nature of the identification of bodies and of the documents in the German report (AM). But AM is the central evidentiary document that sustains the "official" version of Katyn, that the Soviet killed the Poles.

Sakharov draws the following conclusion:

> На основании вышеизложенного мы можем утверждать, что находившиеся в руках германской полиции какие-то документы, бумаги и даже предметы, использовались ею, во-первых, в качестве заменителей реально не существующих трупов и, во-вторых, для «идентификации» трупов, изначально фигурировавших как «неопознанные».

Translated:

> On the basis of the aforementioned evidence we can affirm that some documents, papers, and even objects in the hands of the German police were utilized in place of bodies that in reality did not exist and for the "identification" of bodies which had originally been classed as "unidentified."

This implies that some of the documents found on bodies *may* have really belonged to that person – but we have no idea which do and which do not.

We do not know how the Germans determined the nationality of bodies dressed in civilian clothes. Some are listed as "in uniform" without specifying *what* uniform. In light of the statements by Soviet partisans recorded in the summer of 1943 these could have been bodies not of Polish but of Soviet soldiers. Appendices 2 through 5 of Sakharov's article reproduce these accounts of partisans. All accuse the Germans of disinterring bodies of Soviet soldiers as well as of civilians. There is no basis to question the genuine nature of these documents. We have obtained one of these documents and reproduced it above.

Conclusion

Sakharov concludes his article with the following remarks:

> The manipulation cited above of the corpses and materials by the German authorities who had "researched" the "Katyn affair" exclude any "taking on faith" of any fact, taken by itself, of establishing a connection between them [the bodies and the materials].

Sakharov's research, the contradictions internal to AM, and the identification of many of the corpses found at Katyn (Koz'i Gory) as POWs who were shipped to Kalinin or Khar'kov but clearly not shot there – all these results deal a fatal blow to the *bona fides* of the German Report (AM) as an objective body of evidence. These results also mean that, because it relies heavily upon the German Report (AM), the "official" version of Katyn loses its evidentiary foundation.

Chapter 10. The Burdenko Commission Report

In this chapter we begin to consider the accounts of the Katyn massacre that appeared between the German AM of 1943 and the emergence of CP in 1992, and in which new evidence was set forth. These are: the report of the Burdenko Commission (BU) of January, 1944; the Nuremberg trial of 1946; and the Madden Committee of 1952. We begin with the report of the Burdenko Commission.

The Burdenko Report (BU)

The works that set forth the "official" version of Katyn say little about the Burdenko Commission and refer the reader to other critiques. In several cases they assert that these other critiques are "devastating" to the Burdenko Commission's findings.

Here we examine the two major studies by Cienciala and Sanford, and the critiques of BU to which they refer: an essay by M. IU. Sorokina; an essay by Natalia Lebedeva; a chapter in a book by Henri De Montfort; and the chapter on BU in the book *Katynskaia drama*.

We begin with a brief consideration of an essay by Sorokina. This essay has been put online by two prominent Russian supporters of the "official" Soviets-did-it version, Sergei Romanov and Aleksei Pamiatnykh. Presumably they have made it available because they believe it is worthy of consideration.

Sorokina:

> M.IU. Sorokina. "Operatsia 'umelye ruki", ili chto uvi-
> del akademik Burdenko v Orle." ("Operation 'Skillful

Hands', or what Academician Burdenko Saw in Orel."),
2005[1]

Sorokina's 2005 essay is an attempt to discredit Burdenko's contention that the Germans were the guilty party at Katyn. Burdenko reached this opinion by comparing the German AM with his own experience investigating sites of German mass murders, including in Orel.

Sorokina accepts that the "official" version of Katyn is true without questioning it. She is sarcastic, even contemptuous, of Burdenko and his commission. But she is unable to present any evidence at all that Burdenko's analysis was at fault in any respect.

The whole essay is an exercise in logical fallacies: "begging the question" (accepting the "official" version without questioning it); argument by scare quotes instead of by evidence; *ad hominem* argument by attempting to find negative information about Burdenko and the other commission members – although she is finally unable to find any such material.

Her only real conclusion is that, based on his broad experience with German mass murder sites, Burdenko himself was indeed convinced that the Germans had shot the Poles. Burdenko wrote:

> Я в бытность мою в Орле, как член Правительственной комиссии, раскопал почти 1000 трупов и нашел, что 200 расстрелянных советских граждан имеют те же самые ранения, что и польские офицеры. Достаточно тщательно сопоставить описание немецких протоколов и протоколов наших вскрытий, чтобы убедиться в тождестве и обнаружить "умелую руку"... Таким образом, установленное тождество "метода" убийств в Орле и Катынском лесу является знаменательным и дает несомненное доказательство, что "умелая рука"

---

[1] . Online at http://katynfiles.com/content/sorokina-burdenko-orel.html

была одна и та же и обличает немцев как виновников катынской трагедии.

Translated:

When I was in Orel, as a member of the Government Commission, I unearthed almost 1000 corpses and found that 200 Soviet citizens shot to death have the same wounds as the Polish officers. It is enough to compare the description of the German protocols and protocols of our autopsies to make sure of identity and to discover the "skillful hand" ... Thus, the established identity of the "method" of murders in the Orel and Katyn forest is significant and gives unquestionable evidence that the "skillful hand" was the very same and exposes the Germans as the perpetrators of the Katyn tragedy.

Sorokina fails to point out that Burdenko had the very experience – that of examining numerous sites of mass murder – that the members of the commission of medical experts brought to Katyn by the Germans lacked.

De Montfort

Sanford writes as follows:

De Montfort, *Masakra w Katyniu*, pp. 109-19 unravels the inconsistencies and falsehoods in the Soviet report very convincingly. (Sanford, 153 n. 93)

Here Sanford cites the Polish translation of the book by Henri de Montfort, *Le massacre de Katyn: Crime Russe ou Crime Allemand?* (Paris: Editions de la Table Ronde, 1966). For some reason Sanford cites the French edition, not the Polish translation, in his bibliography on page 240.

De Montfort discusses the Burdenko report in Chapter X, pages 117-130 of the original French book. This is also Chapter X (Rozdział X), pages 109-119, in the Polish translation. I have ob-

tained the Polish translation of de Montfort's book and have verified that it is simply a translation of the French original, so here I
will use the French text.

De Montfort did not study AM carefully. He says there were 4145
bodies. (109) In fact there are many gaps in the numbers assigned
to corpses in AM.

De Montfort certainly did not read the BU carefully either. He
states:

> Elle prit donc le parti de soutenir que les documents
> recueillis par les enquêteurs d'avril et de mai 1941
> étaient tous, sans exception, des documents falsifiés.
> (119)

> *Translated:*

> It [the Burdenko Commission] therefore decided to
> maintain that the documents collected by the [Ger-
> man] investigators of April and May 1941 [sic; de
> Montfort must mean 1943] were all, without excep-
> tion, falsified documents.

As evidence for this statement he cites his own translation of BU:

> ...ils retirèrent des vêtements des officiers polonais,
> tués par eux, tous les documents portant une date
> postérieure à avril 1940, date à laquelle, selon la thèse
> provocatrice des Allemands, les Polonais auraient été
> tués par les Bolcheviks...

> ... they [the Germans] removed from the Polish offic-
> ers' clothing, killed by them, all documents bearing a
> date after April 1940, the date on which, according to
> the provocative thesis of the Germans, the Poles were
> killed by the Bolsheviks...

Here, in de Montfort's own translation, we read that BU accuses
the Germans of removing all documents dated after April 1940.
But then de Montfort says this:

Comment les Allemands auraient-ils pu faire fabriquer à l'avance des documents aussi divers, aussi variés, que ceux trouvés sur les cadavres? (119)

Translated:

How could the Germans have produced in advance documents as diverse and varied as those found on corpses?

De Montfort repeats this accusation:

Si, par simple hypothèse, j'admettais momentanément la véracité de la thèse présentée par la Commission d'enquête soviétique, c'est-à-dire l'exécution, par les Allemands, des prisonniers de guerre polonais, entre septembre et décembre 1941, puis l'exhumation des cadavres de ces prisonniers en mars 1943 pour substituer de faux papiers portant des dates antérieures à avril 1940 à leurs vrais papiers portant des dates postérieures à avril 1940... (123-124)

Translated:

If, by mere hypothesis, I were to admit for a moment the veracity of the thesis presented by the Soviet Commission of Inquiry, that is to say the execution by the Germans of the Polish prisoners of war between September and December 1941, then the exhumation of the corpses of these prisoners in March 1943 to substitute false papers bearing dates before April 1940 for their real papers bearing dates after April 1940..

...les Russes ont formellement accusé les Allemands d'avoir fabriqué ces documents ... (127)

Translated:

> ...the Russians formally accused the Germans of hav-
> ing fabricated these documents ...

De Montfort accuses BU of claiming that the Germans *falsified in advance* the documents found on the corpses. Chapter XI of his book is titled "Impossibilité d'introduire de faux documents sur les cadavres" ("impossibility of placing false documents on the corpses").

But BU never states any such thing. Even in de Montfort's own translation BU states that the Germans *removed* documents *later* than 1940 – "**retirèrent** des vêtements des officiers polonais ... tous les documents portant **une date postérieure à avril 1940**."

De Montfort goes on to accept the claim in AM that no insects were found on the corpses:

> l'absence sur un cadavre de ce que le Professeur
> Lacassagne appelle « les travailleurs de la mort » est «
> une indication aussi précieuse que leur présence et
> permet d'établir que la mort a eu lieu pendant l'hiver.»
>
> On voudra bien se rappeler que la Commission des
> Représentants des Instituts de Médecine légale et de
> Criminologie a certifié dans son rapport qu'elle n'avait
> trouvé, sur les cadavres des fosses qu'elle avait vis-
> itées, aucune trace de ces insectes que le Professeur
> Lacassagne appelle « les travailleurs de la mort».
> (134-135)

Translated:

> The absence on a corpse of what Professor Lacassagne
> calls "the workers of death" is "an indication as valua-
> ble as their presence and makes it possible to estab-
> lish that death took place during the winter."
>
> It will be remembered that the Commission of Repre-
> sentatives of the Institutes of Forensic Medicine and
> Criminology certified in its report that it had not

found on the bodies of the graves which it had visited, any trace of these insects that Professor Lacassagne calls "the workers of death."

De Montfort is in error. In our discussion of AM we have seen that there was clear evidence of insects in the corpses examined by two of the doctors.

As a critique of BU de Montfort's chapter is both dishonest and incompetent. That Sanford believes it to be "very convincing" shows that he has been blinded by his own bias. Cienciala, to whose study we turn next, does not mention de Montfort's book at all.

Cienciala:

Anna M Cienciala; Natalia S. Lebedeva; Wojciech Materski. *Katyn: a crime without punishment.* New Haven: Yale University Press, "Annals of Communism" series, 2007.

This book represent the most authoritative account of the "official" version. At 561 pages it is also the longest. Hence we devote more attention to it. We will refer to it as "Cienciala."

> For the next forty-seven years successive Soviet governments claimed that the Germans were guilty of the Katyn massacre. They engaged in a series of cover-ups, the most elaborate of which were the **fabricated** report of the Soviet Commission of Inquiry into the Katyn Massacre (the Burdenko Commission) in January 1944 and the **fabricated** Soviet case for German guilt at the International War Crimes Tribunal held at Nuremberg in 1945–1946. **Although the Soviet charge was disproved**, German guilt was proclaimed by all Soviet and other communist governments for almost half a century. (Cienciala 2)

This claim by Cienciala is false. Cienciala cites no evidence that anything in the BU was falsified in any way, that the Soviet case at Nuremburg was "fabricated," or that "the Soviet charge was disproved."

> It is worth noting that most of the locals who gave tes-
> timony to the Germans and the IMC reversed them-
> selves under NKVD pressure when they **"testified"** be-
> fore the Soviet State (Burdenko) Commission in Janu-
> ary 1944. (135)

Here Cienciala employs the propaganda technique of "argument by scare quotes." The scare quotes signal that Cienciala wishes to suggest that the witness testimony to the BU was deliberately false – fabricated by the Soviets or by the witnesses themselves, per- haps after being threatened. But Cienciala has no evidence that this was so. By implication Cienciala also assumes that that the witnesses' testimony to the Germans as true – another example of "begging the question" by *assuming* that which should be proven, not assumed.

Nor does Ciencala have any evidence that the BU witnesses were lying. So, rather than admitting this, she uses "scare quotes" in hopes that the reader will not notice that she has no evidence to support her accusation.

Cienciala's bias could hardly be more blatant. In Cienciala's ac- count only the Soviets "pressured" the witnesses – though she has no evidence at all that they did so. Cienciala fails to inform her readers that the BU witnesses who also testified for the Germans said that they did so because the Germans threatened and beat them. She does not put the witness testimony on behalf of the Germans into scare quotes.

> The details of this NKVD preparatory work became
> known in 1990, when the investigators of the Russian
> Federation Main Military Prosecutor's Office learned
> that the operational workers sent from Moscow **had
> prepared forged documents with dates later than
> May 1940** and placed them in the clothes of selected
> victims. (227)

Note 55 to this paragraph, which is on page 500 of Cienciala, reads: "On the NKVD preparation of documents and witnesses, see KD2, pp. 430–432." On p. xxiv Cienciala identifies "KD2" as the volume *Katyn: Mart 1940 g.– Sentiabr 2000 g.*

Here is the relevant part of that source:

> Следователи Главной военной прокуратуры (ГВП) Российской Федерации в начале 90-х гг. самым тщательным образом изучили методы проведения предварительного расследования, предшествовавшие работе Комиссии Н.Н. Бурденко. **Они доказали, что прибывшие из Москвы оперативники изготовили поддельные документы с более поздними датами**, подложили их в извлеченные из могил останки, а также подготовили лжесвидетелей. (KD2 430)

> *Translated:*

> Investigators of the Main Military Prosecutor's Office (GVP) of the Russian Federation in the early 90's studied in the most painstaking manner the methods of conducting the preliminary investigation, which preceded the work of N.N. Burdenko. **They proved that operatives arriving from Moscow produced counterfeit documents with later dates**, put them in the remains of the graves, and prepared false witnesses.

This is an important conclusion! But KD2 gives no evidence for this statement. Cienciala, of course, knew this.

Furthermore, we know that this statement is false – a deliberate lie. Pamiatnykh has published the notes of the Burdenko investigators about the documents they found on the corpses. As we have seen one of them – that of Kozietulski – is so fragmentary that the investigators read it incorrectly, failed to recognize its importance for the Soviet case and so never used it. It is one of the pieces of our "unimpeachable evidence." It cannot have been "planted" by the Soviets.

Therefore "KD2" is lying. Cienciala should have checked this, as we have done. It is the job of every responsible scholar to double-check her sources.

> According to a Soviet decree of 19 April 1943, these people were liable to the death penalty for the crime of "cooperating with the enemy," so when interrogated by NKVD officers, they agreed to say whatever they were told. (227)

There was such a decree – naturally enough. Collaboration with the enemy was illegal in every country.[2] But Cienciala is dishonest here as well. There is no evidence that any of the Burdenko Commission witnesses were threatened with prosecution. Moreover, by the same logic she should have discounted the testimony of the witnesses who confirmed the German version.

There are contradictions in the testimony of the witnesses in the German AM. Witness testimony to the Burdenko Commission claimed German threats and beatings. Valentin Sakharov has published the signed witness statements prepared by the Germans. All are in German, not in Russian. This corroborates the testimony of one witness that he had to sign something he did not understand. We have discussed all this in a previous chapter.

> Between 5 October 1943 and 10 January 1944, NKVD investigators interrogated ninety-five persons and **"verified" (that is, formulated)** seventeen statements later made before the special state commission.[55] (227)[3]

---

[2] For an article in Russian discussing this decree see
https://ru.wikipedia.org/wiki/Указ_«О_мерах_наказания_для_немецко-фашистских_злодеев...» For the text of the decree see:
https://ru.wikisource.org/wiki/Указ_Президиума_ВС_СССР_от_19.04.1943_№_39

[3] Cienciala's note 55, on p. 500, contains no evidence for this statement that the NKVD investigators "formulated" – composed, fabricated – the testimony of the witnesses they called.

More argument by scare quote! Moreover, this statement is a logical fallacy: it "begs the question" – assumes that which must be proven. Cienciala has no evidence that the witnesses' testimony was faked or the result of threats. Therefore, Cienciala is lying. Why not likewise *assume* the Germans threatened *their* witnesses?

> It is not known how many of its members knew or suspected the truth at the time, but Burdenko may have done so. Shortly before his death in 1946, he reportedly admitted to a family friend—Boris Olshansky—that as a doctor, he knew the graves were four years old, which would have dated them to 1940. He also said he believed the NKVD comrades had made a "great blunder." Burdenko's daughter-in-law allegedly confirmed this statement to Yuri Zoria, son of the Soviet deputy prosecutor at the Nuremberg Trials, who died a mysterious death at Nuremberg in May 1946.[56] (228)

At note 56 (page 500) we read:

> On Burdenko's admission to Boris Olshansky, Jr., see Zawodny, *Death in the Forest*, pp. 158 and 167 n. 57. Burdenko's daughter-in-law told Yuri Zoria that when Burdenko was very sick, he admitted that the NKVD had falsified documents, including the dates of the Katyn crime; see Inessa Jazborowska, Anatolij Jablokow, and Jurij Zoria, *Katyń: Zbrodnia Chroniona Tajemnicą Państwową* [Katyn: The Crime Protected as a State Secret] (Warsaw, 1998), p. 299. This is a more popular, Polish version of the later Russian work by Inessa S. Yazhborovskaia, Anatolii Yu. Yablokov, Valentina S. Parsadanova, titled *Katynskii Sindrom*.

This tale is also noted by Sanford (139-140). Let's check this story.

Katyń: Zbrodnia Chroniona... p. 299:

> Sam Burdenko, ciężko chory, wyznał później, że NKWD sfałszowało dokumenty, między innymi daty

zbrodni katyńskiej. Potwierdziła to synowa Burdenki
w rozmowie z Jurijem Zorią.

Burdenko himself, seriously ill, confessed later that
the NKVD falsified documents, including the date of
the Katyn massacre. This was confirmed by Burdenko's daughter-in-law in an interview with Yuri Zoria.

No source is cited for this rumor. Moreover, we know that it is
false. As we have seen, Sorokina shows that Burdenko himself was
firmly convinced of German guilt. Natalia Lebedeva too concludes
that Burdenko believed the Germans were guilty:

Первое заседание Комиссии открылось 13 января
в 13 часов в здании Нейрохирургического инсти-
тута в Москве (ул. Ульяновского, д. 19). Председа-
тельствовал Николай Бурденко, который, по всей
видимости, верил в то, что катынское преступле-
ние было совершено гитлеровцами.

Translated:

The first session of the Commission opened on January 13 [1944] at 1300 hours in the building of the
Neurosurgical institute in Moscow (Ul'ianovskii Street,
19). It was chaired by Nikolai Burdenko who, from all
appearances, believed that the crime of Katyn had
been perpetrated by the Hitlerites. (Lebedeva, at note
39)

Burdenko himself said *none* of Burdenko Commission members
had any doubts of German guilt:

В тот же день Бурденко отправил Меркулову
письмо, в котором разъяснял слова Колесникова,
сказанные тем несколькими днями ранее в разго-
воре с наркомом. Колесников тогда заявил, что
«уже найденными документами от конца 1940 го-

да полностью опровергнута версия немцев о том,
что поляки убиты русскими весной 1940 года. ...
Бурденко писал, что «поэтому он (Колесников —
Н.Л.) и сказал, что очень важно, если мы найдем
документы более позднего периода. Таковые к
счастию и нашлись. Ни у одного из членов Комиссии не получилось ложного впечатления». Катынь
1940 — 2000. С. 512—513.

Translated:

The same day Burdenko sent a letter to Merkulov in
which he explained Kolesnikov's words, spoken a few
days before in conversation with the People's Commissar. Kolesnikov then stated that "the version of the
Germans that the Poles were killed by the Russians in
the spring of 1940 is fully refuted by the documents
we have already found from the end of 1940." ... Burdenko wrote that "therefore he (Kolesnikov – N.L.)
said to that it was very important to find documents
dated from a later period. Fortunately, such documents have been found. Not a single one of the members of the Commission received a false impression." –
Katyn' 1940-2000, pp. 512-513 (Lebedeva, note 78).

Cienciala cites Lebedeva's essay, so there is no excuse for her to
have inserted this rumor that she had to know is contradicted by
Lebedeva. One could hardly wish for a clearer example of the fun-
damental dishonesty of Cienciala's book.

The O'Malley Report

Cienciala:

Sir Owen O'Malley, ambassador to the Polish government-in-exile, had made a convincing case of Soviet
guilt three years earlier in his letter of 24 May 1943 to
Foreign Secretary Sir Anthony Eden and wrote **a devastating critique** of the Burdenko Commission report
in February 1944.[66] (232)

The note to this passage:

> 66. Ambassador O'Malley's letters to Foreign Secretary
> Eden on Katyn in May 1943 and on the Burdenko
> Commission Report in February 1944 were first pub-
> lished in January 1972, in a pamphlet titled *Katyn—
> Dispatches* of Sir Owen O'Malley to the British Gov-
> ernment (London, 1972), with a preface by Lord
> Barnby, a supporter of the Polish cause, and an intro-
> duction by the American journalist Louis FitzGibbon.
> FitzGibbon also published them in his three books,
> *The Katyn Cover-Up* (London, 1972), *Unpitied and Un-
> known* (London, 1975), and *The Katyn Massacre* (Lon-
> don, 1977). See also the British publications listed in
> the next note. (501)[4]

O'Malley was a fanatical anticommunist as witness, for example,
the ferocity of his diatribe against Stalin in his May 1943 report.[5]
In his February 1944 report, the one in which he briefly discusses
BU, he states:

> The Russian story gives no explanation of why in
> these circumstances not a single one of the Poles who
> were allegedly transferred from Kozielsk, Starobielsk
> and Ostashkov to the labour camps Nos. 1 O.N., 2 O.N.,
> and 3 O.N. has ever been seen or heard of alive again.

O'Malley was the U.K. ambassador to the Polish Government-In-
Exile (GIE). He accepts their version of events and repeats their
reasons for rejecting the BU:

---

[4] The O'Malley report of May 24, 1943 is available online at
http://www.polandfirsttofight.besaba.com/malley1.html and several other places. The
O'Malley report of February 11, 1944 is online at http://www.nspm.rs/files/Owen.pdf

[5] See paragraph 17 of the May 1943 report.

* that it was up to the USSR to explain why no Polish POWs escaped the German "round-ups" of Poles after the German capture of the camps;

* that nothing was heard from any of the Polish POWs after they were transferred out of the three POW camps;

* that the Soviet government said nothing about their transfer to Camps 1-ON, 2-ON, and 3-ON before the German announcement about Katyn in April 1943.

In reality we do not know that "nothing was heard from any of the Polish POWs after they were transferred out of the three POW camps." This is the position of the Polish Government In Exile (GIE). Did they check? If so, how? Where is the documentation of their checkup?

More important: how do we know they were telling the truth? After all, if we are going to "believe" the Polish GIE we have already abandoned objectivity and the search for the historical truth just as surely as if we had decided to "believe" the Soviet government.

Were the Germans even delivering mail from the USSR to German-occupied Poland after September 1940, when the Polish POW's mail privileges were restored? O'Malley did not know. Evidently he did not care. He simply took the word of the Polish GIE.

Far from presenting a "devastating critique" of the BU, as Cienciala claims, O'Malley made no valid criticisms at all of the BU. These are "arguments from silence." O'Malley ignores what the BU *did* say, and instead concentrates on what it did *not* say. This is precisely the argument of the Polish GIE.

"The Polish Historians' Expert Assessment"

Cienciala writes:

> At the suggestion of a member of the Soviet group, Professor Oleg Rzheshevsky, who wanted to delay discussion of the Katyn question, the Polish historians

analyzed the Burdenko report, and in May they unexpectedly delivered to their Soviet colleagues a **devastating critique** that deprived it of any credibility…[111] (247)

This statement is, quite simply, false. We discuss this critique fully below.

Here is Cienciala's note to the passage above:

> [111.] Maciszewski, *Wydrzeć Prawdę* , p. 97; the author gives the Polish side of the story, while the chairman of the Soviet group, Professor Georgy Lukich Smirnov, gives his in *Uroki Minuvshevo* [Lessons of the Past] (Moscow, 1997). For another account of the Soviet group and its problems, see Yazhborovskaia, Yablokov, and Parsadanova, *Katynskii Sindrom*, chap. 4; also Jazborowska, Jablokow, and Zoria, *Katyń: Zbrodnia Chroniona*, chap. 2. Yazhborovskaia was a member of the Soviet group. (p. 506)

Cienciala again (248-249):

> The Polish media now increased their pressure for the truth about Katyn. The Polish Party historians' **devastating critique** of the Burdenko Commission report of 1944, handed to their Soviet colleagues in May 1988, was summarized in the 19 August 1989 issue of *Polityka*. Here, Polish historians related the known history of the Katyn crime, concluded that the Burdenko Commission findings were undoubtedly false, and claimed that the NKVD bore full responsibility for the extermination of the Kozelsk prisoners at Katyn, as well as the extermination of the prisoners of Starobel'sk and Ostashkov, even though their burial sites could not be established without access to Russian documents.[113]

The footnote to this passage:

113. *Polityka*, 33/1685 (1989), pp. 13–14. For the full
text of **the Polish historians' expert assessment** of
the Burdenko Commission report, see Jarema Maciszewski, comp. and ed., *Zbrodnia Katyńska: Z Prac
Polskiej Części Wspólnej Komisji Partyjnych Historyków
Polski i ZSRR* [The Crime of Katyn: From the Work of
the Polish Part of the Joint Commission of Soviet-
Polish Party Historians] (Warsaw, 1990; offset); **see
the Russian text in Yasnova, *Katynskaia Drama*,
pp. 179–201.** (p. 506)

Sanford states the same thing (139):

> The weaknesses and inconsistencies in the Burdenko
> Report were dissected in full in the April 1989 Report
> of the Polish members of the Joint Polish-Soviet His-
> torical Commission established to examine 'Blank
> Spots' in their relationship.[96]

> n. 96 p. 153: 'Ekspertyza', *Polityka*, 19 August 1989,
> pp. 13-14.

Cienciala and Sanford cite the same issue article in *Polityka*. Cienciala says we can use the Russian text in *Katynskaia Drama*. Just to
be certain, I have checked the Russian text both against the Maciszewski book *Zbrodnia Katyńska: Z Prac...* cited by Cienciala and
against the Polish version in *Polityka* of August 19, 1989, which
both Sanford and Cienciala cite.

Maciszewski *Zbrodnia Katyńska: Z Prac..* 15-36 (= 'Ekspertyza', *Polityka*); *Katynskaia Drama* pages 179-201 (Maciszewski = M; Katynskaia Drama = KD)

We saw above that Ciencala (248) also calls this a "devastating critique" of BU. This statement is false. As we shall demonstrate, what
Cienciala calls "the Polish historians' expert assessment" offers no
valid critique of BU at all.

It does make some interesting statements.

* M 21 point 4; KD 184:

> "4. Zwłoki z grobów I-VII ubrane były w odzież zimo-
> wą."

> "4. The Corpses from graves I-VII were dressed in win-
> ter clothing."

That means the Polish POWs had been provided with winter clothing by the Polish Army when captured in September 1939. They
would also have had it whether they were shot in April – May
1940, as the Germans claimed, or in September – December 1941,
as the Soviets concluded.

No one captured in Russia – or, for that matter, Western Ukraine
or Western Belorussia – would ever abandon winter clothing, no
matter what time of year it was. When they were transferred from
any camp to any other camp or place – say, to execution at Koz'i
Gory – they would have taken their winter clothing with them. If
they had no baggage – no account, German, Soviet, or Polish, says
anything about baggage – they would have worn what they had.

* M 22 point 8; KD 185:

> W grobach katyńskich znalazły się dokumenty osobi-
> ste pozwalające zidentyfikować 2730 zwłok na ogólną
> liczbę 4151. Radziecka Komisja Specjalna, dokonując
> ponownej ekshumacji, **nie znalazła dalszych doku-
> mentów osobistych.**

> *Translated:*

> In the graves at Katyn were personal documents
> which made it possible to identify 2730 of the remains
> out of a total of 4151. The Soviet Special commission,
> when it carried out a second exhumation, **did not find
> any other personal documents.**

That this statement is false is obvious to us today since we now
have a list of documents found by Burdenko Commission investigators and published by Pamiatnykh. But it was recognizably false

in 1989 too! The final section of BU is titled "Documents Found on the Bodies." This section refers to letters, postcards, a Catholic prayer book, and receipts found. These are "personal documents."

* M 23 point 12; KD 186:

> ... fakt użycia w egzekucjach amunicji produkcji nie-mieckiej, co potem wyjaśniono masowym eksportem tej amunicji do ZSRR **(do roku 1932)** oraz do Polski i krajów nadbałtyckich.

> *Translated:*

> ... the fact of the use in the executions of bullets of German manufacture, which was later explained by **a massive export of these bullets to the USSR (before 1932)** as well as to Poland and the Baltic countries.

This too is a false claim. What's more, the writers of this chapter had to know that it is false. At the Madden Commission Hearings in 1952 Gustav Genschow, president of the company that manufactured the "Geco" ammunition that the Germans found at Katyn, said that there had been **only very small sales of Geco ammunition to the USSR after 1928**.

> Mr. Flood [of the Commission]. Do you know what caliber of ammunition was used and what kind of pistol was used by the NKVD or the GPU from the year 1933 until the end of the war?

> Mr. Genschow. No; I do not know that also, because since 1928 we did not export large quantities of pistol ammunition to Soviet Russia;

> Mr. Flood. Did you export any quantities of 7.65 pistol ammunition to Soviet Russia?

> Mr. Genschow. Yes; before 1928, somewhat larger amounts. But I wish to point out that at that time the stamp on the bottom of the cartridge was different

from the one I stated before, and **after 1928 the quantities which were exported were small.**

Mr. Flood. But there were some quantities shipped to Soviet Russia after 1928, of 7.65 ammunition bearing the "Geco" trade-mark?

Mr. Genschow. Yes.

I wish to point out that the trade-mark which was used before 1933-34, when the latest trade-mark was introduced, also had the word "Geco" in it and "7.65." There was only the addition of two D's slightly underneath the right and left end of the word "Geco." (Madden V 1578-9)

On page 35 of AM we read:

Außerhalb der Gräber wurden eine Anzahl beschossener Pistolenhälsen mit dem Bodenaufdruck „Geco DD 7.65" gefunden..."

Translated:

Outside the graves were found a number of used pistol shell casings with the headstamp "Geco DD 7.65..."

The shells mentioned in AM were the 1928-1931 type show in the middle drawing (see Chapter 3 above). Genschow said that the larger exports to the USSR were before 1928, when the word "Geco" did not appear on the shells, and were small after that, when the "Geco DD 7.65" shells were made.

The authors of "the Polish historians' expert assessment" knew this. They also knew that very few, if indeed any, of those who read their work in 1988 would have had the ability to check the Madden Commission hearings, which were at that time available only in very large libraries in the United States and which must have been much scarcer than that in Eastern Europe.

The "Vetoshnikov" question

A Major Vetoshnikov testified to the Burdenko Commission about the unsuccessful evacuation of Camp 1-ON in July 1941. "Drama" repeatedly suggests that there was no one named Vetoshnikov:

> Wśród wymienianych przez nich urzędników nie było mjr. Wietosznikowa, przedstawionego jako komendanta Nr 1 – ON. (M 23; KD 187)

> ... z załogi ujawniony został tylko świadek mjr Wietosznikow, z którym żaden z internowanych polskich oficerów, który przeżył obozy, nie zetknął się. (M 24; KD 188)

> Potwierdzeniem tego mają być zeznania bliżej nieznanego mjr Wietosznikowa, szęfa obozu Nr 1 - ON. (M 27; KD 1909)

Translated:

> Among the men in authority named by them [former Polish POWs] the name of Major Vetoshnikov, presented [in the BU] as the commander of camp No. 1-ON, is not mentioned.

> ... of the personnel [at camp 1-ON] presented there was only the witness Major Vetoshnikov, with whom not a single one of the Polish officers imprisoned in the camps, had ever come into contact.

> As confirmation of this were to serve the statements of a Major Vetoshnikov, commander of camp No. 1-ON, who was not known to anyone.

Writing years later, Lebedeva also claims that Vetoshnikov never existed:

> Еще одним сфальсифицированным документом был рапорт якобы начальника лагеря № 1-ОН «майора государственной безопасности» В.М. Ве-

тошникова от 12 августа 1941 г., направленный де начальнику УПВИ «майору госбезопасности» Со-пруненко.

Сам Ветошников не фигурирует ни в одном из документов УПВИ или другого управления НКВД. Тем не менее, в сообщении Специальной комиссии имеется ссылка на показания этого мифического майора госбезопасности[32].

Translated:

One more falsified document was the report supposedly by the commander of camps No. 1-ON "Major of State Security" V.M. Vetoshnikov of August 12, 1941, sent, so it was said, to the commander of the UPVI "Major of State Security" Soprunenko.

Vetoshnikov himself does not figure in a single one of the documents of the UPVI or of any other directorate of the NKVD. Nevertheless, in the report of the Special commission [the BU] there is a reference to the statements of this mythical major of State Security.[32]

But in footnote 32 Lebedeva says something different:

В справке Меркулова и Кобулова он, правда, фигурирует как лейтенант госбезопасности (*Военно-исторический архив*. 1990. № 11. С. 29).

Translated:

In the report by Merkulov and Kobulov he [Vetoshnikov], it is true, figures as a lieutenant of State Security (*Voenno-istoricheskii Arkhiv* [sic!] 1990, No. 11, p. 29).

Here is that citation, from *Voenno-Istoricheskii Zhurnal* (*not* "Arkhiv") 11 (1990), p.29:

Начальник лагеря № 1-ОН лейтенант госбезопасности Ветошников В. М., давая объяснения о судьбе порученного ему лагеря, в своём рапорте на имя начальника Управления по делам военнопленных и интернированных НКВД СССР от 12 августа 1941 года пишет: «После того, как я получил от Вас указание подготовить лагерь к эвакуации, я принял к этому необходимые меры.

Translated:

The commander of camp No. 1-ON Lieutenant of State Security Vetoshnikov V.M., explaining the fate of the camp entrusted to him, in his report to the chief of the Directorate of POW and Internee Affairs (UDVI) of the NKVD of the USSR of August 12, 1941, writes: "After I received from you the order to prepare the camp for evacuation, I took the essential measures."

This is good evidence that Vetoshnikov did exist and was indeed the commander of Camp 1-ON in July 1941. It is not likely that, in this document marked "top secret" Merkulov and Kobulov would have fabricated the existence of this man, called him a lieutenant rather than a major, mentioned this fictional person once, and never again.

It is only necessary to *assume* that Vetoshnikov did not exist if one has previously also assumed that no camps 1-, 2-, and 3-ON existed. The Polish "official" version does make this assumption. But the existence of these camps is documented in the list of documents found on the corpses by the Burdenko Commission investigators and published on the Internet by Aleksei Pamiatnykh, a fervent advocate of the "official" Soviets-did-it version:

в) Квитанции лагеря 1-СН от 6 апреля 1941 года о приеме от АРАЛЬБИЧА денег в сумме 225 руб.;

г) Квитанция лагеря 1-ОН от 5 мая 1941 года о приеме от АРАЛЬБИЧА денег в сумме сто два рубля.

б) Квитанция лагеря 1-СН от 18 мая 1941 года о приеме
от ....ого Б. денег в сумме сто семьдосят пять
рублей.

Images 10.1 and 10.2 Burdenko Commission excerpts.

b) Receipt from camp 1-ON of 6 April 1941 for accepting from ARASHKEVICH of money in the sum of ??? rub.;

c) Receipt from camp 1-ON of 6 May 1941 for accepting from ARASHKEVICH of money in the sum of one hundred two rubles.

...

b) Receipt from camp 1-ON of 18 May 1941 for accepting from LEVANDOVSKI E. money in the sum of one hundred seventy-five rubles.[6]

The Account of Boris Men'shagin

Boris Men'shagin was a lawyer in Smolensk who was appointed Mayor by the Germans and served in that post until captured by the Soviets. According to the BU Men'shagin's notebook (*bloknot*) was found after the Soviets liberated Smolensk in September 1943. Some strategic passages from it are reproduced in the BU.

At the end of this Merkulov-Kobulov document we read the following:

Фотоснимки с записей Меньшагина из его блокнота при этом прилагаются.

Translated:

---

[6] Aleksei Pamiatnykh, "Katynskie materialy. Iz neopublikovannykh materialov Kommissii Burdenko" („Katyn materials. From the unpublished materials of the Burdenko Commission."). At http://katynfiles.com/content/pamyatnykh-burdenko-materials.html Pages 18 and 27 of the materials.

Photocopies with Men'shagin's notes from his notebook are attached herewith.[7]

Most of these notations deal with the persecution and impending
murder of Jews. Only one concerns the Polish POWs:

13. Ходят ли среди населения слухи о расстреле
польских военнопленных в Коз[ьих] Гор[ах] (Ум-
нову).

Translated:

13. Are there any rumors among the population concerning the shooting of Polish war prisoners in Kozy
Gory (for Umnov).[8]

Men'shagin did not write "shooting .... by the Germans." Perhaps
someone could argue that Men'shagin might have been asking
about shootings of Poles by the Soviets. The context – the rest of
the note has to do with German actions – makes this very unlikely.

But it speaks to the authenticity of this note by Men'shagin. If the
Soviets had faked a note by Men'shagin, would they have made it
so short and so laconic that it did not directly implicate the Germans? Why would the Soviets have fabricated a lengthy account of
shooting of Jews by the Germans and left the question of who shot
the Polish POWs to a very brief and ambiguous mention at the
end?

Concerning "Umnov" BU continues as follows:

Umnov, who is mentioned in the note, was the chief of
the Russian police in Smolensk during the early
months of its occupation. (BU 234)

---

[7] "Babii Iar pod Katyniu? *Voenno-Istoricheskii Zhurnal* 11 (1990), p. 35 col. 2.

[8] Ibid. Also in BU 234.

After serving a 25-years sentence for collaboration Men'shagin was released from a Soviet prison and wrote his memoirs, which were published by the YMCA Press in Paris in 1988.

If Men'shagin had affirmed what his former assistant mayor Bazilevskii had testified at Nuremberg – that Men'shagin knew that the Germans had killed the Polish prisoners – there would be no "Katyn mystery." Instead Men'shagin says that Bazilevskii's remarks "completely do not correspond to reality." But Men'shagin does say that Bazilevskii's remarks about Men'shagin's wanting to get a friend of his released from the Russian camp were accurate.

> BAZILEVSKY: In the camp for Russian prisoners of war known as "Dulag 126" there prevailed such a severe regime that prisoners of war were dying by the hundreds every day; for this reason I tried to free all those from this camp for whose release a reason could be given. I learned that in this camp there was also a very well-known pedagogue named Zhiglinski. I asked Menschagin to make representations to the German Kommandantur of Smolensk, and in particular to Von Schwetz, and to plead for the release of Zhiglinski from this camp.... Menschagin answered my request with, "What is the use? We can save one, but hundreds will die." However, I insisted; and Menschagin, after some hesitation, agreed to put this request to the German Kommandantur.   (Nuremberg XVII 325).

Bazilevskii testified that Men'shagin told him that the Germans had told him that the Polish POWs would be killed. Two weeks later, at the end of September, Men'shagin told him that the Germans had now killed the Poles.

In his memoirs Men'shagin responded strangely.

> И этот Базилевский сказал, что об убийстве поляков он узнал от меня, что в 41-м году он узнал, что в плен попал и находится в немецком лагере в Смоленске его знакомый Кожуховский. И просил

меня, не могу ли я похлопотать об его освобождении. Я, дескать, охотно согласился на это, написал
ходатайство и сам понес в комендатуру. Вернув-
шись из комендатуры, я сказал: «Ничего не вый-
дет, потому что в комендатуре мне объявили, что
все поляки будут расстреляны». Через несколько
дней, придя оттуда, я снова ему сказал: «Уже расстреляны». Вот те данные, которыми располагал
Базилевский.

Эти сведения, сообщенные Базилевским, совер-
шенно не соответствуют действительности. Слу-
чай его ходатайства за Кожуховского действи-
тельно имел место в августе 1941 года. И я воз-
буждал ходатайство об его освобождении, и через
дня три-четыре после этого ходатайства Кожухов-
ский лично явился, освобожденный, и находился в
Смоленске после этого, имея свою пекарню все
время немецкой оккупации города, а впослед-
ствии я его видел в Минске в 44-м году, где он
точно так же имел кондитерскую. Кожуховского
этого я лично знал, так как он проходил свидете-
лем по делу хлебозавода № 2, разбиравшемуся
Смоленским областным судом в марте 1939 года.
(131)

Translated:

And this Bazilevsky said that he learned about the
murder of the Poles from me, that in 1941 he learned
that his acquaintance Kozhukhovsky was taken prisoner and was in the German camp in Smolensk. And
he asked me if I could request his release. He said that
I willingly agreed to this, wrote a petition and took it
myself to the commandant's office. Returning from the
commandant's office, I said: "Nothing will come of it,
because in the commandant's office I was told that all
Poles would be shot." A few days later, having come

> from there, I again told him: "They have already been shot." These are the facts that Bazilevsky had.

> This information, reported by Bazilevsky, is completely untrue. The case of his petition for Kozhukhovsky really did take place in August 1941. And I filed a petition for his release, and three or four days after this petition, Kozhukhovsky personally appeared, released, and was in Smolensk after that, running his bakery all during the time of the German occupation of the city, and subsequently I saw him in Minsk in '44, where he also had a confectionery. I knew this Kozhukhovsky personally, as he had been a witness in the case of Bakery No. 2, which the Smolensk Regional Court had examined in March 1939.

The editors of Men'shagin's memoirs note that there is no record of any Kozhukhovskii, whereas Zheglinskii (with an "e" instead of an "i"), the name cited by Bazilevskii, is known. Zheglinskii was released from the German camp "undoubtedly through the efforts of Men'shagin." Zheglinskii became involved in the pro-Soviet underground, was found out by the Germans, and killed in September 1942 (226-227). Either Men'shagin's memory about these events was not good or he was dissimulating for some reason.

As for our main interest, the deaths of the Polish POWs, Men'shagin claimed that, when he was interrogated by NKVD investigators during his imprisonment first in Smolensk and later in the Lubianka prison, he had told them that he did not know who had killed the Poles. (132) But the editors of his memoirs set forth evidence that this is not the full story either.

In 1970 Men'shagin, while still in a Soviet prison, was called as a witness in the case of a certain Sviatoslav Karavanskii, who was charged with anti-Soviet agitation and propaganda. Karavanskii had written a "testament" and "farewell" in Men'shagin's name but without telling Men'shagin about this. In them he had stated that the Soviets had murdered the Poles.

At Karavanskii's trial Men'shagin testified as follows:

> Свидетель Меньшагин Б.Г. показал, что связи с за-
> ключенным Караванским он не поддерживал и
> писать от своего имени провокационные заявле-
> ния по так называемому «Катынскому делу» Ка-
> раванскому не поручал. Далее Меньшагин пояс-
> нил, что **ему** как бывшему бургомистру города
> Смоленска **обстоятельства уничтожения поль-
> ских военнопленных офицеров в 1941 году не
> известны, однако он убежден, что польские во-
> еннопленные были расстреляны немецкими
> фашистами.** (149-150)

Translated:

Witness Men'shagin B.G. testified that he had no connection to the prisoner Karavanskii and did not ask
Karavanskii to write in his [Men'shagin's] name the
provocational declarations about the so-called "Katyn
affair." Men'shagin further explained that **he, the
former mayor of the city of Smolensk, did not
know the circumstances of the annihilation of the
Polish officer POWs in 1941. However he was convinced that the Polish POWs had been shot by the
German fascists.**

Men'shagin claimed that he did not know the circumstances of the
murder of the Poles but was convinced that the Germans had done
it. This statement is consistent with Men'shagin's statement in his
memoir. It also does not contradict point 13 in his notebook that
he was asked to report to Umnov whether there was "rumors
among the population about the shootings of Polish POWs in Koz'i
Gory."

Back to "The Polish Historians' Expert Assessment"

Stanisław Kuczyński

In criticism of BU's account of bodies with documents dated after May 1940 Maciszewski writes:

> Jeden z tych dowodów to nie wysłana, kartka poczto-wa, napisana z datą 20 czerwca 1941 r., a nadawcą mial być Stanisław Kuczyński. W istocie rotmistrz tego imienia i nazwiska, wnuk emigranta polskiego, jedne-go z organizatorów armii tureckiej, przebywał wprawdzie w obozie starobielskim, ale już w listopa-dzie 1939 r. wywieziony został w nieznanym kierun-ku, zaginął·o nim wszelki słuch. (33)

Translated:

One of these pieces of evidence is an unsent postcard dated June 20, 1941, the author [literally "sender"] of which was Stanislaw Kuczyński. In fact a colonel of cavalry ("rotmistr" in Russian, "rotmistrz" in Polish) with this first and last name, the nephew of a Polish emigrant, one of the organizers of the Turkish army really was in the Starobel'sk camp, but he had been sent out of it in November 1939 to an unknown desti-nation, after which nothing is known about him.

This is another deliberate deception. For indeed there is *another* Stanisław Kuczyński listed as killed in the Katyn murders. He was a prisoner at Ostashkov. In his Ostashkov list Tucholski records the following (314 col. 1)

Kuczyński Stanisław
Ur. 31 .3.1908, s. Antoniego i Stanisławy.
Funkcj. PP, posterunek Pruszków,
pow. Warszawa. Prawdop. Ostaszków.

The Soviet transit lists record that Stanisław Kuczyński was No. 87 in list 037/3, transferred from Ostashkov on April 20, 1940. (Tucholski p. 851 #87):

> 87. КУЧИНСКОГО Станислава Антоновича, 1908 г.р.

Maciszewski's book is early; perhaps he did not know this. But Cienciala had to be aware that this Stanisław Kuczyński was a prisoner at Ostashkov and that the finding of this 1941 document of his at Katyn constitutes a serious blow to the "official" version, according to which all Ostashkov prisoners were shot at Kalinin and buried at Mednoe. No doubt this is the reason that she withholds this information from her readers.

Tucholski also records the "Turkish" Stanisław Kuczyński mentioned in "drama" at Starobel'sk. (939) This was a different man.

> 1414. КУЧИНСКИЙ-ИСКИНДЕР БЕЙ Станислав Стан. 1903

It appears that like Cienciala the authors of "Drama" wanted to conceal the fact that the body of an Ostashkov prisoner was found at Katyn, and therefore had *not* been shot by the Soviets NKVD at Kalinin, as the "official" version demands.

Jan Zaluska

Maciszewski writes:

> Są w spisie ewidencyjnym pomyłki czy fałszerstwa; m.in. znalazł się na liście niemieckiej jeden dziś zyjący (Remigiusz Bierżanek) i kilku zamordowanych w okupowanym kraju (np. Płk Jan Załuska), ale nie podważa to wiarygodności podstawowego zestawu nazwisk ofiar. (M 34)

Translated:

In the said list there are errors or falsifications. In particular, in the German list there occur: one person living today (Remigiusz Bierżanek) **and several men killed in occupied Poland (for example, Colonel Jan Zaluska).** However, this does not undermine the reliability of the basic list of victims' names.

For the sake of space we will not examine the case of Remigiusz Bierżanek. Everyone agrees that he was put on the list of Katyn victims when in fact he was alive and well in Poland.[9]

But we will consider the case of Jan Zaluska. The text mentions "several [POWs in the German list] killed in occupied Poland (for example, Colonel Jan Zaluska)." He is cited in Tucholski as a Kozel'sk prisoner (626 #82):

> 82. ЗАЛУСКА Яна Александровича, 1889 г.р.

> Załuska Jan Ur. 25.5.1889, s. Aleksandra. Płk piech. sł. st., dowódca obrony plot. DOK II, legionista. PCK (AM) Nr 03488. (Tuch. 255 col. 1-2)

He is in AM on p. 257:

> 3488. Załuska, Jan, Oberst, geb. 25. 6. 89, wohnh.: Lublin.

> Postsparbuch, Visitenkarten, Orden „Virtuti-militari".

The author of this 1988 document, Jarema Maciszewski, says that he knows not only about Bierżanek and Zaluska but about "several" men who are on the German list but were not killed at Katyn but, rather, in occupied Poland. Unfortunately he identifies only Zaluska.

After the publication of Maciszewski's book Zaluska goes unmentioned in the accounts of the "official" version of Katyn. He is listed

---

[9] See Witold Stankiewicz, "Jak żyjący Remigiusz Henryk Bierzanek znalazł się na liście ofiar katyńskich (Glosa do pracy Czesława Madajczyka, *Dramat katyński*, Warszawa 1989)." *Dzieje Najnowsze* XXVIII, No. 4 (1995), 127-130.

in the official "Katyn Cemetery Book" (p. 723) without any indication that he was not shot at Katyn:

Płk **Jan ZAŁUSKA** s. Aleksandra i Agnieszki z Kawalków, ur. 25 V 1889 w majątku Rachodoszcze, pow. zamojski. Żołnierz I i III Brygady Leg. Uczestnik bitwy pod Kostiuchnówką. Od 1918 w sikolnictwie wojskowym WP. Od 1927 zca dcy 82 pp i dca 8 pp Leg. Płk od 1 I 1933. W 1938 dca obrony plot. OK II. Odznaczony VM 5 ld, OOP 4 kl., KW czterokrotnie. Żonaty z Marią z Klimontowiczów, miał dzieci: Zofię, Tadeusza i Jerzego.

CAW. AP 6993, 9449, 9378, 74, ,VM 77-7458, OOP 1/211, KN 6 VI 1931; MiD WTN, L.W. 015/2 z 1940; AM 3488.

Cemetery book entry recreated based upon original entry.

Col. Zaluska is also in Gur'ianov, *Ubity v Katyni* (2013) on p. 338:

Залуска Ян *(Załuska Jan s. Aleksandra I Agnieszki)*, Род. в 1889 г. в имении Радохоще Замойского повята Лю-Блинского в-ва. Полковник, командующий ПВО II корпусного округа, жил в г. Люблин. Женат, имел троих Детей ■ По состоянию на 28.10.1939 содержался в Южском лагере военнопленных, [в ноябре или начале декабря 1939 г. прибыл в Козельский лагерь.], 07-09.04.1940* направлен в распоряжение начальника УНКВД по Смоленской обл. (список-предписание № 015/2 от [05.04.1940]), [расстрелян в период 09.-11.1940*]. ■ Эксгумация: германская суточная сводка от 28.05.1943, № 3488 в списке АМ. ■ N-415-82-1151 Залуска Ян Александрович, N_1-69-132 отч. Александрович, учитель [!], значится в списке военнопленных генералов и старших офицеров от 28.10.1939;V-99-03488; AM-257-3488; РСК: GARF-127-03488. APL,-47-03488, APL,-184-03488,MUZ.,-46-03488;GK-177-3488;NKW-170-03488;MOSZ-213;JT-255; M-1990/(3-4)-428; КС-723; РК розыск 1946. 1949 гг.; RK; RO39-8, 512.

There is no mention here either of his being killed in occupied Poland, as stated in the text recommended by Cienciala.

Cienciala and Sanford certainly knew about this claim of Maciszewski's that Col. Zaluska and other men named in the German AM list were in fact not killed at Katyn but in occupied Poland. But they do not mention it. Why? Why, for example, don't they contest it? They could have claimed that Maciszewski was mistaken, and explained what they believed the real situation to be.

Certainly the Polish proponents of the "official" Soviets-did-it version must have discussed this potentially embarrassing statement by Maciszewski. But they pass over it in silence. This suggests that they do not want anyone to notice it. That is quite likely. An admission that Maciszewski was mistaken would require investigation into what the basis of his statement was. It is yet another admission that the German AM list is not correct.

But the whole "official" version rests upon the reliability of the German AM! Logically a reader would conclude that if Zaluska and "several others" on the German AM list, including Remigiusz Bierżanek, were not shot at Katyn, others on the German AM list might not have been shot there either. Such an admission would threaten to dismantle the "official" version of Katyn.

Alternatively, Cienciala and Sanford could suggest that Maciszewski's statement is incorrect. But that would call into question Cienciala's repeated claim that Maciszewski's document is a "devastating critique" of the BU.

In either case, Cienciala's and Sanford's silence about this statement by Maciszewski, which counters their claims, is intriguing. It is certainly a sign that they wish to hide something.

False charge of falsification

Maciszewski states:

Czy dokumenty tysięcy ofiar mogły zostać generalnie
sfałszowane, jak mogłoby wynikać z "Komunikatun
Komisji Specjalnej?

Translated:

Was it possible [for the Germans] to falsify the documents of thousands of victims, as that can be inferred
from the Report of the Special commission [that is,
BU]?

De Montfort made the same false accusation. As we have already
shown, BU does not at all imply that the Germans "falsified documents of thousands of victims." Rather, BU implies that the Germans took from the corpses all the documents they could find that
were dated after April-May 1940.

Moskovskaia's BU statement

Burdenko Commission witness A. M. Moskovskaia stated that she
hid an escaped Soviet POW named Nikolai Yegorov in her shed and
fed him. Yegorov told Moskovskaia that he and other Soviet POWs
were assigned to take all the documents out of the pockets of the
corpses at Katyn and then replace them. Yegorov was captured by
the Germans. When interrogated by them Moskovskaia told the
Germans that she knew nothing of the Soviet POW's presence in
her shed and was released.

"Drama" states the following about Moskovskaia's testimony:

Zeznanie A.M. Moskowskiej powtarzające relację M.
Jegorowa, radzieckiego jeńca wykorzystanego rzeko-
mo przy obróbce trupów, nie jest przekonywające i
nie ma potwierdzenia w innych zeznaniach. (M 35)

Translated:

The testimony of A.M. Moskovskaia, which repeated
the account of M. Egorov, a Soviet prisoner, who was

allegedly employed in work with the corpses, is un-
convincing and is not confirmed by other testimony.

It is true that Moskovskaia's story is not directly confirmed. But
that does not mean it is false. Rather, it suggests an important
question: Can anything in the Burdenko Commission testimony be
independently confirmed? The answer is: Yes.

Testimony that the Germans Trucked In Bodies from Elsewhere

Testimony that the Germans had trucked towards Katyn corpses
from other sites is given in BU by three witnesses: P.F. Sukhachev,
Vladimir Afanasievich Yegorov, and Frol Maximovich Yakovlev-
Sokolov. (BU 241-242)

This is confirmed by four archival documents cited by Valentin
Sakharov from Soviet partisan groups attesting to reports by escaped Red Army POWs that the Germans had dug up bodies from a
Smolensk cemetery, including bodies of Red Army soldiers killed
in the defense of Smolensk in 1941, and trucked them to Katyn.
Three reports are dated late July 1943. All four documents report
the same thing. In a previous chapter we examined a document
that we independently verified by obtaining a photocopy directly
from the State Library of the Smolensk Oblast'.

Evaluating this evidence

The partisan reports do confirm the testimony of the three witnesses recorded in the BU. No objective student would conclude
that the partisan reports are a fabrication, concocted by the Soviets in a far-sighted attempt to provide documentation for a future
attempt to counter the German AM. The paragraphs cited occupy
less than a page in a 10-page long report of partisan activities. In
July 1943 the Germans were still in Smolensk and also in Katyn,
which is about 25 miles to the west of Smolensk. The partisans
were still engaged in fighting the German occupation. Smolensk
was not liberated until September 25, 1943.

Yet if one does not take the position – unsupported by any evidence – that the partisan reports are fabrications, the genuineness of the German AM is destroyed. And this confirms other evidence that negates any claim to evidentiary validity of the German AM.

Therefore, the partisan reports are *confirmatory* evidence that the German AM has been seriously falsified and is not valid evidence for the "official" version of Katyn. At the same time, the partisan reports are confirmatory evidence in favor of the credibility of BU.

Conclusion about Maciszewski and "The Polish Historians' Expert Assessment"

Cienciala calls this essay a "devastating critique of the Burdenko Commission report." (248; 337; n. 113 p. 506) Sanford (139) echoes this claim. But this claim is entirely without validity.

It is hard to believe that Cienciala and Sanford could really have believed that this document was any kind of critique of the BU, let alone a "devastating" one. But a powerful desire to believe and remain loyal to a preconceived idea – in this case, the "official" version of Katyn – can cloud the reason of otherwise intelligent persons. If one's bias dictates that the "official" version *must* be true, *has* to be true, than it follows that the BU must be false.

It appears that Cienciala and Sanford were deliberately deceiving their readers, counting on the fact that not one in a thousand would study this essay, whether in Maciszewski's book, in *Polityka*, in *Dramat Katyński*, or in Russian in "Katynskaia drama" in order to check to see whether their statements about it were accurate. So one might conclude that Cienciala and Sanford are deliberately lying, deceiving their readers.

But I think it is also possible that, blinded by their bias, they saw what they wanted to see, like the onlookers in the story "The Emperor's New Clothes." Or, perhaps, both. Whatever the case may be, their works are a good negative example of how a lack of devotion to objectivity, to discovering the truth no matter whose preconceived ideas are shattered, ruins any possibility of good re-search.

Kathleen Harriman's Letter

During the Burdenko Commission investigations Kathleen Harri-man went to Katyn with her father Averell Harriman, U.S. ambas-sador to the USSR. On January 28, 1943, she wrote a long account of her trip in a letter to her sister Mary and to Pamela Churchill:

> The Katyn Forest turned out to be a small measly pine
> tree woods. We were shown the works by a big Soviet
> doctor who looked like a chef in white peaked cap,
> white apron, and rubber gloves. With relish he
> showed us a sliced Polish brain carefully placed on a
> dinner plate for inspection purposes. And then we be-
> gan a tour to each and every one of the seven graves.
> We must have seen a good many thousand corpses or
> parts of corpses, all in varying degrees of decomposi-
> tion, but smelling about as bad. (Luckily I had a cold,
> so was less bothered by the stench than others.) Some
> of the corpses had been dug up by the Germans in the
> spring of '43 after they'd first launched their version
> of the story. These were laid in neat orderly rows,
> from six to eight bodies deep. The bodies in the re-
> maining graves had been tossed in every which way.
> All the time we were there, the regular work of ex-
> huming continued by men in army uniform. Somehow
> I didn't envy them! The most interesting thing, and the
> most convincing bit of evidence, was that every Pole
> had been shot through the back of the head with a sin-
> gle bullet. Some of the bodies had their hands tied be-
> hind their backs, all of which is typically German. Next
> on the program we were taken into post mortem
> tents. These were hot and stuffy and smelt to high
> heaven. Numerous post mortems were going on, each
> and every body is given a thorough going over, and we
> witnessed several . . . personally. I was amazed at how
> whole the corpses were. Most still had hair. Even I

could recognize their internal organs and they still had a good quantity of red colored "firm" meat on their thighs . . . You see, the Germans say that the Russians killed the Poles back in '40, whereas the Russians say the Poles weren't killed until the fall of '41, so there's quite a discrepancy in time. **Though the Germans had ripped open the Poles' pockets, they'd missed some written documents. While I was watching, they found one letter dated the summer of '41, which is damned good evidence.**[10]

She must be referring to the Stanisław Kuczyński letter:

9. On body No. 53: An unmailed postcard in the polish [sic] language addressed Warsaw Bagatelia 15, apartment 47, to Irene Kuczinska, and dated June 20, 1941. The sender is Stanislaw Kuczinski. (BU 246-247)

Kathleen Harriman repeated this in the formal report she made after visiting Katyn:

Despite the thoroughness of the pocket ripping by the Germans, out of the seven hundred corpses the Commission have so far investigated 146 items have been found. The earliest date was found on a postcard—March 1940—and the latest—an unmailed postcard dated June 20, 1941. (Madden Vol. 7 p. 2138)

Averell Harriman confirmed this in his memoirs published in 1975.[11]

---

[10] Quoted in Goeffrey Roberts, "The Wartime Correspondence of Kathleen Harriman." *Harriman Magazine*, Winter, 2015, p. 18.

[11] W. Averell Harriman and Elie Abel. *Special Envoy to Churchill and Stalin 1941-1946.* New York: Random House, 1975, p. 302.

At the Congressional Madden Commission hearings held in 1952 – a blatantly anticommunist affair that set out to prove the Soviets guilty – Kathleen Harriman (here called by her married name, Kathleen H. Mortimer) did not admit that she had personally seen the document in question removed from the corpse.

> Mr. Machrowicz. But these exhibits that you referred to as having been found on the corpses, were not taken from the corpses in your presence, they were in a museum at the time?
>
> Mrs. Mortimer. That is right—in Smolensk, which was some distance away.
>
> (Madden Vol. 7 p. 2145).

There is no reason to think that Kathleen Harriman lied in the letter to her sister and to Pamela Churchill of January 1944. Rather, there is every reason to suppose that at the Madden Committee she bent her testimony to the winds of the Cold War, which were blowing hard in 1952. Her father does not mention his daughter's Madden Commission testimony in his memoir account.

Sanford states:

> The silly Harriman girl, however, allowed herself to be used by Roosevelt and the State Department, subsequently, in support of the thesis of German guilt. (139)

To call Harriman's report "silly" is a dishonest attempt at an *ad hominem* argument. Kathleen Harriman's report of January 1944 is quite critical of the Soviet attempt to persuade the correspondents and others present, and rather skeptical of the Soviet performance in general. She was certainly no "dupe."

Neither Cienciala nor Sanford can explain the documents found on the corpses except to suggest that they were "planted." We have demonstrated that the Kozietulski documents could not have been planted, and that this fact strongly suggests that the rest of the documents found on the bodies by the Burdenko Commission investigators are also genuine.

Conclusion on the Burdenko Commission

Both Cienciala and Sanford claim that the BU has been refuted. This is a false claim. There have been several attempts to refute it. All are incompetent, dishonest, or both, and can be shown to falsify and prevaricate, as we have done here.

In reality, BU has never been disproven on any essential points. It remains the single most accurate account to date of the mass murders of Polish prisoners at the Katyn (Koz'i Gory) site.

Chapter 11. Nuremberg, the Madden Commission

Nuremberg

Dr Marko Markov of Bulgaria had been one of the medical experts in the team assembled by the Germans to go to Katyn and endorse their version of events. He testified at the Nuremberg trials on July 1, 1946.

Cienciala:

> ...three witnesses were heard for the prosecution: the former deputy mayor of Smolensk, Boris Bazilevsky, a professor of astronomy; the Bulgarian forensic medicine expert Professor Anton Marko Markov, **who had testified in support of Soviet guilt in 1943** but now testified in support of German guilt; and Victor Prozorovsky, a Soviet professor of forensic medicine and a member of the Burdenko Commission. (232)

The statement in boldface above is false. Markov did not "testify in support of Soviet guilt in 1943." Here is everything that Markov stated in the German Report (AM):

> Aus den Zeugenaussagen, den bei den Leichen aufgefundenen Briefschaften, Tagebüchern, Zeitungen usw. ergibt sich, daß die Erschießungen in den Monaten März und April 1940 stattgefunden haben. (118)

> *Translated:*

> From the witness testimony and the correspondence, diaries, newspapers, etc. found on the corpses, it follows that the shootings took place in the months of March and April 1940.

This is not testimony of any kind, let alone scientific testimony based on examination of any of the corpses. At Nuremberg Markov stated that he neither spoke to any of the witnesses nor read any of the documents. Here he and the other scientists simply repeated what the Germans clearly demanded from them.

Here is Markov's only conclusion in the German Report based on his examination of a corpse:

> Wegen der teilweisen Verseifung der Leiche muß man annehmen, daß der Tod um **mehr als 1 Jahr zurück-liegt**. (128)

> *Translated:*

> Because of the partial saponification of the corpse, one must assume that death had occurred **more than one year earlier.**

"More than one year" could indicate either German or Soviet guilt. We shall see below that Markov really thought that the body could not have been buried for more than 18 months. He could hardly write this when he was at the mercy of the Germans. And even if, careless of his own safety, he had done so, the Germans certainly would not have printed it.

Cienciala had to know all this. It is hard to avoid the conclusion that she was deliberately lying here. She had studied the German report, so she knew that Markov had never "testified in support of Soviet guilt."

But Cienciala says nothing about the testimony of any of the three Nuremberg witnesses who *supported* German guilt at Katyn. In particular she has nothing to say about Markov's testimony, which is indeed devastating – but to the "official" version, not the Soviet, case.

Markov's Nuremberg Testimony[1]

In his Nuremberg testimony Markov dispelled any illusions about the supposedly scientific evidence given in the report by the medical experts called to Katyn by the Germans.

1. Only eight corpses in all were examined.

> The only part of our activity which could be characterized as a scientific, medico-legal examination were the autopsies carried out by certain members of the commission who were themselves medico-legal experts; but there were only seven or eight of us who could lay claim to that qualification, and as far as I recall only eight corpses were opened. Each of us operated on one corpse, except Professor Hájek, who dissected two corpses. Our further activity during these 2 days consisted of a hasty inspection under the guidance of Germans. It was like a tourists' walk during which we saw the open graves; ...

2. The scientific team never examined any of the documents from the graves.

> The documents which we saw in the glass cases had already been removed from the bodies before we arrived ... We did not carry out any scientific examination of these papers. As I have already told you, these papers were exhibited in glass cases and we did not even touch them.

3. Markov concluded that the bodies had been buried for no more than 12 – 18 months.

---

[1] Markov's testimony is in *Trial of the Major War Criminals* Vol. XVII. It is available online: http://avalon.law.yale.edu/imt/07-01-46.asp (towards the end) and http://avalon.law.yale.edu/imt/07-02-46.asp

MR. COUNSELLOR SMIRNOV: I would like you to answer the following question. Did the medico-legal investigations testify to the fact that the corpses had been in the graves already for 3 years?

MARKOV: As to that question I could judge only from the corpse on which I myself had held a post mortem. The condition of this corpse, as I have already stated, was typical of the average condition of the Katyn corpses. These corpses were far removed from the stage of disintegration of the soft parts, since the fat was only beginning to turn into wax. In my opinion these corpses were buried for a shorter period of time than 3 years. I considered that the corpse which I dissected had been buried for not more than 1 year or 18 months.

... Yes, quite right. I had the impression that they had been buried for not more than a year and a half. (Trial 337-8)

4. Markov could not say this while at Katyn because it would have contradicted the German version.

MR. COUNSELLOR SMIRNOV: Was a deduction contained in the record you made regarding the autopsy?

MARKOV: My record of the autopsy contained only a description without any conclusion.

MR. COUNSELLOR SMIRNOV: Why?

MARKOV: Because from the papers which were given to us there I understood that they wanted us to say that the corpses had been in the ground for 3 years ... Inasmuch as the objective deduction regarding the autopsy I performed was in contradiction with this version, I did not make any deductions.

MR. COUNSELLOR SMIRNOV: Consequently you did not make any deduction because the objective data of the autopsy testified to the fact that the corpses had been in the ground, not 3 years, but only 18 months?

MARKOV: Yes, that is quite correct.

MARKOV: Most of the members of the delegation who performed the autopsies in the Katyn wood made their deductions without answering the essential question regarding the time the corpses had been buried ... The only one who gave a definite statement in regard to the time the corpses had been buried was Professor Miloslavich from Zagreb, and he said it was 3 years. However, when the German book regarding Katyn was published, I read the result of his impartial statement regarding the corpse on which he had performed the autopsy. I had the impression that the corpse on which he had performed the autopsy did not differ in its stage of decomposition from the other corpses. This led me to think that his statement that the corpses had been in the ground for 3 years did not coincide with the facts of his description.

Dr. Ferenc Orsós and his Notion of "Pseudocallus"

Dr Ferenc Orsós was the only medical expert whom the Germans called both to Katyn and to Vinnitsa, the Ukrainian city where the Germans staged a similar exhumation with expert witnesses and a report.

We noted above that Orsós was "pro-German." In fact he was a pro-Nazi fanatic. According to István Deák, himself a very anti-communist historian:

Orsós was not only a medical expert but also an outright fascist and an anti-Semite, who demanded that there be no Jewish doctors at all in a profession about one half of whose members were Jews. Nor was Professor Orsós satisfied with fighting the Jewish threat.

On July 18, 1941, during a debate in the Hungarian Upper House on the third anti-Jewish Law forbidding marriage as well as sexual intercourse between Jews and Christians, Orsós demanded that the ban be extended to marriage and intercourse between Gypsies and Hungarians. In presenting his case, Orsós used the typical National Socialist argument that while "pure" Gypsies were Aryans and therefore members of an acceptable race, Gypsies of mixed blood turned out to be the worst criminals, and therefore their procreation must be stopped. As we know, the SS deported and killed during the war mostly such Gypsies whom it judged to be of mixed racial heritage.

Unfortunately for Orsós, the largely aristocratic members of the Upper House made fun of his argument, and did not take action against Gypsy-Hungarian love affairs. Nor was the anti-Nazi Minister of Interior Ferenc Keresztes-Fischer amenable to Orsós's call that Jewish doctors be kept away from christian patients. Jewish doctors remained free to treat Christian patients until after the German occupation of Hungary on March 19, 1944. Orsós and the MONE then submitted to the Gestapo a list of Jewish doctors, many of whom died as a result. As in Nazi Germany, the Hungarian medical profession was heavily Nazified, whereas the legal profession, for instance, remained considerably more independent throughout the war.

One might think that Professor Orsós deserved some punishment for his deeds, perhaps even the execution that, according to Professor Thuróczy, was his regrettable fate. In fact, however, Orsós was not executed. On December 6, 1944, he left Budapest with the retreating German army and settled in Halle am Saale, from where he moved to the University of Mainz in West Germany in 1946. There he lived as a respected

Professor of Artistic Anatomy until his retirement in
1955. Orsós died in Mainz on July 25, 1962.[2]

This criminal history did not prevent the Madden Commission
from calling the Nazi Orsós as a witness.

Neither Cienciala, nor Sanford – nor, to my knowledge, *any* of the
other works that set forth the "official" Soviets-did-it version of
Katyn – even mention Orsós' Nazi collaboration. To do so would
compromise the supposed "objectivity" of the conclusions of the
medical commission, headed by Orsós, which was called by the
Nazis to Katyn.

It is clear from AM that Orsós was summoned because of a single
article he had published in a Hungarian medical journal in 1941. In
it he concluded that the presence in the skull of a corpse of a hard
substance he called "pseudocallus," formed from the decomposition of brain matter, proved that the skull had been buried for at
least three years.[3] This fact, and even the word "pseudocallus" itself, was unknown to Markov and, Markov believed, to all the other
scientists as well.

> SMIRNOV: [Turning to the witness.] Were there many
> skulls with signs of so-called pseudocallus shown to
> the members of the commission? Will you please give
> an exact explanation of this term of Professor Orsós.

> MARKOV: Professor Orsós spoke to us regarding
> pseudocallus at a general conference of the delegates.
> That took place on 30 April, in the afternoon, in the

---

[2] Letter to the editor, *New York Review of Books*, March 24, 1994.

[3] Orsós Ferenc. "A halál utáni csontmészelenedés, - szuvasodás és pseudocallus." *Orvosi
hetilap.* - 85. (1941) 11. , p. 140-141. ("Post mortem decalcification, callus, and pseudocallus
on bones.") I obtained this article from the George F. Smith Library of Rutgers University
Medical School in Newark, NJ. My thanks to my friend Laszlo Berkowitz, who orally translated this article for me in 1988. Since then I have located and studied this article in its
German translation from 1954: F. Orsós, "Postmortale Decalcination, Caries und Pseudocal-
lusbildung." *Deutsche Zeitschrift für Gesamte Gerichtliche Medizin* 434 (1-2) 1954, pp. 47-53.

building where the field laboratory of Dr. Butz in Smolensk was located.

Professor Orsós described the term pseudocallus as meaning some sediment of indissoluble salt, of calcium, and other salts on the inside of the cranium. **Professor Orsós stated that, according to his observations in Hungary, this happened if the corpses have been in the ground for at least 3 years.** When Professor Orsós stated this at the scientific conference, none of the delegates said anything either for or against it. **I deduced from that that this term pseudocallus was as unknown to the other delegates as it was to me.**

MR. COUNSELLOR SMIRNOV: Tell me this, please. Did you notice any pseudocallus on the skulls of the corpses on which you and your colleagues performed autopsies?

MARKOV: On the skull of the corpse on which I performed an autopsy, there was some sort of pulpy substance in place of the brain, but I never noticed any sign of pseudocallus. The other delegates after the explanation of Professor Orsós likewise did not state that they had found any pseudocallus in the other skulls. **Even Butz[4] and his co-workers, who had examined the corpses before our arrival, did not mention any sign of pseudocallus.**

Later on, in a book which was published by the Germans and which contained the report of Butz, I noticed that Butz referred to pseudocallus in order to give more weight to his statement that the corpses had been in the ground for 3 years.

---

[4] Correct spelling: Buhtz.

MR. COUNSELLOR SMIRNOV: That is to say, that of the 11,000 corpses only one skull was submitted to you which had pseudocallus?

MARKOV: That is quite correct.

The Conditions under which Markov Signed the Report

Markov stated that he felt he had no choice but to sign the report.

MR. COUNSELLOR SMIRNOV: Yes, Mr. President.

I would ask you, Witness, to interrupt the reply to this question and to answer the following one: At the time you signed this general report of the commission, was it quite clear to you that the murders were perpetrated in Katyn not earlier than the last quarter of 1941, and that 1940, in any case, was excluded.

MARKOV: **Yes, this was absolutely clear to me** and that is why I did not make any deductions in the minutes which I made on my findings in the Katyn wood.

MARKOV: Around noon we arrived at the airport which was called Bela. The airport was apparently a military airfield because of the temporary military barracks I saw there. We had dinner there and immediately after dinner, notwithstanding the fact that we were not told that the signing of the minutes would take place on the way to Berlin, we were submitted copies of the protocol for signature. During the signing a number of military persons were present, as there were no other people except military personnel on this airfield. **I was rather struck by the fact that on the one hand the records were already completed in Smolensk but were not submitted to us for signing there, and on the other hand that they did not wait till we arrived in Berlin a few hours later. They were submitted to us for signing at this iso-**

lated military airfield. This was the reason why I signed the report, in spite of the conviction I had acquired during the autopsy which I had performed at Smolensk.

MR. COUNSELLOR SMIRNOV: That is to say, the date and the locality which are shown in the protocol are incorrect?

MARKOV: Yes, that is so.

DR. STAHMER: Did you consider the task you had to carry out there a political one or a scientific one?

MARKOV: I understood this task from the very first moment as a political one and therefore I tried to evade it.

Markov Noted that the German Report Lied about Insect Remains

We have already noted the issue of insect remains as one of the many contradictions in the German Report (AM). Markov noted this too.

MARKOV: As to the insects and their larvae, the assertion of the general report that none were discovered is in flagrant contradiction to the conclusions of Professor Palmieri, which are recorded in his personal minutes concerning the corpse which he himself dissected. In this protocol, which is published in the same German White Book, it is said that there were traces of remains of insects and their larvae in the mouths of the corpses.

Markov Testified He Had Signed the Report Under Duress

DR. STAHMER: Witness, at the beginning of my examination you stated that you were fully aware of the political significance of your task. **Why, then, did you**

desist from protesting against this report which was not in accord with your scientific conviction?

MARKOV: I have already said that I signed the protocol as I was convinced that the circumstances at this isolated military airfield offered no other possibility, and therefore I could not make any objections.

DR. STAHMER: Why did you not take steps later on?

MARKOV: My conduct after the signing of the protocol corresponds fully to what I am stating here, I repeat. I was not convinced of the truth of the German version ... Because of the political situation in which we found ourselves at that moment, I could not make a public statement declaring the German version was wrong.

There is no evidence that Markov was "forced" to testify at Nuremberg. If he had wanted to do so he could have claimed political asylum while he was in West Germany. He did not, so there is no reason to think that his testimony at Nuremberg was compelled in any way. Markov states repeatedly that he felt compelled to sign the report in AM which concluded that the Katyn corpses had been buried three years earlier although this contradicted his own view.

Cienciala certainly knew that Markov's testimony was indeed devastating — but to the German and Polish anticommunist version that the Soviets were guilty. If Cienciala had been an objective, responsible historian she would have examined Markov's testimony, conceded that it contradicts the "official" version, and moved on. Instead, she dishonestly conceals this from her readers, who will not know it.

Hájek

Cienciala does not mention Dr. František Hájek's testimony at all! His name does not even appear in her book. Yet Hájek, a member of the German Commission, published a book with his criticisms of the German Report:

František Hájek *Důkazy Katynské* [Katyn Evidence].
[Praha], [Spolek českých lékařů], [1946][5]

Hájek repeated the main points of this 1945 book in shorter form
in an interview of March 9, 1952 in the Czech newspaper *Lidova
demokracie*, in which he criticized the US Congress's Madden
Commission hearings. It was reprinted in the Soviet newspaper
Pravda on March 12, 1952.[6]

Hájek's criticism of the German AM could accurately be described
as "devastating." Neither Cienciala nor Sanford discuss it or Markov's critiques of the German report. Neither Hájek's book nor his
interview have been published in English translation.

Some sources claim that Hájek was arrested by Soviet authorities
and forced to write the book in which he refutes the German report. I can find no evidence that this happened. Evidently, Hájek
himself never made this claim, for surely the anticommunist Czech
writers on Katyn would have mentioned it. But Hájek did claim
that he acted out of fear of the Germans, both at Katyn and upon
his return to German-occupied Czechoslovakia.

Here I reproduce a few quotations from Hájek's book and his 1952
article that show how damaging Hájek's testimony is to the "official" version of Katyn.

> Snad nekdo namítne, že moje úvaha nemá také
> významu, ponevadž z vdecnosti k Rusum, kterí náš
> národ osvobodili, nemohu jinak mluviti. Mne však jde
> o to, aby historik, který by chtel otázku katynskou
> rešiti, mel podklad v duvodech, které uvedu. Kdybych
> mlcel, zdálo by se, že souhlasím s Nemci a že tedy

---

[5] OCLC # 14747046 It can be downloaded in a dual-language Russian-Czech side by side
version at http://katynbooks.narod.ru/Hájek/Hájek_rus_cz.html

[6] The Russian translation of this article was reprinted in the Soviet journal *Voenno-
Istoricheskii Zhurnal* 8 (1991) pp. 68-69, now online at http://www.katyn-
books.ru/archive/vizh/1991-08_01.html

trvám na svém podpisu, t. j. na tom, že popravy polských dustojníku byly provedeny na jare 1940. (6)

Translated:

Perhaps some may argue that my idea is not important because, in gratitude to the Russians who liberated our nation, I cannot speak otherwise. But my
point is that the historian who would like to solve the
issue of Katyn, has a basis in evidence that I will cite. If
I had remained silent, it would seem that I agree with
Germans and maintain with my signature [on the expert report in AM], i.e. the fact that executions of
Polish officers were carried out in the spring of 1940.

Ve výpovedi tohoto svedka je plno rozporu. Jiní sved-
kové udávali, že lesík byl ohražen 2 m vysokým
drátem, že byl strežen ozbrojenou stráží a nikdo ne-
mel do neho prístupu. Tento svedek tvrdí, že v okolí
zámku se nesmely v ony dny sbírati houby. Ostatne je
težko veriti, že by v dubnu nebo v kvetnu v tech
místech rostly houby. Také je nepravdepodobné, že by
ze vzdálenosti 50 m vecer nebo v noci mohl rozpozna-
ti typicky židovské obliceje. (10)

Translated:

In the confessions of this witness there were many
contradictions. Other witnesses testified that the little
woods was secured by two-meter barbed wire, guard-
ed by armed men, and that no one could enter it. This
witness asserts that around the castle in those days
one could gather mushrooms. Also, it is hard to believe that in April or May there were mushrooms
growing there. It is also unlikely that a distance of 50
m in the evening or at night one could recognize a typ-
ically Jewish face.

Jest podivné, že nemecká správa, když již si dala tolik práce, nevypátrala a nevyslechla onech 10 polských delníku, kterí v léte 1942 nalezli první hroby a neptala se jich, od koho se od nich dovedeli a proc to tehdy neoznámili nemeckým úradum. Polští delníci nemeli prece duvodu vec zatajovati. (11)

Translated:

It is also strange that the German administration, despite the fact that they devoted so much work on this affair, did not seek out the 10 Polish workers who first found the graves in the summer of 1942, and did not ask them from whom they found out about the graves and why they did not report their find to the German authorities at that time. The Polish workers had no reason to keep this affair secret.

6. Dukaz petiletými borovickami.

Jako dukaz uvádí Nemci také mladé petileté borovicky, které byly nasázeny na nasypaných pahorcích. My jsme jich sami nevideli, nebot hroby byly již otevreny, nám byla jen jedna borovicka ukázána. Rez jedné borovicky byl vyšetren vertikálním iluminátorem. Zjišteno. že je nejméne petiletá a na rezu blíže stredu bylo lze videti málo znatelný temnejší pruh. Zavolaný lesmistr von Herff prohlásil, že takový pruh vzniká, když je rust borovicky necím zabrzden, na pr. presazením a soudil, že borovická byla presazena pred 3 lety. Sám však uznal, že borovicky jsou špatne vyvinuté, rostoucí ve stínu velkých stromu — mohl tedy býti tento pruh zavinen také vlivem jiným a ne jen presazením. (15)

Translated:

6. The evidence of the five-year-old small pine trees

As evidence the Germans also refer to the small five-year-old pine trees that had been planted on heaped-up mounds. We did not see them ourselves because the graves were already opened, we were only shown one little pine. A section of the pine was examined with a vertical illuminator. It was determined that the treeling was at least five years old and in the section near to the center was a faint dark stripe. The forestry expert von Herff who had been summoned stated that a dark stripe like this arises when something stops the treeling's growth, for example, in the case of transplanting, and assumed that the little pine had been transplanted three years earlier. However, he also admitted that the treelings were poorly developed, were growing in the shade of other trees, and that the stripe in question could therefore arise from other causes and not only from transplantation.

[Concerning the diary of Adam Solski]

Tento deník jsem sám nevidel. Poslední jeho práve popsaná stránka byla uverejnena v Bílé knize. Jedosti podezrelý svým obsahem a v rozporu s výpovedmi svedku i jinými okolnostmi. 9/4. Mluví o tom, že prišli do lesa v 8.30 ráno, ac podle svedka Silvestrovova byli do lesa odváženi vecer a v noci. Podezrelé jest, že mohl býti psán až takrka do posledního okamžiku pred po-pra-[va]. Nemá uveden rok, nýbrž jen den a mesíc. Má dvakráte datum vou, nehlede ani k tomu, že deníky se psávají vecer o událostech predcházejících. Také není podán dukaz, že by byl psán vlastní rukou. (16)

Translated:

I did not see this diary myself. The last page of it, reproduced above, was published in the German Report [lit. "White Book."] Its contents are rather suspicious and are in contradiction to the testimony of witnesses and other circumstances. 9/4 states that they arrived in the woods at 8:30 a.m., although according to the confessions of the witness Sil'vestrov they were carried off into the woods in the evening and at night. It is also suspicious that the diary could have been written in, so to speak, until the last moments before execution. No year is given, only the day and month. One date is entered twice, despite the fact that diaries are normally written in the evening about the events of the past day. There is also no evidence that it was written in the hand of the [stated] author.

I když pripustíme, že pro menší množství vzdušného kyslíku byl proces oxydacní v katynských mrtvolách zpomalen, prece nelze pripustiti, že by byly ležely v hrobech 3 roky. Stav mrtvol by poukazoval, že tam ležely nekolik mesícu a vzhledem k menšímu množství vzdušného kyslíku a zlenenému procesu oxydacnímu, že jam ležely nejvýše 1.5 roku. (18)

Translated:

While acknowledging that because of smaller amounts of atmospheric oxygen the oxidation process was slowed in the Katyn corpses, one cannot concede that they were lying in the graves for three years. The condition of the corpses would suggest that they had lain there a few months and, due to the reduced amount of oxygen in the air and the slower process of oxidation, that they had lain there 1.5 years at most.

Rozsah adipociru rovnež svedcí, že mrtvoly ležely v hrobe asi 1.5 roku. ...Nález na šatstvu a na kovových soucástkách i cigaretách mluví rovnež proti tomu, že by mrtvoly byly bývaly ležely v zemi 3 leta. (31)

Translated:

The extent of adipocere also indicates that the corpses lay in the grave for about 1.5 years.... Analysis of the garment and of the metal parts and cigarettes also speak against the corpses having lain in the earth for three years.

Hájek too rejected Dr. Orsós' idea of "pseudocallus" as evidence that a corpse had been buried for at least three years:

Prof. Orsós z Budapešti upozornoval na to, že v lebce jedné mrtvoly nalezl na povrchu mozkové kaše tvrdou, jako vápenatou, vrstevnatou inkrustaci, která podle jeho zkušeností je pozorována teprve po 3 letech pobytu mrtvoly v hrobe.

Translated:

Prof. Orsós from Budapest pointed out that in the skull of one corpse he found on the surface a brain mush hard as a calcium deposit, which in his experience is observed only after the corpse has lain 3 years in the grave.

Tomu však nebývá až po 3 letech, nýbrž nekdy i mnohem dríve, nebot záleží na množství a koncentraci kyselin, které zpusobují odvápnení a zmeknutí kostí a koncentrace ta je urcite ruzná. Prof. Órsós prohlédl radu lebek a jen v jedné nalezl podobné zmeny v nepatrném stupni, u jiných nikoliv.(20)

Translated:

But this happens not just after three years, but sometimes much earlier, since it depends on the amount and concentration of acids that cause decalcification and softening of the bones and this concentration varies. Prof. Orsós looked at a series of skulls and in only one of them found such changes in a slight degree, and not in others.

Hájek Testified that His Real Opinion Was Censored

Když jsem se vrátil a úredne byl uverejnen Katynský protokol, dostavili se ke mne redaktori tehdejších deníku „Polední list" a „Vecerní Ceské slovo"'. Pravili, že dostali pokyn, aby si u mne vyžádali rozhovor, že mé odpovedi budou uverejneny ve všech denních listech. Zodpovedel jsem jim jejich otázky a rekl po pravde, co jsem v Katynu videl a slyšel, ale následujícího dne jsem byl velmi roztrpcen, když jsem cetl neco zcela jiného a když mi byly dány do úst výroky, jichž jsem vubec neucinil a uciniti nemohl. (21)

Translated:

When I returned [from Katyn] and the Katyn protocol was officially published the editors of the dailies "Poledni list" and "Vecerní Ceské Slovo" came to me. They said they had been instructed to interview me and that my answers would be published in all daily papers. I answered their questions and told the truth about what I had seen and heard at Katyn, but the next day I was very embittered when I read something totally different and when remarks were put into my mouth which I had not made and could not make.

Za nekolik dnu jsem byl požádán tiskovým šéfem pro t. zv. protektorát, Wolframem von Wolmarem, abych o svých zkušenostech prednášel pred zástupci tisku v Presseklubu. Ucinil jsem tak, ale opet jen objektivne a po prednášce vytkl jsem dosti ostre zmíneným redaktorum jejich zpusob psaní, jak také nyní konstatovala ceská tisková kancelár. (Viz „Práce" ze dne 11.

cervence 1945.) Zduraznoval jsem tehdy, že lékar
nemá práva dotýkati se viny nebo neviny obviněných,
nýbrž podávati vecný posudek, spadající do
lékarského oboru. Redaktori poukazovali na censuru.
(21)

Translated:

Several days later I was asked by the press chief of the
so-called Protectorate, Wolfram von Wolmar, to lecture about my experiences before the press in the
Press club. I did so, but again only objectively, and after the lecture I criticized the editors rather sharply
for their way of writing, as the Czech News Agency has
recently confirmed. (See "Prace" of 11 July 1945). I
pointed out then that a doctor has no right to judge
the guilt or innocence of defendants but give an objective judgment within the medical field. The editors referred to the censorship.

Hájek Was Forced to Sign the German Report

Na tretí otázku, proc jsem podepsal katynský protokol,
jsem odpovedel:

„Každému z nás bylo jasno, kdybychom protokol,
který vypracovali prof. Buhtz z Vratislavi a prof. Orsós
z Budapešti, nepodepsali, že by se letadlo s námi urcite nebylo vrátilo. (22)

Translated:

To the third question, why I had signed the Katyn protocol [the expert statement in AM] I answered:

"It was clear to all of us that if we did not sign the protocol composed by Prof. Buhtz of Bratislava and Prof.
Orsós of Budapest, our airplane would certainly not
return."

In his 1952 article Hájek added that when he tried to beg off the trip to Katyn on grounds of illness he was threatened by the Ministry of Internal Affairs of the "Protectorate of Bohemia and Moravia," the puppet state under German occupation, with being accused of "sabotage" and sent to a concentration camp.

Hájek also stated that a number of the medical experts called to Katyn by the Germans did not know German very well. Buhtz, the German professor, wrote the report, read it out loud, and the rest of the scientists signed it.

Polish Observers at Katyn Who Retracted Their Testimony

Sanford claims in one sentence that Dr. Adam Szebesta and Edmund Seyfried, who had been members of Polish delegations at Katyn, retracted their testimony after the war. (206)

Seyfried was imprisoned by the postwar pro-communist government for collaboration. The article concerning Seyfried by Stanisław Jankowski, to which Cienciala refers, states that he had made some kind of statement at the request of the Germans:

> Edmund Seyfried przyznaje, że przed opuszczeniem
> miejsca ekshumacji uczestnicy delegacji „na prośbę
> Niemców opowiedzieli swoje wrażenia"...[7]

Translated:

> Edmund Seyfried admits that before leaving the place
> of exhumation the members of the delegation "stated
> their opinions at the request of the Germans..."

---

[7] Stanisław M. Jankowski, "Pod Specjalnym Nadzorem, przy Drzwiach Zamkniętych: Wyroki Sądowe w PRL za Ujawnienie Prawdy o Zbrodni Katyńskiej" [Under Special Surveillance, with Doors Closed: Sentences in People's Poland for Revealing the Truth about Katyn], in Marek Tarczyński, ed., *Zbrodnia Katyńska: Polskie Śledztwo* [The Crime of Katyn: The Polish Investigation], *Zeszyty Katyńskie*, no. 20 (Warsaw, 2005), 106 n. 44.

A document of the Polish underground reproduced in translation in volume 4 of the Madden Commission hearings states the following:

> Seyfried, after inspecting the graves, with the permission of the Germans, made the following speech, whose contents were affirmed by another delegate: "I call upon you gentlemen to take off your hats, bow your heads, and pay tribute to these heroes who gave their lives that Poland might live." The Germans saluted. The entire proceedings were filmed, photographed, and sound-recorded. The participants have expressed * * * a sound recording was also made. (Madden Vol. 4 p. 717; confirmed on p. 846. The three asterisks are in the original)

Neither Cienciala nor Sanford give any indication where Seyfried's retraction can be found. It would be interesting to read both what Seyfried said or reported in 1943 and what he said in his retraction, evidently in 1945.

Seyfried was apparently jailed in 1948. We do not know whether his role at Katyn was the only charge against him, or whether he was charged with other instances of collaboration with the Germans. We do know that the Polish delegations that visited Katyn at German invitation in April 1943 could not have had any more evidence of Soviet guilt than the Germans did. As we have seen, even months later, when the German Report was published, the Germans did not have any such evidence either.

Sanford helpfully identifies Dr. Szebesta's retraction (152 n. 56). Sanford claims that Szebesta was "forced to recant his wartime testimony." Sanford gives no evidence that this testimony was "forced." But he does identify an interview with Szebesta in the Polish communist newspaper *Trybuna Ludu* of March 20, 1952, which I have obtained. In this interview Szebesta said that the Germans had obviously demanded and staged the visit of the Polish officials as a propaganda stunt.

Szebesta claimed that he was sent by the German authorities straight to the airport, without being able even to say goodbye to his wife. He stated that they were always accompanied by some Germans, always under guard, and had no freedom of action at all. In fact, he said that they were at Katyn for only one hour! They were continually told by the Germans that only the Soviets could have done such a terrible thing. Szebesta thought it particularly ironic that the Germans told him that Germans could never have committed such a massacre!

He says that the German doctor who accompanied them told him that the cartridge shells found at Katyn were of the caliber of weapons used by the Soviets.

> Oprowadzający nas lekarz niemiecki pokazywał różne przestrzelone czaszki tłumacząc, że kaliber broni od- powiada tej, jaka jest używana w ZSRR.

Translated:

> The German doctor who accompanied us showed us various used shells and explained that the caliber of weapons corresponded to that used in the USSR.

This is evidence that the Germans had initially planned to claim that Soviet guns were used to shoot the Polish prisoners at Katyn. Szebesta and the other Polish delegates were at Katyn in early April. It was not until the end of the month that the Germans decided that they had to admit that German shells had been found at Katyn.

Goebbels thought that the presence of German shells in the Katyn graves should have been enough to convince the Allies that the Germans had shot the Poles at Katyn. But Goebbels was mistaken! The issue of the German shells has been blithely passed over by all those eager to blame the Soviets, beginning with the Polish GIE. Goebbels underestimated the Allies' anticommunist zeal.

Like other witnesses Szebesta was convinced that the corpses and the other materials in the graves were far too well preserved to have been buried three years earlier, in 1940. Szebesta's remarks about the corpses are similar to those of Markov and Hájek.

Cienciala and Sanford are bluffing – in plain language, lying – about Seyfried and Szebesta. Did the Germans, or the Soviets, or both, "force" Seyfried and Szebesta to make whatever statements they made? Were their retractions compelled by the Nazis, or the communists? Or were made voluntarily and out of conviction? An objective study would identify and examine the circumstances surrounding them, in an attempt to determine which, if any, of their statements were valid, and if unsuccessful, would say as much. But neither Sanford nor Cienciala does.

The Phillimore Note

Lt Col Harry Phillimore was Secretary of the British War Crimes Executive (BWCE) at Nuremberg. He reported to Patrick Dean, legal adviser to the Foreign Office. His report is available online.[8]

Neither Cienciala nor Sanford mention Phillimore's note of July 6, 1946. This omission is probably due to the fact that Phillimore concluded that the Soviet case set forth at Nuremberg was a convincing one, particularly as set forth by Professor Prozorovsky of the Burdenko Commission,

> The third witness was the principal member of the
> Soviet investigation [Prozorovsky]. He was undoubt-
> edly a most effective witness and testified to having
> personally exhumed some 5,000 bodies at Kiev, Khar-
> kov, Smolensk and other places. He spoke in great de-
> tail of the condition of the bodies and of the very care-

---

[8] I have put the Phillimore report online at
http://msuweb.montclair.edu/~furrg/research/phillimore.pdf It was formerly available at:
http://collection.europarchive.org/tna/20070206143611/http://fco.gov.uk/files/kfile/an nexf.pdf At is still available at the Internet Archive:
https://web.archive.org/web/20160913024024/http://collection.europarchive.org/tna/2 0070206143611/http://fco.gov.uk/files/kfile/annexf.pdf

ful investigation made. His commission had made a
most careful autopsy of 925 bodies, only 3 of which
had apparently been perfunctorily examined previously. He explained the condition of the clothing,
which had been searched and gave details of a few
documents found. They included receipts dated April
and May 1941 and a letter from a wife to the Soviet
Red Cross, bearing a Warsaw and Moscow postmark
in September 1940 as well as postmark with the
stamp of the Tarnopol Post Office dated 13 November
1940. He has personally discovered a letter dated 20
June. His mastery of the details of these documents
was complete and his evidence delivered confidently
and quickly, but obviously not parrot wise. He went on
to deal with the bullet cases, which were found in the
graves, which were those of a calibre which the German witnesses had admitted applied to the German
pistols and which, he stated, bore the initials of a German firm GECO. This evidence was greatly fortified by
a captured document produced by the Americans being a telegram dated May 1943 from an official of the
Government General to the defendant Frank's office in
Poland stating that members of the Polish Red Cross
who had been visiting Katyn at the invitation of the
Germans had been very much disturbed at finding bullet cases marked GECO, a well known German firm.
The conjunction between this document showing
German bullet cases found in the graves in May 1943
by the Poles and by the Soviet commission a year later
in January 1944, was most convincing. He went on to
give reasons why the bodies could not have been buried as early as 1940 and concluded by comparing the
method of killing with that in the many other cases
which he had personally investigated where German
action was not disputed. **Altogether, although not of
course conclusive the evidence emerged strongly
in favour of the Soviet case and the German report**

was largely discredited and their evidence unimpressive.

Sanford:

> The most important Soviet witness, Dr Markov, the
> Bulgarian member of the International Commission,
> agreed to all Prosecutor Smirnov's leading questions.
> [109] His evidence that the International Commission
> had been presented with already exhumed bodies and
> had signed only under German pressure was to be **refuted later by Drs Naville and Tramsen**. (140)

This statement by Sanford is a lie. It is a reference to Naville's and Tramsen's testimony to the US Madden Commission in 1952 (neither testified at Nuremberg). There they did not refute anything that Markov said. We discuss their testimony below.

The Madden Commission

Cienciala says little about the Madden Commission and nothing about the testimony given there. In particular, she does not point out the following testimony:

* Gustav Genschow, whose armaments firm manufactured the Geco 7.65 DD ammunition found at Katyn, testified that only small amounts of this ammunition were exported to the USSR – "only two to three thousand rounds" after 1928, a truly insignificant quantity. (Madden V, 1578-9)

* Dr. Francois Naville of Switzerland, the only medical expert at Katyn who was from a neutral country, discounted Dr. Ferenc Orsós's theory of "pseudocallus". (Madden V, 1612) This was the sole medical evidence set forth by the Germans that the bodies had been buried for three years, and even Orsós claimed to have found it in only one corpse.

* Kathleen Mortimer, Averill Harriman's daughter, had been at Katyn. As we have seen, she had attended the Burdenko Commission investigation and had written a private letter in

which she stated that she had witnessed a document dated the summer of 1941 as it was taken from the pocket of a corpse.

It is notable that in her testimony to the Madden Commission she did not deny this. She was not directly asked about it because this detail was not in her 1944 report from Katyn. Nor did she volunteer it. She did insist that she had been present at post-mortems, and that the documents she saw at a museum in Smolensk "had been taken from bodies that had been buried a considerable length of time." (Madden VII, 2145) This partially corroborates what she wrote to her sister.

The importance of this, once again, is that the presence of documents dated in the second half of 1940 or any time in 1941 proves that the Soviets did not shoot the Poles, regardless of any other evidence. The "official" Soviets-did-it version assumes that all the Polish POWs were shot shortly after they were transferred from the three POW camps to the NKVD in Smolensk, Kalinin, and Khar'kov in April and May, 1940.

Sanford

> Dr Palmieri confirmed that all the signs indicated that
> the Poles had been killed between March and May
> 1940. (142-3)

Sanford is being untruthful again. In reality Palmieri said he based his conclusion on Orsós's conclusion alone.

> Mr. Machrowicz. Was Dr. Orsós' conclusion that the
> deaths occurred not later than April or May 1940?
>
> Dr. Palmieri. Yes.
>
> Mr. Machrowicz. Did you agree?
>
> Dr. Palmieri. Yes, based on the researches that Dr.
> Orsós had made.

Palmieri specifically declined to reach any conclusion based on his own experience.

> Mr. Machrowicz. From your own experiences and ex-
> periments at Katyn did you come to any conclusion as
> to the time of death of the persons found in these
> graves?
>
> Dr. Palmieri. I can say no more than when a person is
> buried between 18 and 30 months to establish the ex-
> act time of burial is difficult. (Madden V 1619)

The Germans' claim – now the "official" version – is that the Poles POWs had been shot and buried in April and May, 1940, between 35 and 37 months prior to the April-June German excavation. That means that here Dr. Palmieri *explicitly refused to confirm* that, as Sanford claims, "all the signs indicated that the Poles had been killed between March and May 1940." On the contrary: Palmieri's statements support the Soviet account! But the Madden Commission members failed to mention this fact.

Sanford:

> Dr Tramsen testified that the mummification of the
> bodies caused by the pressure of sand and of other
> bodies on them confirmed beyond all doubt that the
> Poles had been buried in the winter clothing in which
> they had been killed. (Sanford 143)

Tramsen did say that (Madden V 1455). But it proves nothing. The Poles had been captured in September, 1939. Therefore, they had their winter clothing with them at that time. Therefore they could have been wearing it in the fall – September to December 1941 – as well as in April or May 1940. The fact that some of the Poles whose corpses were disinterred at Katyn were dressed in winter clothes says nothing about the time of year they were murdered.

Of the Madden Committee report Sanford states:

The British FO deprecated the inconclusive, one-sided and contradictory evidence on which it was based. The committee had 'an obvious political bias and has not been drawn up in an exclusively judicial fashion'. ... The Republicans used Roosevelt's conspiracy of silence, and worse, over Katyn as part of their 1952 election campaign designed to win over East European ethnic voters away from the Democrats. (143-144)

Cienciala more or less agrees:

The Madden Committee failed to achieve its main goal, a trial of the Katyn case by the United Nations or some other international tribunal....the Madden Committee was unpopular in Democratic circles not only because it seemed to align itself with McCarthy, but also because many prominent members of the Roosevelt and Truman administrations were charged with suppressing information on Katyn. The same circles also had a generally negative attitude toward the exiled Polish government in London, which was pushing for a trial of the Katyn case. For all these reasons, the hearings received wide publicity in Polish-American but not in mainstream American media. (239)

Conclusion

BU has not been called into doubt in any way by the defenders of the "official" version of Katyn or in any of the critiques they have cited. Much less has it been refuted.

BU remains the most accurate account of the killings at Katyn. Cienciala and Sanford have been blinded by their anticommunist bias; are deliberately lying; or both. Despite their repeated claims, none of the documents they cite refute the BU or the Soviet case as it was set forth at Nuremberg.

Chapter 12. The Excavations at Volodymyr-Volyns'kiy

On August 27, 2014, the following story appeared in The Telegraph of London, UK:

> "Stalin-era mass grave found in Ukrainian castle"
>
> Polish and Ukrainian scientists have unearthed a mass grave containing up to a thousand victims of Stalinist terror in a castle once used as a secret police prison.
>
> Among the victims found in the grave are Polish soldiers, and the Polish press has already called the find a "new Katyn" in reference to a massacre of thousands of Poles by Stalin in 1940. The Katyn massacre still clouds Polish-Russian relations.
>
> The grave was found in the grounds of the Kazimierz the Great castle in the town of Volodymyr-Volynsky in western Ukraine, close to the Polish border.
>
> Although the NKVD had a base on the remains of the 13th-Century castle from 1939-1956—except when it was occupied by the Germans—scientists say the victims were killed between 1940 and 1941.
>
> http://www.telegraph.co.uk/news/worldnews/europe/ukraine/11059224/Stalin-era-mass-grave-found-in-Ukrainian-castle.html

In the fall of 2013, a few months after my article in *Socialism and Democracy*[1] was published, the end of the excavations at Volodymyr-Volyns'kiy was announced. According to newspaper reports the chief Polish archeologist, Dr. Dominika Siemińska, said that 57 bodies had been exhumed and reburied. In a video interview of Dr. Siemińska two additional badges of Polish policemen are shown. They are badges 1154/III and 639/VII. The first is from the Kiel police district, the second from the Pomorsk district. The Polish language video interview is here:

https://www.youtube.com/watch?v=gPGFcvETG1Q

The important issues here are the following:

* The Polish report by Dr. Siemińska has been taken off the Internet. The Report was originally online here:

http://www.kresykedzierzynkozle.home.pl/attachments/File/Rap.pdf

It is still available at the Internet Archive:

https://web.archive.org/web/20130203224105/http://www.kresykedzierzynkozle.home.pl/attachments/File/Rap.pdf

* Polish and Ukrainian media accounts continue to identify thIs as a Soviet NKVD mass shooting. The fact that 96% - 98.67% of all the shell casings found there are German and manufactured in 1941 is no longer mentioned. Instead the claim is made that shell casings from the Soviet Tokarev pistol have been found, though no evidence or even numbers are given to substantiate this claim.

The Claim that Soviet Pistol Shells Were Found at V-V:

Dr. Siemińska:

---

[1] Grover Furr. "The "Official" Version of the Katyn Massacre Disproven? Discoveries at a German Mass Murder Site in Ukraine." *Socialism and Democracy* 27(2) (August 2013): 96-129.

Znalezione na miejscu łuski z pistoletu TT wskazują, że zostali zabici przez NKWD w 1940 i 1941 roku.

Translated:

Shells from the TT[2] pistol found at this place show that they were killed by the NKVD in 1940 and 1941.

Both the Polish and the Ukrainian archeological reports from V-V state that the shells found in the mass graves were overwhelmingly from 9 mm. weapons.

In the video interview given as the excavations were being completed Dr. Siemińska stated that the ammunition found in Grave No. 4 is "smaller than 8 mm."

W przebadanych do tej pory... um, ponad dwustu czaszkach... eh, z mogiły numer cztery... eh, jest około sto pięćdziesięciu... eh, no, śladów, wlotów ...eh, um... po pociskach... no, i świadczą one o tym, że amunicja, którą te osoby zostały rozstrzelane to jest kaliber mniej niż osiem milimetrów, bo te otwory mają około - wlotowe - około ośmiu milimetrów, więc zostały zrobione... eh, amunicją poniżej ośmiu milimetrów.

Translated:

In the more than two hundred skulls examined up till this time ... eh, from grave number four ... eh, there are about one hundred fifty... he, well, traces, entry holes ... eh, well, after missiles ... well, and they testify to the fact that the ammunition with which these people were shot is of a caliber less than eight millimeters, because these openings

---

[2] „Śladami bestialstwa totalitaryzmu." Dziennik Kijowski No. 2 (January-February 2015), p. 5. At http://kresy24.pl/wp-content/uploads/2015/03/Dziennik_Kijowski_2_2015.pdf (TT = Tokarev pistol. See the Wikipedia entry at https://en.wikipedia.org/wiki/TT_pistol)

have entry holes of about eight millimeters, and so they were made by ammunition of less than eight millimeters.

- https://www.youtube.com/watch?v=gPGFcvETG1Q

The Tokarev TT pistol takes a 7.62 mm cartridge. This is clearly an attempt to place the blame on the Soviets. She says that "few shell casings were found" in this grave ("Również dość mała ilość łusek znalezionych"). But they are not identified. This too is a false statement. As we have already seen, the Polish archeologist's report counts several hundred shell casings, more than 96% of them German and dated 1941.

As late as September, 2013, Polish reports were still admitting that the victims were shot by Germans in 1941, although the archeologists were expecting to find NKVD victims:

> Znaleziono wówczas szczątki 343 osób, a podczas prac w roku kolejnym - 512 osób. Byli to jak oceniamy w większości miejscowi Żydzi, prawdopodobnie zamordowani przez Niemców latem 1941 r. po wejściu do miasta. **Generalnie poszukiwaliśmy w tym miejscu ofiar NKWD, jednak podczas oględzin szczątków okazało się, że sposób mordowania wskazuje na Niemców. Są tam pogrzebane całe rodziny, w większości kobiety i dzieci, czego NKWD jednak raczej nie robiło, wysyłając ich zwykle na Syberię.** Szczątki były niemal pozbawione ubrań i przedmiotów osobistych. Wskazywałoby to na Niemców, którzy rozstrzeliwali ludzi wpędzonych do dołu śmierci. **Sprawstwo hitlerowskie wydaje się też potwierdzać odnaleziona niemiecka amunicja z 1941 r.** - opowiadał naczelnik wydziału zagranicznego Rady Ochrony Pamięci Walk i Męczeństwa Maciej Dancewicz.[3]

---

[3] „Ludzkie szczątki odkryte we Włodzimierzu Wołyńskim. 'Zamordowani strzałem w głowę'" At http://www.tvn24.pl/wiadomosci-z-kraju,3/ludzkie-szczatki-odkryte-we-wlodzimierzu-wolynskim-zamordowani-strzalem-w-glowe,354815.html (Accessed June 16 2015)

Translated:

They found at that time the remains of 343 people, and during the work in the next year – 512 people. They were as we believe, mostly local Jews, probably murdered by the Germans in the summer of 1941 when they entered the city. **Generally we were looking for the victims of the NKVD at this site, but during the examination of the remains it turned out that the manner of killing points to the Germans. There are buried entire families, mostly women and children, what the NKVD did not do; they usually sent them to Siberia.** The remains were almost devoid of clothes and personal items. This would point to the Germans, who shot down people whom they drove to the death pit. **Nazi perpetration also seems to be confirmed by German ammunition from 1941 that has been found**. – said the head of the foreign department of the Council for Protection of Memory of Combat and Martyrdom Maciej Dancewicz.

In *Nasz Dziennik* of September 24, 2013 Dr. Siemińska is still talking about "the identification of a person on the Mednoe list" and that "most shell cases are also of German production":

Tu również udało się zidentyfikować osobę, która była na liście z Miednoje – zaznacza dr Dominika Siemińska.

„Większość łusek również produkcji niemieckiej, z tej samej serii, co poprzednio,..."

Translated:

Here we also managed to identify a person who is on the Mednoe list – says Dr. Dominika Siemińska.

"Most of the shells are also of German production, from the same series as before…"

- „Kim są ofiary z Włodzimierza?" - Nasz Dziennik – Sept.24 2013. At http://www.naszdziennik.pl/polska-kraj/54675

Research published by Prof. Ivan Katchanovski that these victims were shot by the Germans and by their Ukrainian Nationalist allies is ignored.

> "Katyn in Reverse in Ukraine: Nazi-led Massacres turned into Soviet Massacres." -
> http://www.opednews.com/articles/Katyn-in-Reverse-in-Ukrain-by-Ivan-Katchanovski-121212-435.html

> "ОУН(б) и нацистские массовые убийства летом 1941 года на исторической Волыни." ("Mass murders by the OUN(b) and the Nazis in the summer of 1941 in historic Volhynia.") - http://www1.ku-eichs-
> taett.de/ZIMOS/forum/docs/forumruss22/15Kachanovskij.pdf

> "Owning a massacre; 'Ukraine' Katyn'. Open Democracy 10.26.2011. - https://www.opendemocracy.net/od-russia/ivan-katchanovski/owning-massacre-ukraines-katyn

The Polish archeologists' report, written and signed by Dr. Dominika Siemińska herself in November 2011 is simply not mentioned. That report concluded that the mass murders at Volodymyr-Volyns'kiy were committed by the Germans, not by the Soviets,

* Two more badges of Polish policemen were found before the excavations were shut down.

> Znaleźliśmy polskie guziki wojskowe... znaleźliśmy fragmenty mundurów policyjnych... no, ale najważniejsze znaleziska to są... um, znaki ewidencyjne policjantów polskich. Dwa są zachowane w całości i wiemy, że jeden należał do... eh, funkcjonariusza z komen... z okręgu... eh, pomorskiego a drugi z okręgu... eh, kieleckiego. Trzeci – niestety! – zachował się tylko we fragmencie i jest... eh, ułamany w ten sposób, że zachował się tylko fragment numeru, więc nie możemy nawet powiedzieć z jakiego okręgu.

...Um, jeden to jest... um, ten z okręgu... um, pomorskiego: to jest sześćset trzydzieści dziewięć; ten z okręgu kieleckiego to jest tysiąc sto pięćdziesiąt cztery, a ten zachowany w kaw... we fragmencie numer to jest osiemset trzydzieści sześć.

Translated:

We have found Polish military buttons ... we found fragments of police uniforms ... but the most important finds are ... um, registration marks of Polish policemen. The two are preserved in their entirety, and we know that one belonged to ... eh, an officer of the Pomorsze [Pomeranian] district and the other from the district... eh, of Kielce. The third - alas! – is preserved only in a fragment and is ... eh, chipped in such a way that only a fragment of the number has been preserved, so we cannot even say from which district.

...Um, one is ... um, the one from the ... um, Pomorsze [Pomeranian] district: it is number six hundred thirty nine; the one from the Kielce district is one thousand one hundred fifty-four, and this preserved in fragments is eight hundred thirty six.

Images 12. 1 and 12.2 Artist's rendering of addittional Polish policemen's badges unearthed at Volodymyr-Volyns'kiy. Polish officials have refused to identify them.

But the owners of these badges have not been publicly identified by Polish authorities. Earlier, before the significance of the Volodymyr-Volyns'kiy excavations for the Katyn issue was fully recognized, Ludwik Małowiejski's and Józef Kuligowski's badges were quickly associated with their owners.

We should remember that the badges of Kuligowski and Małowiejski were found in the same mass graves in 2010 and 2011. According to the "official" version these two Polish policemen were shot at Kalinin (now Tver') and buried nearby at Mednoe. Memorial plaques bearing their names are displayed at the memorial graveyard at Mednoe along with more than 6300 other such plaques. The discovery of their badges at Volodymyr-Volyns'kiy, Ukraine, 700 miles (1200 km) away, led to some publicity. This in turn led to the initial article by Sergei Strygin, in Russian, and my own more detailed article in English, pointing out that this discovery undermines the "official" version of Katyn.

Today a "curtain of silence" has descended over these discoveries. There are many more than 57 bodies in these mass graves – hundreds, in fact. But the excavations have been ended. The evidence that the victims were murdered by the Germans and Ukrainian fascists, not the Soviets, is hushed up. Soviet guilt is simply stated as a "fact" rather than investigated. The question of the shell casings is no longer mentioned.

This revealing sentence can be found in an article in a Lublin (Poland) newspaper dated October 21, 2013, at the same time that the excavations at Volodymyr-Volyns'kiy were concluded:

> Archeolodzy odnaleźli pojedyncze policyjne odznaki z numerami funkcjonariuszy, ale te, które odnaleziono do tej pory, należały do policjantów, którzy, jak wskazują zachowane dokumenty, zostali zabici przez Sowietów w zupełnie innym miejscu - w Twerze.

Translated:

Archeologists have found individual police badges with numbers of officers, but those that have been found so far belonged to policemen who, according to documents that have been preserved, had been killed by the Soviets in a completely different place – in Tver'.[4]

This story appeared at the same time as the interview with Dr. Siemińska, the Polish archeologist – the same interview where the two additional Polish policemen's badges, numbers 1154/III and 639/VII are pictured (see above).

It is possible that these badges too belong to supposed "Katyn massacre" victims. If they are not, then why haven't the policemen to whom these badges belonged been publicly identified?

But this information has not been made public. The whole matter is being hushed up, kept quiet. This in itself is evidence, if not a virtual admission, that the Polish and Ukrainian governments know that the "official" Soviets-did-it version has been seriously compromised by the discovery of these badges.

All the newspaper articles that report on the ending of the excavations at Volodymyr-Volyns'kiy claim, without evidence of any kind, that the Poles who were shot there were shot by the Soviet NKVD while the Jews and other civilians were shot by the Germans. As we have seen, according to all the evidence the Poles too were murdered by the Germans and their Ukrainian allies. Most articles from the fall of 2013 ignore the Katyn connection completely.

A joint Polish-Ukrainian ceremony presented the bodies as victims of the NKVD, despite a multitude of evidence strongly indicating that these were victims of the Germans and their Ukrainian na-

---

4 "Wojskowe guziki w masowej mogile. Odkrycie na Wołyniu." *Gazeta.pl* Lublin October 21, 2013. At
http://lublin.gazeta.pl/lublin/1,48724,14812213,Wojskowe_guziki_w_masowej_mogile_Od
krycie_na_Wolyniu.html

tionalist collaborators. These collaborators are celebrates as national heroes by today's Ukrainian state.

The YouTube interview of Dr. Siemińska carries the following paragraph:

> Znalezione polskie odznaki policyjne w kolejnych mogiłach we Włodzimierzu Wołyńskim mogą pomóc w ustaleniu nazwisk ofiar. Odznaka o numerze 1154 należała do policjanta z okręgu kieleckiego, natomiast o numerze 639 to policjanta z okręgu pomorskiego. Skala mordów, odkrywane nowe pochówki powodują, że badania polskich i ukraińskich archeologów muszą być kontynuowane w przyszłym roku. Tematem jest również zainteresowana Fundacja Niepodległości, która wspiera prace poszukiwawcze ofiar komunizmu w Polsce.

Translated:

> The Polish police badges found in subsequent graves in Volodymyr-Volyns'kiy can help in establishing the names of the victims. The badge number 1154 belonged to a policeman from the Kielce district, while number 639 was a policeman from the Pomeranian district. The scale of murders and the new burials discovered mean that the research of Polish and Ukrainian archaeologists should be continued next year. This topic is also of interest to the Independence Foundation, which supports the search for victims of communism in Poland.

It appears that the Polish and Ukrainian governments do not want to find more "Katyn victims" where they are not supposed to be.

* The excavations and exhumations have been stopped.

* No DNA testing has been reported.

* The names of Kuligowski and Małowiejski are not mentioned any longer in connection with the Volodymyr-Volyns'kiy excavations. This despite the fact that the discovery of their badges is by far the

most historically significant, as well as the most newsworthy, aspect of this excavation.

* It is now conceded that Jews shot by the Nazis were also buried in these mass graves. But the fact that the Polish materials, including the policemen's badges, were buried in the same mass graves, is now passed over in silence.

* The claim is now made that the Poles were shot by the NKVD as the German army was advancing. This claim, like any claim, requires demonstration – evidence, proof – not a simple assertion. But no evidence is given.

* The "Sardinenpackung" form of burial of the victims in one mass grave, characteristic of the Nazi Einsatzkommando group led by Jeckeln, identified by the Polish archeologist Dr. Dominika Siemińska in the now-suppressed Polish archeological report, and clearly evident in the photograph reproduced in that report, is no longer mentioned.

This cruel method of execution and burial, in which victims were forced to lie down in rows on top of other victims who had been executed before and were then shot, was characteristic of a German SS killing squad's methods.

* We noted in a previous chapter that Ukrainian archeologist Oleksei Zlatohors'kiy protested this finding because it cast doubt on the preconceived notion that the NKVD had murdered the Polish POWs at Katyn.

The vital point is that Kuligowski and Małowiejski were in Volodymyr-Volyns'kiy in 1941 at all. Their presence means that the Polish POWs named in the Soviet "transit" or "shipment" lists, published by Tucholski, of Poles shipped out of the three POW camps in April and May 1940 were not being shipped to execution.

The "official" version of the Katyn massacre rests on the assumption that the POWs were shipped to execution and were executed in April and May 1940. This is only an assumption. The corpses of those supposedly shot by the Soviets at Kalinin (Tver') and Kharkiv have never been found, much less counted or identified. Kuli-gowski's and Małowiejski's memorial tablets remain at Mednoe outside of Tver' even though they were in fact murdered more than a year later and more than 700 miles away in Volodymyr-Volyns'kiy and the Polish authorities, who know this, have not re-moved them. They are "pretending" that the discoveries at Vo-lodymyr-Volyns'kiy never happened.

The fact that their bodies are not there suggests that the bodies of the other Polish POWs are not there either. *There is no evidence that any of these men whose names are recorded on the thousands of memorial tables at Mednoe and Piatykhatky, were in fact executed there and are buried there.*

The fact that Kuligowski and Małowiejski were buried in a mass grave associated with German ammunition dated 1941 and in a location associated with German mass executions of Jews and oth-ers constitutes very strong evidence that they and others were shot by the Germans. But no matter who shot these Polish police-men in Volodymyr-Volyns'kiy in 1941, they were not shot at Kali-nin (Tver') in April-May 1940. This alone fatally undermines the "official" Soviets-did-it version of the Katyn massacre.

We should understand this cover-up, this "conspiracy of silence," as an admission that the Volodymyr-Volyns'kiy excavations have dismantled the "official" version of the Katyn massacre. There is no other version involving Soviet guilt.

The only other version of the massacres of Polish POWs that is known as "Katyn" is that of the Burdenko Commission, which con-cluded that the Germans shot the Polish POWs at Katyn. At this point, the only hypothesis supported by the evidence now availa-ble is that the Germans were guilty of the mass murders known as the "Katyn massacre."

As the "official" version of Katyn becomes more and more called into doubt there may be some attempt in the future to "reinter-pret" the Volodymyr-Volyns'kiy discoveries to try to account for the presence of Kuligowski's and Małowiejski's badges. Documents may be fabricated and brought forward in a fraudulent attempt to "prove" that Kuligowski and Małowiejski were among a small number of "exceptions" who were not executed at Kalinin in 1940. Or some other attempt will be made to salvage the "official" version.

Whatever subterfuge may be invented in future, we can confidently predict that the truth will be denied. The "official" version is too valuable as a stick with which to beat Stalin, the Soviet Union and the communist movement, to let the truth get in the way.

Chapter 13. The 'Ukrainian Trail of Katyn'

Cienciala introduces the "Ukrainian trail" as follows:

> While much is known about the fate of the prisoners
> of war in the three special camps, the same does not
> apply to those held in the NKVD prisons of the west-
> ern regions of Ukraine and Belorussia who were
> transferred to NKVD prisons in Kiev, Kharkov, Kher-
> son, and Minsk following Beria's order of 22 March
> 1940 **(doc. 53)**. According to Beria's resolution, ap-
> proved by the Politburo on 5 March, these prisoners
> were also to be shot. Beria stated that out of a total of
> 18, 632 persons arrested and held in the NKVD pris-
> ons, 10,685 were Poles **(doc. 47)**. However, in a doc-
> ument of March 1959, the number of those shot in the
> prisons was given as 7,305 **(doc. 110)**. **The lists of
> victims shot in Ukraine have been found; the total
> number is 3,435, more than 2,000 of whom have
> been identified.** Their burial sites are unknown, but
> since Beria ordered them to be moved to NKVD jails in
> Kiev, Kharkov, and Kherson, presumably they were
> buried in or near each of these cities.[27] The lists must
> have included at least some of the prisoners whom
> Merkulov ordered on 22 February 1940 to be taken
> out of the three camps and transported to NKVD pris-
> ons (doc. 42). Most, however, seem to have been ar-
> rested and jailed in western Ukraine (East Galicia),
> which was part of interwar Poland. (Cienciala 136)

Note 27, page 481 to this passage reads:

> 27. See Zuzanna Gajowniczek, ed., *Ukraiński Ślad
> Katynia* [The Ukrainian Trail of Katyn] (Warsaw,

1995); the identifications were made by Gajowniczek.
This publication, made possible by the cooperation of
the Ukrainian and Polish Security Services, contains
thirty-four lists of victims. The lists were sent with a
cover letter dated 25 November 1940 by GB 1st Lieutenant Feodor A. Tsvetukhin to the head of the NKVD
1st Special Department, Moscow, GB Major Leonid F.
Bashtakov. Tsvetukhin, head of the 1st Special Department, Ukraine, 1939–1940, wrote that he was en-
closing 3,435 files in five sacks (p. xxii). **The list numbers are from the same series as those for the
three special camps** that Gorbachev gave to General
Jaruzelski in Moscow on 13 April 1990, when the Soviet news agency TASS admitted Soviet guilt for the
Katyn massacre (doc. 117).

Document 53 (Cienciala 154-156) is Beria's order of March 22,
1940, to transfer 3000 prisoners from prisons in the Western
Ukraine to prisons in Central Ukraine. There is, of course, nothing
said about murdering them. Nor does it even say that the prisoners
are Poles. As we shall see, many of them were not.

Western Ukraine, part of Poland since 1921 when it was taken by
the Polish army from a weakened Soviet Russia, was reunited with
the Eastern Ukraine in October 1939. The population was made up
of Ukrainians, Poles, Jews, and a smattering of other nationalities,
with Poles being a minority.

Beria's order of March 22, 1940, unlike the "Beria Letter" (document 47), which is one of the forgeries in CP, is not concerned with
the nationalities of the prisoners at all. It does contain this interesting passage:

> 6) USSR Deputy People's Commissar of Internal Af-
> fairs, Divisional Commander Com. Chernyshov, shall
> within ten days' time remove from their NKVD places
> of imprisonment in the Ukrainian SSR **and send to
> USSR NKVD correctional labor camps 8,000 con-**

victed prisoners, including 3,000 from the Kiev, Kharkov, and Kherson prisons.

Jósef Kuligowski and Ludwik Małowiejski, Polish policemen who had been transferred out of Ostashkov POW camp to the NKVD in Kalinin, Russia, ended up in the Western Ukraine, where they were killed by the Germans and their Ukrainian Nationalist allies. They were probably in a correctional labor camp, along with other Polish POW, perhaps many of them, who are now fraudulently listed as "Katyn victims."

The "Beria Letter" in CP states:

> In the prisons of the western oblasts of Ukraine and Belorussia a total of 18,632 arrested people (including 10,685 Poles) are being held...

However, the "Shelepin Letter" of March 1959 – also one of the CP documents – gives a different the number of persons shot in western Ukraine and western Belorussia:

> On the basis of the decision by the special Troika of the NKVD USSR, a total of 21,857 persons were shot; of these ... 7,305 persons were shot in other camps and prisons of western Ukraine and western Belorussia. (Cienciala 332)

It is no wonder that 11,000 (or 10,685), the number of prisoners in W. Ukraine and W. Belorussia to be shot according to the "Beria Letter", and 7305, the number "shot" according to the "Shelepin Letter," are very different. All the evidence we have suggests that these two forgeries were done at very different times: the "Beria Letter" during the Gorbachev years, the "Shelepin Letter" during Khrushchev's time.

Cienciala states: "The lists of victims shot in Ukraine have been found." This is false. There is no indication in the book in question, Zuzanna Gajowniczek, ed., *Ukraiński Ślad Katynia*, that the prisoners on these lists were shot. These are simply lists of names, many of them recognizably Ukrainian.

The only thing that suggests any relation to what we know as "Katyn" is the fact that the NKVD list numbers are in the same sequence as the NKVD file numbers of the Polish POWs shipped out of Kozel'sk, Starobel'sk, and Ostashkov. But we know that the prisoners shipped to the Smolensk, Khar'kov, and Kalinin NKVD were not shot there, because many of the Starobel'sk and Ostashkov prisoners turned up dead at Katyn, and at least two Ostashkov POWs turned up dead in Volodymyr-Volyns'kiy.

The list numbers appear to be related to NKVD Convoy troops. Abarinov discovered that Convoy battalion No. 136 transported prisoners to Ukraine as well as to Smolensk. According to Abarinov:

> Изучая книгу приказов по 136-му батальону, я изумился числу конвоев, отправившихся в апреле-мае 1940 года по одному и тому же маршруту: Смоленск западные области Украины и Белоруссии.[1]

Translated:

> Studying the book of orders of the 136th battalion I was struck by the number of convoys that set out in April-May 1940 on one and the same route: Smolensk to and from Western Ukraine and Western Belorussia.

There are actually two editions of this "Ukrainian trail of Katyn." *Listy Katyńskiej Ciąg Dalszy* (Warsaw: Zeszyty Katyńskie, 1994), and the Gajowniczek book mentioned above, *Ukraiński Ślad Katynia* (Warsaw, 1995). The first gives the names of the prisoners in alphabetical order, citing the list number in each case as well. The second orders them according to the list number.

---

[1] Vladimir Abarinov. *Katynskii labirint.* Mosow: Novosti, 1991, p. 75.

The SBU List

We are fortunate to have yet one more list, albeit a partial one. This is an original archival list from a branch state archive of the Ukrainian SBU, the Security Service of Ukraine, the equivalent of the Russian FSB. It contains a little more than 900 names. But it gives much more detail than the two published lists above. Sergei Romanov, who discovered this list, has helpfully scanned it and made it available online for downloading.[2]

We can learn a lot about the nature of this "Ukrainian list" by comparing Romanov's archival SBU list with the two published lists we have. The SBU list has page numbers in the upper right-hand corner. We will refer here to these numbers for reference. For the Ukrainian list we will use Gajowniczek, ed., *Ukraiński Ślad Katynia*, abbreviated US, and *Listy Katyńskiej Ciąg Dalszy*, abbreviated LK.

Romanov notes that 4 of the 6 men mentioned as Trotskyists on SBU 17-18 "are on the Ukrainian list." In reality 5 are on the Ukrainian list: Stefan Bojko (#243, LK 8, US 174); Michal Jacuszko (#3453, LK 34, US 171); Wlodzimierz Kuliniak (# 1593, LK 50 US 173); Iwan Jurkiw (#3378, LK 37 US 171). Iwan Kozar' is also on the list (#1459, LK 46 US 114).

Five of these six men are listed as "Ukrainian." All are identified as, and were no doubt arrested as, "active members of a Trotskyist organization in the Dorogobych raion."

So the so-called "Ukrainian list" contains names of persons who were not even Poles. There is also no evidence that they were shot. Only investigations and interrogations about their Trotskyist activities are mentioned.

Clearly, none of these men had anything to do with Katyn. This invalidates the whole idea of a "Ukrainian list." But we would never

---

[2] At http://katynfiles.com/content/gdasbu-1.html

know this from the entries in LK and US. We know it only because Romanov found this later archival documentation.

In LK the published "Ukrainian list" is subtitled:

LISTA OBYWATELI POLSKICH ZAMORDOWANYCH NA UKRAINIE NA PODSTAWIE DECYZJI BIURA POLI-TYCZNEGO WKP (b) I NACZELNYCH WŁADZ PAŃ-STWOWYCH ZSRR Z 5 MARCA 1940 ROKU.

Translated:

List of Polish citizens murdered in Ukraine on the basis of the decision of the Politburo of the AUCP(b)[3] and the government of the USSR of 5 March 1940.

This subtitle is yet another lie. There is no evidence that these men were killed. The Polish editors chose this name so that it would appear to confirm the "official" version.

The archival document (p. 18) states that on May 5 and 7, 1940, the six accused Trotskyists were transferred from the Ukrainian NKVD to the NKVD of the USSR. Thereafter, whatever happened to them happened outside the Ukraine.

Page 78 of the archival list concerns Vladimir Filaretovich Perventsev who, along with his case file, was transferred to the NKVD of the USSR – again, outside the Ukraine. He is in LK 72, US 203. He is described on the archival list, p. 197, #233, as a "leader of Russian nationalists." A two-part article online about Russian émigrés in Poland identifies Perventsev as a regional leader of an anti-Soviet Russian organization.[4]

---

[3] All-Union Commuist Party (bolshevik), the formal name of the Bolshevik party from December 1925 until October 1952.

[4] Sergiy Tkachov, "Rossiiskaia emigratsiia v mezhvoennom Pol'she." (The Russian emigration in Interwar Poland), at http://www.mochola.org/russiaabroad/tkachref1.htm and following. Perventsev is mentioned at

Romanov says that Perventsev was "shot as a Polish citizen." This is a lie. There is no evidence that he was shot, or of what became of him. Whatever happened to him most likely happened because he had been a leading organizer of an anti-Soviet group of Russian émigrés, not "as a Polish citizen."

Page 100 of the archival document identifies two persons who were not shot: Boleslav Vladimirovich Turovskii and Vladimir Iosifovich Goninchak. Turowski, Uk. List #2989 (LK 100 US 16) was not shot. A note on LK 100 states that Turowski was sentenced on March 8, 1941, to 5 years in a corrective labor camp and later released "for permanent residence."

Goninchak is, more accurately, Haninczak. He is also on the "Katyn" Starobel'sk list published by Tucholski: (p. 929 #929 [sic] and p. 415 col. 2):

929: ГАНИНЧАК Владимир Юзефович

Haninczak Włodzimierz
Prezes lub wiceprezes Sądu Okręgowego we Lwowie
(President or Vice-President of the District Court in
Lwów.).

This entry from Tucholski is reproduced on page 159 of the "Khar'kov Cemetery Book," *Księga Cmentarna Charków* (Warsaw, 2003).

Włodzimierz HANINCZAK s. Jósefa, ur. 1883. Preyes lub wicepreyes Sądu Okręgowego we Lwowie, bdd.

L.S. 929, J. Tucholski, Mord w Katyniu.

---

http://www.mochola.org/russiaabroad/tkachref4.htm and
http://www.mochola.org/russiaabroad/tkachref5.htm

So, according to the "official" version Haninczak was murdered at Khar'kov and buried at Piatykhatky. The Polish Wikipedia article on him also claims that he was killed "in the Spring of 1940" (https://pl.wikipedia.org/wiki/Włodzimierz_Haninczak) This is another example of how dishonest the whole "official" version of Katyn is.

There is no evidence that Haninczak was executed at all! Quite the contrary: page 100 of the archival document states that there was an investigative file on Haninczak dated February 24, 1941, which has been destroyed. This suggests that Haninczak was still alive as of about that date. We know that Turowski, who is discussed on the same page, was not shot at all.

Moreover, there is no evidence that *any* of the persons on this list were executed! This is simply "assumed" by defenders of the "official" version.

Persons on the Archival List Arrested Long After the "Beria Letter"

At least 9 prisoners on this archival list, and on the "Ukrainian list," were arrested in late 1940 or in 1941. They are:

*Uk. list #285 (LK 285 US 14) – Filimon BOJAR, this list p. 171 #312. Arrested October 20 1940 as a "Polish spy"

* Uk. list #286 (LK 9 US 31) – Wawrzyniec Brażuk, this list p. 202 #286 [sic]. Arrested December 21 1940 as a "former officer of the White Army."

* Uk. list #3089 (LK 12 US 50) – Wiktor CHAJES, this list p. 203 #295 – arrested November 15 1940 as a member of an organization of "Zionists" (quotation marks in original).

* Uk. List #2329 (LK 74 US 191) – Edward Podgórski, this list p. 205 #6. Arrested October 10 1940 as a (civilian) Polish policeman.

* Uk. list #3292 (LK 96 US 16) – Karol Szynkowski, this list p. 206 #12. Arrested December 3 1940 as a former White émigré.

* Uk. List #2441 (LK 78 US 198) – Stanislaw Ratajczak, this list p. 223 #149. Arrested September 18 1940 as a (civilian) Polish policeman.

* Uk. List #2502 (LK 78 US 52) – Kazimierz Rodziewicz, this list p. 232 #224. Arrested September 26 1940 as "an agent of the Polish police."

* Uk. List #930 (LK 18 US 187) – Josef Dołbniak, this list p. 144 #37. Arrested April 21 1941 as a Polish policeman.

* Uk. List missing (not in LK or US) – Mechislav Kulianda, this list p. 236 #258, Arrested November 30 1940 as a "large-scale merchant and member of the "OZN" party

All the men listed above were arrested much later than March 5, 1940. One, Josef Dołbniak, was not even arrested until April 1941. Obviously none of them could have had nothing to do with any decision taken on March 5 1940 even if the "Beria letter" were genuine.

In addition, one prisoner, arrested in 1939, was charged with a criminal offense (Uk. list #3418; LK 38 US 197) – Bolesław Janicki, this list p. 207 #19. Arrested on October 7 1939 "as a participant in a counterrevolutionary Polish organization, a police agent, who committed a murder [of someone] for revolutionary activity, transferred to the NKVD of the USSR on May 28, 1940."

US does not mention the reason for Janicki's arrest. It just states that he was "a gymnasium teacher in Tarnopol'" (Ukraine). This appears to be a cover-up – an attempt to make an accused murderer look like an innocent victim.

List Numbers

Bolesław Janicki is #46 in on list 64/1 (US 197). He was arrested on October 7, 1939. Stanislaw Ratajczak is #60 on the same list,

64/1. He was arrested on September 26, 1940, almost a year after Janicki.

Since these numbers are those of the NKVD convoys – the defenders of the "official" version say they are, and it is logical to assume this – that means that *all 100* of the men on this list were alive as of late September – early October 1940. (US 143-148)

Edward Podgórski is #98 on list 66/2. He was arrested on October 10, 1940. Josef Dołbniak is #20 in list 66/2. He was arrested on April 21 1941, more than six months later than Podgórski. They were both in the same convoy, therefore, and this convoy did not depart until May 1941 or later. That also means that *everyone on the list – 100 men –* was alive as of May, 1941. (US 186-191)

The same conclusion must be drawn for everyone whose name is on a list with one of the men above who was arrested long after March 1940. What's more, there is no evidence that any of these men were executed at any time.

Naturally, these lists of names could not have had any relation to the "Beria Letter," which complains about anti-Soviet sentiments among prisoners as of early March 1940. We know from other evidence that the "Beria Letter" is a fake.

Other Matters of Interest:

* Uk. List #29 (LK 2 US 44) – Edmund Ambicki, this list p. 202 #284. Arrested as a German spy. This detail is not mentioned in LK or US.

* Uk. List #1016 (LK 36 US 26) – Władisław Jędrzejewski – this list p. 202 #287. Arrested in Lvov as "leader of a fascist military plot." US says "organizer of the civic guard in Lwów in September 1939."

The Polish Wikipedia page on him —
http://pl.wikipedia.org/wiki/Władysław_Jędrzejewski_(generał)
— claims he either died in Prison in Lwów in March 1940 or was shot in 1939. This is simply a lie. The Poles have no information

about any of this. It is part of the fictional "official" version of Katyn.

* Uk. List #2184 (LK 71 US 135) – Abrasim Pawełka – this list p. 208 #28 – Uk. Ślad p. 135 #3 - "former OUN organizer, took part in Jewish pogroms" Neither LK nor US say anything about him.

Not only viciously anti-Semitic, the OUN was murderously anti-Polish. In 1943 OUN forces murdered about 100,000 Polish civilians in Western Ukraine in order to "ethnically cleanse" it of non-Ukrainians.

This little-known mass murder – an instance of true genocide, as it was an attempt to wipe out the Polish population – is called the "Volhynia Massacre" (Polish: *rzeź wołyńska*). To this day the Ukrainian nationalists prefer to call this the "Volhynian Tragedy" (*Волинська трагедія*), as though it were some unfortunate event other than Ukrainian nationalist mass murder. The forces that committed this genocide are officially declared "heroes" of the Ukrainian nation today.

* Uk. List p. 73 #2311 (LK 73 US 193) – Stefan Piśmienny – this list p. 234 #249. Arrested as "chief of the military chancellery of the Petliura government, chief of a Polish counter-revolutionary organization." («начальника военной канцелярии правительства Петлюры, начальник польской к-р организации».) US identifies him as "zam. wieś Żarzyna pow. Równe" – a resident of the village of Żarzyn in the county (powiat) of Równe. That is, just an ordinary citizen.

This appears to be another cover-up. Simon Petliura was leader of an anti-Bolshevik nationalist army during the Civil War. His forces organized a number of pogroms against Jews. He was assassinated by a Jewish man whose family had been killed in anti-Jewish pogroms and who considered Petliura responsible. Ukrainian nationalists consider him a hero. The Bolsheviks considered him a criminal. They would naturally have considered Piśmienny a criminal too.

Who Are the People On This List?

My study of the 900 or so entries on the archival list published online by Romanov shows that the following are the most common identifications of the persons arrested:

> Policemen; Polish army officers or former army officers; members of Polish nationalist groups (OZON, Związek Strzelecki, Związek Walki Zbrojnei, ZWZ)[5]; members of Ukrainian nationalist groups (OUN, Petliurists); Polish General Staff; employees of the Polish judicial system (e.g. judges); jailers; border crossers; members of other "c-r [counterrevolutionary] groups"; business and factory owners; landowners; merchants; Polish intelligence; Polish government employees; former White officers; Zionists; people who were actively anti-Soviet; *osadniki*; Polish politicians.

> Plus: one Russian nationalist; one German spy (Ambicki, above)

The *osadniki*, or "settlers," were persons, often military men, sent to "settle" Western Belorussia and Western Ukraine after they had been taken from Soviet Russia in the Polish-Soviet war of 1918-1921. These areas had a minority Polish population. These "settlers" constituted the imperialist infrastructure sent to "polonize" – "make more Polish" – these areas. They were in charge of the intense cultural and political oppression conducted by the prewar Polish government against the native Belorussian, Ukrainian, and

---

[5] OZON -- Obóz Zjednczenia Narodowego (English: Camp of National Unity) – was a fascist, militarist, anti-Semitic organization. (See
https://pl.wikipedia.org/wiki/Obóz_Zjednoczenia_Narodowego ;
https://en.wikipedia.org/wiki/Camp_of_National_Unity) For "Związek Strzelecki" see
https://pl.wikipedia.org/wiki/Związek_Strzelecki ;
https://en.wikipedia.org/wiki/Riflemen's_Association For Związek Walki Zbrojnei see
https://pl.wikipedia.org/wiki/ Związek_Walki_Zbrojnej;
https://en.wikipedia.org/wiki/Union_of_Armed_Struggle

Jewish populations. After the Soviets retook these areas in September 1939 and reunited Belorussia and Ukraine they deported the "settlers" and their families.

Conclusion

This so-called "Ukrainian List of Katyn" list is a fraud. It has nothing to do with Katyn. It is not a list of persons executed or to be executed. It is just a list of persons who were convoyed from one place to another. It is not comprised only of Poles. There are many non-Poles – Ukrainians and Jews – on it, including anti-Polish persons (OUN members) and anti-Semites.

The occupations given on this list suggest that this is largely a partial list of the many Poles residents who were considered to be part of the Polish imperialist infrastructure within Western Ukraine. This is the kind of people the Soviets arrested and deported after they retook possession of the Western Ukraine in September 1939.

Forged "Ukrainian Documents of Katyn"

In the summer of 2009 on the official internet site of the Ukrainian State Security (SBU) there appeared three documents that purport to be letters of high officials of the 1960s Ukrainian KGB. These were published by the "Memorial Society," a ferociously anticommunist organization whose officials have been involved in a number of falsifications.

> http://memorial.kiev.ua/images/stories/2009/06/05
> _001_arhivna_sprava.pdf

> http://memorial.kiev.ua/images/stories/2009/06/05
> _002_harkiv_shelestu_1969.pdf

> http://memorial.kiev.ua/images/stories/2009/06/05
> _005_andropov_harkiv.pdf

> http://memorial.kiev.ua/images/stories/2009/06/05
> _008_andropov_znyschennia_slidiv.pdf

In two of the letters, under the stamp "Top Secret, Eyes Only" (*sovershenno sekretno, tol'ko lichno*) the Chairman of the KGB of the Ukrainian SSR V. Nikitchenko informs Petro Shelest, first secretary of the Central Committee of the Communist Party of the Ukraine and the Chairman of the KGB of the USSR Iurii Andropov that in the woods near the village of Piatykhatky children had accidently discovered "a mass grave." Nikitchenko also states that it had been "determined that in this place in 1940 the UNKVD of Khar'kov oblast' had buried a considerable number / several thousand / officers and generals of bourgeois Poland who had been shot..."

In the third letter, also marked "Top Secret" (*sov. sekretno*), dated June 1959, general-major P. Feshchenko, chief of the Directorate of State Security of Khar'kov oblast', informs Nikitchenko about the destruction of the graves at Piatykhatky by means of caustic soda (sodium hydroxide), capable of completely dissolving human remains, clothing, and documents. However, during exhumations in the 1990s at the special cemetery of the UNKVD at Piatykhatky Polish archeologists did not find any traces of caustic soda. Moreover, they remarked on the "amazingly good" preservation of the remains of uniforms and of paper documents found in the graves.

Nevertheless, supporters of the "official" version judged these letters to be evidence of traces of the Katyn killings in Ukraine. Evidently none of them noticed that in the left corner of Feshchenko's letter there is the following handwritten resolution of Nikitchenko's: "reported to Comrade Shelest P.E." and dated, in the same handwriting, 2008!

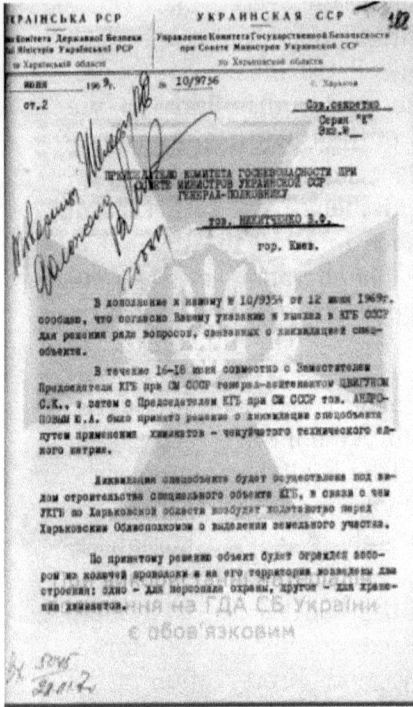

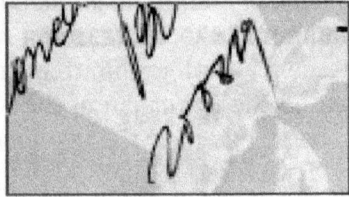

Images 13.1 and 13.2 "Ukrainian Documents of Katyn"

The date (enlargement, at right) reads "2008 gd" – "the year 2008." These documents are definitely a fraud. Perhaps one of the forgers had a guilty conscience over this fabrication and deliberately made an error to embarrass the falsifiers?

These letters are a good example of how easily a modern state, with all its resources, can falsify official documents. If it were not for this obviously bogus date these documents would still be cited by supporters of the "official" version as evidence of "the Ukrainian trace of Katyn."

Chapter 14. Conclusion - The Katyn Forest Mystery Solved

The primary source evidence is unambiguous. The Germans, not the Soviets, shot the Polish POWs in the various mass murders known to history as "Katyn."

The reader who knows little about Katyn may suspect that I have biased this study "by omission." Bias by omission involves leaving out, remaining silent about, ignoring, not informing the reader of, evidence that does not support the writer's preconceived conclusion. That reader may suspect that I have simply omitted the evidence that the Soviets were guilty, or that the Germans were innocent.

To such a reader I say: Inform yourself! Start with the Wikipedia page on Katyn: Read the "mainstream" books on Katyn. Read Cienciala and Sanford! If you can find better, more complete, more recent studies that assert the "official" version – I don't know of any – read them. Only then you will be an informed reader. And only then will you know that I have not omitted any evidence that supports the "official" Soviets-did-it version.

Readers who come to this book with some knowledge of Katyn but yet – and this is essential – are able to question what they have heard and to be objective, what is often called "open-minded" – will see that I have discussed the evidence they have heard about, and a lot of material that they probably did not know existed.

But they will still wonder: How is it possible that so many people could have been so mistaken for so long?

Everybody knows that a murder mystery requires a careful, objective investigation during which the investigator gathers all the facts, identifies and collects all the evidence, studies it in a scientific manner, and draws conclusions based on the evidence. The "Katyn Forest Murder Mystery" is no different.

The first prerequisite for any investigator of this or any other mystery is *objectivity*. It is inevitable that anyone who seriously approaches the Katyn mystery will not only have heard about it but will also have formed some idea about it. Almost inevitably, that idea will be that the Soviets are guilty, because that is the version of Katyn that has dominated scholarly, political, and public discourse about it since at least 1992.

Since there is no way to "erase" one's preconceived biases and ideas from one's brain, a serious investigator has to consciously adopt an attitude of objectivity. She must recognize that she inevitably has a bias. This can only be done by clearly articulating – stating – that bias, first of all, to herself.

Then she has to adopt an attitude of constant mindfulness. She has to employ a strategy of compensating for her bias by *giving an especially generous reading* to any evidence that seems to go counter to what she already believes about the case – for she does already believe something. Likewise, she must develop a strategy of *giving an especially skeptical reading* to evidence that tends to support her bias or preconceived idea.

Historian Michael Schudson has said: "Objectivity is an ideology of the distrust of the self." (Schudson 71) This is vital. It is no use to claim to be objective without operationalizing that determination to be objective in the way one identifies, gathers, studies, and draws logical conclusions from, the evidence.

If one is not determined to do everything in one's power to be objective, then one will not be objective. And then what you discover will not be the truth. The history of the "official" version of Katyn illustrates this clearly. Both the Germans and the Polish Government-In-Exile were interested only in a conclusion that indicted the Soviets. Neither made any effort to be objective, and neither was. The Nuremburg Trial produced some testimony that contradicted the German AM but little else. The Madden Committee hearings were never a serious attempt to be objective.

The Gorbachev regime believed that blaming the Stalin-era USSR would help to improve relations with a still-friendly Poland. Today's anticommunists embrace the notion of Soviet guilt at Katyn as good propaganda for their cause. For Polish nationalists, Katyn is one of the foundation stones for their reconstruction of a right-wing version of nationalism and a cover-up for atrocious actions of the prewar Polish regimes, the wartime Home Army, and the postwar underground anticommunist terrorists.

Why the "Official" Version of Katyn Is Wrong

Some readers will wonder how it can be that the "official" Soviets-did-it version is false. The scholarly world and the governments of all the countries involved assert just the opposite: that the Soviets, not the Germans, are the guilty party. In the spheres of scholarly, political, and public discourse, the "official" version of Katyn is a "closed case." Soviet guilt – "Stalin's" guilt – is accepted so universally that it is almost never questioned.

Our analysis of the definitive accounts of the "official" version, Cienciala/Materski and Sanford, reveals that they never attempted to "solve the mystery" – to determine just who it was who murdered the Polish prisoners. Instead, they committed the logical fallacy of *petitio principii* or "begging the question:" *they assumed that which they should have been attempting to prove.* In effect, they assumed that someone else had already done the job of examining all the evidence and, on that basis, proved Soviet guilt.

Having assumed – rather than demonstrated – that the German Report was truthful and that the Burdenko Commission report had been refuted, they and all other accounts that support the "official" version have simply *declared* the Soviet case to be false and the evidence supporting it to be fraudulent.

* They ignored the contradictions in the German Report. Likewise they ignored or slandered, but never analyzed, all the evidence not contained in the German Report that proves how invalid it is.

* They assumed that the Soviet citizens who testified for the Germans told the truth while those who testified for the Soviets had been forced to lie.

* They dismissed or ignored altogether the testimony of Drs. Markov and Hájek, both of whom denounced the German Report after the war.

* They ignored or distorted the testimony given at Nuremberg and at the Madden Committee that undermined the case for Soviet guilt.

* They declared that the critiques of BU by defenders of the "official" version are "devastating." In reality these critiques are not only invalid but dishonest. There is still no evidence that BU investigation is faulty, let alone fraudulent in any way.

* They ignored the fact that a number of Ostashkov and Starobel'sk POWs were killed at Katyn, including a number of those named in the German Report itself. They had all the evidence necessary to uncover this fact – all the evidence we have today. But they either never investigated this question at all, or they hushed it up.

* They knew about the suspicious origins of "Closed Packet No. 1" and about the arguments of some researchers that these documents are forgeries. But they never seriously investigated the possibility of forgery. They failed to acknowledge the obvious fact that that *although the documents cannot be proven false by analysis of the documents alone, neither can they be proven genuine.* Much less ought they be *assumed* to be genuine.

Cienciala and Sanford committed these offenses against responsible scholarly practice because they did not set out to discover who had murdered the Poles in the first place. They never made any attempt to be objective. From the outset they chose to "believe" the Polish anticommunist version—which means they believed the German Nazi version. Then they set out to collect all the arguments they could to support this preconceived idea and to ignore any and all evidence inconsistent with it. This is called "cherry-picking" or the fallacy of incomplete evidence, similar to confirmation bias[1] – and they did it with a vengeance.

After that it was all downhill. They continued to look with special favor upon everything that seemed to be evidence supporting Soviet guilt. They distorted, belittled, dismissed, or ignored anything that appeared to be evidence pointing away from Soviet guilt.

Given their determination to abandon objectivity and their strong anti-Soviet and anticommunist bias it was impossible for Cienciala and Sanford to arrive at the truth in this mystery. They refused to understand that it *is* a mystery in the first place. Once a researcher commits the cardinal error of deciding the result of the investigation in advance, she is trapped.

* * *

All recent books on Katyn, including all of those mentioned in this book, contain a great deal more information than is in the present book. In particular, the works by Shved, Prudenikova and Chigirin, and Mukhin, and the excellent website formerly maintained by the late Sergei Strygin, http://www.katyn.ru/ , have detailed comparisons and criticisms of the documents in "Closed Packet No. 1".

I have argued that it is not possible through internal analysis alone to tell whether these documents are forgeries or are genuine. However, now that we know that the version of Katyn reflected in them is a false one, the contradictions in them that careful internal examination reveals confirm that which, without that external evidence, we could only suspect – that these documents are fabrications. This analysis is interesting, and some of it is brilliant.

For the person unable to read the Russian works I have cited in Chapter One my own page "The Katyn Forest Whodunnit." In that chapter I also cite the "Katynmassakern" and "Mythcracker" websites. I do not agree with all of the points made there. But it gives

---

[1] See the Wikipedia article at https://en.wikipedia.org/wiki/Cherry_picking

an idea of the kind of analysis that has been carried out. I have omitted this kind of analysis here because it is not essential to identifying the guilty party. This book is a "Whodunnit." The mystery had to be solved and the guilty party identified through the collection and study of other evidence.

This book does not offer a point-by-point examination and critique of every false assertion in Cienciala/Materski's and Sanford's books. I have included only the amount of criticism of these works that I think is necessary for the purpose of solving the mystery of Katyn. Both of these books contain a great many more false statements, lies, and fallacious conclusions than can be examined here. A detailed critique of either of these works would be of some interest in itself since they enjoy a high reputation that is utterly undeserved. But such a detailed critique is beyond the limits of this book.

* * *

I look forward to reading the reactions, positive and critical, from scholars who, like myself, have been fascinated by what I have irreverently called the "Katyn Forest Whodunnit." In future editions of this book I will include corrections, with my thanks to the readers who have pointed them out.

By the same token those who are interested not in the truth (though they will never admit it) but in arraigning Stalin and the Soviets will condemn and attack me. This is called "shooting the messenger," an all-too-common fallacy among those who do not wish their illusions shattered.

But shattering our illusions is what honest research is all about. For this reason I anticipate such attacks as indirect recognition of the research I have done and welcome criticism from all readers.

Appendix 1. Testimony of Soprunenko, Syromiatnikov, Tokarev

During 1990 – 1992 the Soviet prosecutors' office located three aged and long-retired NKVD men who were involved in some way with the Polish POWs. They were:

> * Petr Karpovich Soprunenko, in 1940 Chief of Office for Prisoners of War and Internees;

> * Mitrofan Vasil'evich Syromiatnikov, in 1940 senior supervisor in the block of the inner prison of the Directorate of the NKVD of Khar'kov district with the rank of lieutenant;

> * Dmitrii Stepanovich Tokarev, in 1940 Acting Chief of the Directorate of the NKVD of Kalinin region.

Before the publication of Closed Packet No. 1 these confessions were the only evidence that the Soviets had shot the Polish POWs, aside from the German Report (AM).

In 1990-1992 each of these men were questioned by representatives of the Soviet, and then of the Ukrainian, investigative services. In addition Syromiatnikov was interviewed by Polish writer Jerzy Morawski.

We do not have the former NKVD men's exact words. Although the interrogations were all conducted in Russian they are available only in Polish translation. The Russian originals have never been made public.[1] In addition, the Polish transcript was made from

---

[1] Except for the excerpts in Russian published by S.M. Zavorotnov in his book *Khar'kovskaia Katyn'* ("The Khar'kov Katyn") of the interrogations of Syromiatnikov of June 20, 1990, and March 6, 1992. However, there is no indication of the provenance of these excerpts in Russian. It is possible that they are simply partial retranslations into Russian of the Polish texts.

sound recordings. In the Polish text there are several lacunae where the sound recording was indecipherable to the persons who transcribed the interrogations.

In Tokarev's case there was at least one interrogation that took place before the one we have. No transcript or any information about that interrogation has been published. We do not know whether there are, or were, unpublished interrogations of Soprunenko and Syromiatnikov. However, the sole interrogation we have of Soprunenko bears the subtitle "Pierwsze przesłuchanie" – "first interrogation." This suggests that other interrogations of Soprunenko did take place. But we do not have them.

These confessions are very contradictory in ways that often do not reinforce the "official" version. None of these men was at Katyn where the 4000+ bodies of Polish POWs were unearthed by the Germans in 1943, and none of them has anything to say about this, the most famous of the execution/burial sites subsumed under the rubric "the Katyn massacre."

All three men were threatened repeatedly with criminal prosecution if they failed to "tell the truth." In addition, they were told that Soviet guilt had already been established. In reality, this was a lie. In 1990 – 1991 there was no evidence other than the German AM Report alleging Soviet guilt. The documents from "Closed Packet No. 1" had not yet been published.[2]

It is therefore possible that out of fear of prosecution the former NKVD men gave answers they believed their interrogators wanted. So it does appear that the confessions of these three old men were not entirely voluntary. Many of the interrogators' questions were "leading" questions. Of course this is common in criminal investigations. But it would have been obvious what answers the investi-

---

[2] There is at least one account by an alleged actual witness – that of Petr F. Klimov. It was published in the November 16, 1990 issue of the newspaper *Moskovskie Novosti*. Cienciala calls it an "alleged" account and Polish sources do not use it.

gators wanted to hear. That kind of atmosphere is fatal to obtaining trustworthy testimony.

The Polish translations of the interrogations of Soprunenko, Syromiatnikov, and Tokarev were published in Polish journals and then republished in the official Polish government collections *Zeszyty Katyńskie* and *Katyń. Dokumenty Zbrodni* (KDZ) volume 2. One additional interrogation of Syromiatnikov was published by Jerzy Morawski, a director of documentary films, in one of his books. These interrogations are seldom referred to any longer. Perhaps this is due to the problems that we identify in this chapter.

Soprunenko October 25, 1990

Soprunenko, who was in overall charge of the Office of POWs and Internees, should certainly have been one of those who knew about the executions, if they had taken place. Many documents signed by him relating to the Polish POWs survive. They are reprinted in the Polish-language KDZ series and in a similar Russian-language collection. None of these documents mention anything about Poles being executed.

Soprunenko's testimony is very contradictory. On the one hand he claimed that he knew nothing about any NKVD orders to shoot the Poles (428) and knew nothing about any shootings. (430) In fact he claimed that he only heard about the Katyn shootings in April 1990, when Polish President General Jaruzelski visited Moscow. (429) On the other hand Soprunenko also said that in 1940 he had heard "rumors" (*słuchy* and *pogłoski*) about a Central Committee decision signed by Stalin that had been the basis for shooting the Poles.

The sole interrogation that we have of Soprunenko is titled „Pierwsze przesłuchanie", "first interrogation." This suggests that there were more of them. But only this one, dated October 25, 1990, has been published.

Syromiatnikov

There are six interrogations of Syromiatnikov. We use the five from KDZ volume 2, and the sixth from Jerzy Morawski's book *Ślad Kuli* (Warsaw and London, 1992). In the following, page numbers preceded by the letter M denote pages in Morawski's book; numbers alone denote pages in KDZ volume 2.

Syromiatnikov testified that he had just heard about the Katyn massacres from the mass media. (475, 476) He said that, when the Poles were brought down to the cellar of the NKVD building, there was always a prokuror (prosecutor) present. (477; 484; M 113, 124) Syromiatnikov also said that the Polish prisoners whom he accompanied were interrogated. (M 124)

The prokuror and interrogations imply the charge of a criminal offense, an investigation, and an attempt to make sure that the individual being executed was the person against whom a sentence had been passed. It does not fit the notion of a mass killing of all POWs. Syromiatnikov stated several times that he was told that the Polish prisoners had been involved in a rebellion in a Soviet camp. (478; M 110, 120)

Syromiatnikov stated repeatedly that only about 200 (385) or 300 (487) prisoners were shot while he was working at the prison. Thereafter he fell sick and when he returned the Poles were no longer there. (M 117-9) When two of the Russian interrogators, Snezhko and Tretetskii, insisted that 4000 Poles were killed at Khar'kov Syromiatnikov said that he did not know how many Poles were involved in all but thought that neither the Khar'kov NKVD prison nor, more to the point, the burial site at Piatykhatky could hold 4000. (M 121-2)

In an interesting contradiction Syromiatnikov first testified that one woman was among the Polish prisoners and that she was certainly shot (480; 489) But in the later interview with Morawski Syromiatnikov retracted this statement and claimed that he did not know whether the woman was a Pole or a Russian (M 114)

Syromiatnikov's testimony is consistent with the idea that some Poles were tried and executed for some anti-Soviet crimes or other. He claimed to know about executions of only 200-300 Poles. In short, Syromiatnikov's testimony does not confirm the "official" version of the Katyn massacre.

Tokarev October 25, 1990

Dmitriy S. Tokarev was Acting Chief of the Directorate of the NKVD of Kalinin region and directly in charge of the prison in Kalinin to which Polish POWs from Ostashkov camp were sent. Tokarev's interrogation is the longest and most interesting since Tokarev claims that he knew that the Soviets had shot the Polish prisoners. We'll briefly review what he says.

Problematic aspects and contradictions in his account include the following issues:

> * Tokarev clearly refers to a previous interrogation (433, 446) that we do not have. Why don't we?

> * In this previous interrogation Tokarev repeatedly says he was told about a Politburo decree, "postanovlenie Politbiuro." (433, 435, 447; 468) His Soviet interrogators agree with him.

This would appear to be impossible. The "Politburo decree" is in "Closed Packet No. 1" which was not even discovered until late in 1991 (according to Gorbachev). Yet here is Tokarev stating, and the Soviet interrogators agreeing, that he was told about it in a previous interrogation, i.e. previous to October 25, 1990, when the present interrogation took place.

There's no reason to believe that Tokarev is lying here, especially since the Russian interrogators agree with him. This means that somebody knew about the Politburo decree long before Gorbachev or his right-hand man Iakovlev supposedly knew about it. It appears that someone knew that the Politburo decree would be forthcoming.

How can this be? Unless the forgery was in the process of preparation and would be produced at some point, and that the Soviet investigators knew this. This is further evidence suggesting that "Closed Packet No. 1" is a forgery.

> * Tokarev claimed that he did know that 14,000 Polish POWs were to be shot. First he said that Bogdan Kobulov told him this (435) A few pages later he claimed that Soprunenko told him (447) But Soprunenko claimed that he did not know anything about any shootings.

> * Tokarev stated twice that he knew that 6000 Polish policemen were shot at Kalinin. (462, 471) He even argues with Iablokov, one of the Soviet interrogators. Iablokov claimed that 6287 Poles were shot at Kalinin but Tokarev said that he remembered the number 6295.

We know that many Ostashkov POWs who were shipped to the NKVD in Kalinin – that is, to Tokarev – were not shot there because their bodies turned up in the German and Soviet exhumations at Katyn and at Volodymyr-Volyns'kiy, Ukraine. Therefore Tokarev must have been lying to please his Soviet interrogators who insist that all the Ostashkov POWs were shot at Kalinin and are buried at Mednoe.

Why would Tokarev lie? Probably because he was warned of serious consequences – criminal prosecution – if he did not tell the truth, and because he had been informed that the Soviets were guilty. As we have seen, he was also told that a Politburo decree had ordered that the Poles be shot, even though no such decree was known when Tokarev was interrogated.

Therefore something else must have taken place before this interrogation as a result of which Tokarev had decided to say what his interrogators wanted him to say. We should recall that prior interrogation to which Tokarev refers but which has never been made public.

> * Tokarev testified (441-442) that NKVD executioner
> Blokhin arrived at Kalinin with a "suitcase full of Wal-
> thers [German automatic pistols]."

It is sometimes stated in books about Katyn that this meant
Blokhin did not have confidence in the Soviet pistols, the Tokarev
"TT" and Nagan (the latter is a revolver). In fact it means the opposite. A single pistol of average quality should be capable of shooting 6000 shots. The Tokarev automatic was famous for being very
rugged.

In short, there was no reason for an NKVD man to use Walthers at
all, much less many of them. However, only German ammunition
was found in the mass graves at Katyn. Presumably it was useful to
enhance the credibility of the "official" version that there be at
least one more instance of the Soviet NKVD using German weapons. We already know that Tokarev lied about the number of
Polish POWs shot at Kalinin. Evidently he lied about the "Walthers" as well.

> * Interrogator Iablokov did not seem to know that in 1940
> the "Osoboe Soveshchanie" ("Special Commission") of the
> NKVD did not have the authority to sentence anyone to exe-
> cution.

> > Jabłokow: Dmitriju Stiepanowiczu, wyjaśnijcie, kto
> > kierował sprawy śledcze przeciwko polskim jeńcom
> > wojennym, głównie rozpatrywał sprawy śledcze do
> > decyzji Kolegium Specjalnego? Kto mógł to kierować?
> > (445)

> > Jabłokow: Dmitriju Stiepanowiczu, znacie taki tryb
> > wykonania wyroków, Še zwykle odczytywana jest de-
> > cyzja. Wówczas była decyzja uchwały Kolegium Spe-
> > cjalnego. Czy im odczytywano uchwałę Kolegium Spe-
> > cjalnego? (446)

> > Yablokov: Dmitriy Stepanovich, please explain who
> > led the investigation of the case against the Polish
> > prisoners of war, who chiefly dealt with the matter of

> investigation before the decision of the Special Com-
> mission? Who could it have been?
>
> Yablokov: Dmitriy Stepanovich, you know the mode of
> execution of the judgments that usually is read the de-
> cision. Then there was a decision of a resolution of the
> Special Commission. Did they read the resolution of
> the Special Commission?

Is it possible that Iablokov, a military procurator and lieutenant colonel of Justice, did not know that in 1940 the "Osoboe Sovesh-chanie" could not sentence defendants to more than eight years of confinement?

> * Tokarev said that he saw no bodies of anyone who was
> shot. (458) This would be hard to believe if 6300 men had in
> fact been shot at his facility. He said that no officers were
> shot (448) *and that hardly any of the Poles were in uniform.*
> (451) By "officers" he *may* mean *military* officers, and this
> was true – the prisoners at Ostashkov were policemen, not
> military. However, Polish policemen wore uniforms too. All
> but a few bodies disinterred by the Germans at Katyn were in
> uniform, while shreds of Polish uniform were found in the
> mass graves at Volodymyr-Volyns'kiy.
>
> * Tokarev was asked whether treelings were planted over the
> mass graves at Mednoe. (461) Iablokov asked him, presuma-
> bly because, according to the Germans, treelings were plant-
> ed over the mass graves at Katyn. Iablokov probably did not
> know that Burdenko wrote that the planting of treelings over
> the mass graves of their victims was a feature of the German
> mass murders he had investigated (see chapter 9)
>
> * During the interrogation of Tokarev Col. Iablokov quoted
> from a number of case files of Polish POWs who were, ac-
> cording to Iablokov's remarks, charged with criminal offens-
> es. These case files might be important, since they indicate an
> individualized approach to the Polish POWs that contradicts
> the notion that all of them were sentences to death with ei-

ther minimal or no investigation at all. But none of these criminal case files have been published.

Conclusion

None of these interrogation-confessions can withstand careful scrutiny. The witnesses had been threatened, and either claimed to remember too much (Tokarev) or hardly anything (Soprunenko, Syromiatnikov) There are many unanswered questions about them: previous interrogations that are not published; whereabouts of the transcripts of the Russian originals; and the many contradictions and outright falsifications contained in them. They are seldom cited today. Certainly the "official" version of Katyn cannot be based on them alone.

Appendix 2. Image Attribution

Image 2.1 AM p. 304 Bild 34, bottom. (German Report)

Image 2.2 Genshow firm drawing. (Pamiatnykh. Source: http://katynfiles.com/content/pamyatnykh-genschow.html Burdenko Commission files, GARF = State Archive of the Russian Federation f. 7021. op. 114.)

Image 3.1 Burdenko Commission inventory excerpt (Pamiatnykh, At http://katynfiles.com/content/pamyatnykh-burdenko-materials.html)

Image 4.1 The Shelepin document (detail).

Image 5.1 Artist's rendering of badge of Constable Police Constable Jósef Kuligowski unearthed at Volodymyr-Volyns'kiy

Image 5.2 Jeckeln during the war. (Wikipedia)

Image 5.3 Jeckeln in Soviet captivity. (Wikipedia)

Image 5.4 Memorial plaque of Kuligowski at Mednoe Cemetery. (Courtesy of Aleksandr Zenin of Tver' and his colleagues.)

Image 5.5 Memorial plaque of Małowiejski at Mednoe Cemetery. (Courtesy of Aleksandr Zenin of Tver' and his colleagues.)

Images 5.6 and 5.7 Artist's rendering of shells of the type found in graves No. 1 and 2. Artwork by Nuclear Heat Graphics, 2018.

Image 9.1 "How the Germans fabricated the Katyn escapade" photocopy. Courtesy of colleague Vladimir L. Bobrov. (GANISO = State Archive of Contemporary History of the Smolensk Oblast' f. 8. op. 2. d. 960. l. 38)

Images 10.1 and 10.2   Burdenko Commission excerpts. (Pamiatnykh)

Images 12. 1 and 12.2 Artist's rendering of addittional Polish policemen's badges unearthed at Volodymyr-Volyns'kiy. Polish officials have refused to identify them. Artwork by Nuclear Heat Graphics, 2018. Based on source photos in interview of Dr. Dominika Siemińska.

Image 13.1 and 13.2 "Ukrainian Documents of Katyn" (Memorial Society, Kiev – Ukrainian government documents)

Bibliography, Photographs, Errata

The **bibliography** may be found here:

https://tinyurl.com/furr-katyn-biblio

Images of the badges and headstamps, shown as drawings in the published book, may be viewed here:

https://tinyurl.com/furr-katyn-images

Errata are noted here:

https://tinyurl.com/furr-katyn-errata

Index.

xxx